ArtScroll Tanach Series®

A traditional commentary on the Books of the Bible

Rabbis Nosson Scherman/Meir Zlotowitz
General Editors

Yonah

Translation and commentary by
Rabbi Meir Zlotowitz

Overview:
Jonah, Repentance, and Yom Kippur
by
Rabbi Nosson Scherman

THE TWELVE PROPHETS:

Jonah

JONAH / A NEW TRANSLATION WITH A COMMENTARY ANTHOLOGIZED FROM TALMUDIC, MIDRASHIC AND RABBINIC SOURCES.

Published by
Mesorah Publications, ltd.

FIRST EDITION
First Impression . . . August, 1978

SECOND EDITION
(Revised and Corrected)
First Impression . . . July 1980
Second Impression . . . August 1981
Third Impression . . . May 1988
Fourth Impression . . . August 1994

Published and Distributed by
MESORAH PUBLICATIONS, Ltd.
4401 Second Avenue
Brooklyn, New York 11232

Distributed in Europe by
J. LEHMANN HEBREW BOOKSELLERS
20 Cambridge Terrace
Gateshead, Tyne and Wear
England NE8 1RP

Distributed in Israel by
SIFRIATI / A. GITLER – BOOKS
4 Bilu Street
P.O.B. 14075
Tel Aviv 61140

Distributed in Australia & New Zealand by
GOLD'S BOOK & GIFT CO.
36 William Street
Balaclava 3183, Vic., Australia

Distributed in South Africa by
KOLLEL BOOKSHOP
22 Muller Street
Yeoville 2198, Johannesburg, South Africa

THE ARTSCROLL TANACH SERIES®
YONAH / JONAH

ISBN:
0-89906-081-1 (Hard cover)
0-89906-082-X (Paperback)

Typography by CompuScribe at ArtScroll Studios, Ltd.
4401 Second Avenue / Brooklyn, N.Y. 11232 / (718) 921-9000

Printed in the United States of America by Noble Book Press Corp.
Bound by Sefercraft, Quality Bookbinders, Ltd. Brooklyn, N.Y.

וַאֲנִי בְּקוֹל תּוֹדָה אֶזְבְּחָה לָּךְ
אֲשֶׁר נָדַרְתִּי אֲשַׁלֵּמָה,
יְשׁוּעָתָה לַה׳.

As for me, with a cheer of gratitude
I will bring offerings to You,
what I have vowed I will fulfill,
for the salvation which is HASHEM's.

— Jonah 2:10

This volume is dedicated to

ישראל ונחמה בלייר קמט

Israel and Naomi Blair Comet

of Beachwood, Ohio

Their passion belongs to Torah.

Their affection to those who spread its word.

Their vision crosses the ocean to the vibrant Torah centers of Israel.

Their support is extended to the people and institutions who planted its seed in America's soil and nurtured it to luxuriant growth.

הסכמת הגאון האמיתי שר התורה ועמוד ההוראה
מורנו ורבנו מרן ר׳ משה פיינשטיין שליט״א

RABBI MOSES FEINSTEIN
455 F. D. R. DRIVE
New York 2, N. Y.

ORegon 7-1222

משה פיינשטיין
ר״מ תפארת ירושלים
בנוא יארק

בע״ה

בע״ה

הנה ידידי הרב הנכבד מאד **מוהר״ר מאיר יעקב בן ידידי הרב הגאון ר׳ אהרן זלאטאוויץ שליט״א,** אשר היה מתלמידינו החשובים בהישיבה, וכל העת מתנהג בכל הענינים כראוי לבני תורה ויראי השי״ת. כבר איתמחי גברא בחבורים הרבים שחיבר על כתבי הקדש שכולם חשובים, בשפה האנגלית המדוברת ביותר במדינה זו, אשר קבץ דברים יקרים ופנינים נחמדים מספרי רבותינו נ״ע אשר הם מעוררים לאהבת התורה וקיום המצות וחזוק האמונה בהשי״ת. ונתקבלו אצל ההמון עם ההולכים בדרך התורה ויש מזה תועלת לקרב לב הקוראים אף מאלו שנתרחקו קצת לאבינו שבשמים ולקיים מצותיו.

ועתה חבר ספר כזה על ספר יונה שהוא ספר אשר עיקרו הוא לעורר לתשובה ודברי כבושין שאומר הזקן בתעניות הוא מקבלת השי״ת את תשובתם, ולכוונה זו מדפיסו עתה קרוב לימי התשובה דאלול וימי הרחמים אשר ג״כ ענין רחמי השי״ת הוא עיקר בספר יונה וכ״ש על ישראל עם הקודש. וכבר ראה אותו בני הרה״ג ר׳ דוד שליט״א ושיבחו מאד, אשר על כן דבר טוב הוא מה שמדפיסו ומוציאו לאור עולם להגדיל אהבת השי״ת ותורתו הקדושה ולעורר לתשובה שנזכה ע״י לגאולה שהובטח לנו מהשי״ת ע״י משיח צדקנו בקרוב. ויתברך ידידי הרב המחבר לחבר עוד ספרים חשובים כאלו וכן ידידי הנכבד מאד **הרב ר׳ נתן שערמאן שליט״א** עבור מאמרו בפתיחת הספר בדברים המושכין את הלב לתשובה ולאהבת התורה ויראת השי״ת יתברך בהצלחה בכל מעשיו לקדש שם שמים וע״ז באתי על החתום בכ״ו תמוז תשל״ח

נאום משה פיינשטיין

מכתב ברכה מאאמו״ר
הגאון הרב אהרן זלאטאוויץ שליט״א

בעזהשי״ת

הרב אהרן זלאטאוויץ

Rabbi Aron Zlotowitz

CONGREGATION ETZ CHAIM ANSHEI LUBIN
EXECUTIVE DIRECTOR: BOARD OF ORTHODOOX RABBIS OF BROOKLYN

RESIDENCE:
1134 EAST 9 STREET
BROOKLYN, N.Y. 11230
(212) 252-9188

ביום שנכפל בו כי טוב לסדר ,,כי ברוך הוא״ י״ג תמוז ה׳תשל״ח

מאד ישמח לבי ת״ל שבני היקר והחביב **הרב ר׳ מאיר יעקב שליט״א** שבס״ד חיבר מקודם ספרים טובים ויקרים על חמש מגילות ועל ספר בראשית באנגלית. וכעת ת״ל חיבר ספר יקר על ספר יונה הנביא. ות״ל שאחר יגיעה רבה אסף בצרור המור להיות לאחרים בידו דברי רבותינו הקדושים ז״ל כמו בחיבוריו הקודמים. וג״כ הוסיף משלו בבינה ודעת. ביחד עם המחנך המפורסם ומרביץ תורה על פי מסורה ידידי **הרב ר׳ נתן שערמאן שליט״א.**

וכמה גדולה כח התשובה שהמתודה ומתחרט על המעשים שעשה ומקבל על עצמו מכאן ולהבא לילך בדרך החיים של תורה ולקיים המצות. וחיברו הספר הנ״ל באנגלית כדי שכל אחד ואחד יוכל להבין. וכבר איתמחי גברא בחיבוריו שהוציא לאור עד כאן וקבלו אותם בשבע רצון וברכה להמחבר שליט״א. ובטחון להקב״ה שג״כ הספר הנ״ל יקבלו בשבע רצון וילמדו להאמין בהקב״ה ולקיים בכל דרכיך דעהו.

באו״ח סימן תרכ״ב איתא שמפטירין ביונה במנחה ביוהכ״פ לפי שיש בו כח התשובה. ועיין שם בט״ז ס״ק ד׳ ושאין יכולים לברוח מהשי״ת. ואיתא בגמרא נדרים ל״ח-א׳ ששילם בעד הנסיעה על הספינה ד׳ אלפי דינרים של זהב וכו׳ מזה נראה שכמה היה נפשו חשקה לברוח מלפני השי״ת. ומה היה הסוף שהשליכו אותו לים והוא היה בודאי שבע רצון מזה שנתקיים מחשבתו לברוח. אבל רבות מחשבות בלב איש ועצת ה׳ היא תקום שהזמין השי״ת דג גדול ובלע אותו וחי במעיו של דג כמה ימים ועשה תשובה וחרט על מעשיו ואח״כ פלט הדג אותו ליבשה. וכדאיתא בתהלים קל״ט אם אסק שמים שם אתה אשכנה באחרית ים גם שם ידך תנחני ותאחזני ימיניך. שאין שום איש יכול לברוח מהשי״ת.

ואיתא באו״ח משנה ברורה סימן תרכ״ב בשער הציון ס״ק ו׳ בזה הלשון: כי האדם חושב כמה פעמים לייאש את עצמו שאין יכול לתקן בשום אופן וע״כ יתנהג תמיד באופן אחד ואם יגזור עליו הקב״ה למות ימות אבל טעות הוא שסוף דבר יהיה כל מה שהקב״ה רוצה מנפשו שיתקן מוכרח הוא לתקן ויבא עוד פעם ופעמים לעוה״ז ובע״כ יוכרח לתקן. וא״כ למה לו כל העמל למות ולסבול חיבוט הקבר ושאר צרות ולחזור עוד הפעם. וראיה מיונה שהקב״ה רצה מאתו שילך וינבא והוא מיאן בזה ונס לים מקום שלא ישרה עליו עוד השכינה לנביאות כידוע וראינו שנטבע בים ונבלע בדג והיה שם במעיו כמה ימים ולפי הנראה בודאי לא יוכל להתקיים דברי השי״ת. ומ״מ ראינו שסוף דבר היה שרצון השי״י נתקיים וילך וינבא כן הוא האדם בעניניו. וזהו שאומרים באבות ואל יבטיחך יצרך שהשאול מנוס לך. עד כאן לשונו.

והנני מברך את בני ממקור לבי, יהי רצון שחפץ ה׳ בידו יצליח להגדיל תורה ואמונה ועוד יפוצו מעינותיו חוצה באורך ימים ושנים ונחת וכל טוב וכל אשר יעשה יצליח אמן.

אהרן זלאטאוויץ החותם

מנהל ומזכיר ועד הרבנים דברוקלין יצ״ו
וסגן נש״א דאגודת הרבנים דארצות הברית וקנדא.

מכתב ברכה
ממרן הגאון ר׳ מרדכי גיפטר שליט״א

הרב מרדכי גיפטר
ראש הישיבה

ישיבת טלז
קרית טלז־סטון
ירושלים

בע״ה

ב׳ פנחס, תשל״ח

לידידי האהובים הרבנים הנעלים **ר׳ מאיר יעקב זלטוביץ ור׳ נתן שרמן,** נר״ו, שלום וברכה נצח לכם ולכל הצוות אשר אתכם!

לשמחה רבה היתה לי הידיעה שהנכם מתכוננים להוסיף חולי׳ חדשה בשרשרת הקדש של עבודתכם הפורי׳ בכתבי הקדש, הפעם ספר יונה, הסובב והולך על ענין התשובה, אשר על כן נתיחד זה הספר להפטרת המנחה של יום הכפורים, הוא יום התשובה והטהרה.

מושג התשובה באספקלריא של תורה שונה הוא תכלית שינוי מכל מה שדנו בזה בכל הזמנים בכל הדתות. כל חיינו עלי אדמות הם החיים שלאחר החטא של אדה״ר ועבודת האדם מכוונת ע״פ התוה״ק לשוב לאותו האור הנפלא שלפני החטא. אשר לפי״ז גם הצדיק גמור עוסק הוא בעבודת התשובה, ומבחינה זו „אין צדיק בארץ אשר יעשה טוב ולא יחטא״ שבכל שיעשה נמצא עטיו של נחש.

הרי רגיש אדם בזה יכיר שאין להתיאש מכל חוטא, יהי׳ מי שיהי׳, ולכל אחד יש לו מקום — כפי מעמדו אשר בו נתיחד — בעולם התשובה, ומבטן שאול יוכל להתרומם לשמי רום, מתוך מה שיסד הבורא ב״ה בסדרי הבריאה שהבא לטהר מסייעין אותו.

ויסוד הבחירה שהוא משרשי תורת ישראל מתברר הוא בכל זהרו בעבודת התשובה, עיין רמב״ם פ״ה מתשובה ה״ב, ועיין ס׳ „הרהורי תשובה״ פ״ו מתשובה, ה״א, אות ד׳.

מובטחני שתוציאו מתחת ידכם דבר נאה ומתוקן כפי חזקת חבר שכבר הוחזקתם בה, וכל המעיינים בספר יתעוררו ברגשות קדש לעבוד את ה׳ וליראה אותו.

מנאי, אוהבכם מלונ״ח, המצפה לישועה

מרדכי גיפטר

מכתב ברכה
ממרן הגאון ר׳ שניאור קוטלר שליט״א

RABBI SHNEUR KOTLER
BETH MEDRASH GOVOHA
LAKEWOOD, N. J.

שניאור קוטלר
בית מדרש גבוה
לייקוואוד, נ. דז.

בע״ה

אשרי חלקם של החברים הנכבדים הנותנים נפשם להצליח בשליחותם הנשגבה, להקים את דברי התורה ו,,להראות פני כתיבתה לעם״ ולשימם לפניהם ובפניהם כשלחן ערוך ומוכן לאכול, ב,,**לשון למודים לדעת לעות את יעף דבר**״, וגו׳, [ישעי׳ נ׳ ד׳], כמשמעו וכפירושו, לדעת לעות — ,,להשיג ללמד לפי העת והזמן״ [מצודת דוד]. את יעף — צמא לשמוע את דבר ה׳ כמו לשתות העיף במדבר. ר״ל הצמא, וכן ,,**בארץ צי׳ ועיף בלי מים**״. [רד״ק] —ולהעיר אזן ולב לשמוע כלמודים. ויתרון חשיבות למשימה זו בהשתרע המדבר, ארץ פרי למלחה, וארצות תבל נגובות מטובה — ויחד עם זה זכינו לראות בהתנוצצות השתלחות הרעב והצמא לדבר — מה גדולה הזכות לנטוע אשל ולחפור בארות מים חיים, להחיות רוח שפלים ולהרוות נפשות צמאות.

באר חפרוה שרים כרוה נדיבי העם במחוקק במשענותם, [במדבר כ״א י״ח], וברש״י ,,כל נשיא וכו׳ נוטל מקלו ומושך אצל דגלו ומחנהו, ומי הבאר נמשכין דרך אותו סימן, וכו׳, ע״פ משה שנקרא מחוקק״. וכבתקופת יצירתו ועיצוב צורתו של כלל ישראל, שבה נסללה דרך אשוריו לדורות, וכל מאורעותי׳ הם לא רק סימן לבנים אלא ,,יצירה לזרעם״ כל׳ הרמב״ן — אף זו דרך סלולה לעתיד — לשלח מעינים בנחלים, לכרות עריצים ואפיקים למשוך אליהם ועל־ידם את זרם המעינות אל תוך הדגלים והמחנות — ואליהם ישובו ללכת. —

יישר חילו של מע״כ ידידי הנעלה, איש אשר רוח בו, הרה״ג, איש האשכלות, **מוה״ר נתן שרמן שליט״א**, אשר להורות נתן בלבו [עי׳ אב״ע ואוה״ח שם], לחשוף מים ממעינות, ולחתות אש התורה ונשמות ישראל מיקוד — ללבות גחלים עוממות ולהדליק נר מצוה באור תורה. — ואפריון נמטי למע״כ ידידי הרה״ג יקר רוח **מוה״ר מאיר יעקב זלטוביץ שליט״א** המנצח על המלאכה, שתרגם ופירש ספר זה, מפורש ושום שכל.

והדעת **לעות את יעף דבר** מיוחדת בספר יונה, שמצב הדור משתקף בו, ביציאתם לפועל של כחות ההרס, ההורסים להוריד את דרגת האדם ולטשטש את הצלם והדמות העליון שבו, ומשתערים לנתק את מוסרות האדם למהותו העליונה ולשעבדו ליצריו ורצונותיו, בהשתוללות ללא רסן, עד ש,,עלתה רעתם״ והגיעה ר״ל עד לאבדן זכות הקיום וכח העמידה — ונשמעה קריאת הנביא לתשובה ולתפלה — ואמנם במצב זה פתוחה האזן יותר לשמוע את הנביא ,,צווח ואומר״ את דברו [כל׳ המס״י], ועלול הדור לראות את עצמו באספקלרית נבואה זו, שהוצרכה, ונאמרה, לדורות — ולהגיע לתשובה שלמה, אכי״ר.

יזכו לראות שכר לפעולתם בשיבת בנים לגבולם, ולמקורם, ולמעלת אבותם [כל׳ הרמב״ן], ונזכה כולנו לראות בקיום ההבטחה כי תמלא הארץ דעה כמים לים מכסים, בבוא גואל לציון בב״א.

הכו״ח לכבוד התורה, אור ליום ו׳ עש״ק מטו״מ, ר״ח מנחם אב התשל״ח

יוסף חיים שניאור קוטלר

בלאאמו״ר הגר״א זצוק״ל

Table of Contents

Preface

The Book of Jonah *is part of* תְּרֵי עָשָׂר, the Twelve Prophets, *and, while* Jonah *is neither the first nor the largest of the twelve, it is undoubtedly the best-known. One of the smallest books in Scripture — only four chapters and forty-eight verses — it is read in its entirety as the Haftarah of the Yom Kippur afternoon service. It is indelibly identified with the solemnity of the day and with repentance and atonement. Indeed, Jonah is a classic text of repentance and of God's eagerness to bestow His mercy upon those who return to Him.*

Because of this familiarity with the Book and its always vital and universal message of repentance, Mesorah Publications presents it separately in a self-contained volume as part of the forthcoming Twelve Prophets set. We sincerely hope that the commentary and Overview will help present a perspective on the Book, Yom Kippur, and the theme of repentance.

Jonah, like such other Books as Esther, and Ruth appears simple on the surface; unfortunately, therefore, too many think of it as the 'story of Jonah and the whale,' an association that is at once wrong, superficial, and unconducive to an understanding of the depth and profundity that are present in every part of Torah, whether its language is difficult or simple, whether it is 'prophecy' or narrative.

This work, like all the others in the ARTSCROLL TANACH SERIES, *is an attempt to present Scripture in the light of the Sages and the classic commentators. May Hashem Yisborach help us succeed in this task of revealing, to whatever degree, the wonders of His Torah.*

ACKNOWLEDGMENTS

Two names sign this work and, naturally are responsible for any errors or blemishes, but a larger group of dedicated mentors, colleagues, and co-workers share much of the credit for its content and quality.

MARAN HAGAON MORDECHAI GIFTER, שליט״א, *the Telsher Rosh Hayeshivah, who is presently building a new Torah citadel in Kiryat Telshe-Stone, Israel, has long been a source of encouragement and guidance. His counsel was of vital importance during the development of this work.* HARAV DAVID FEINSTEIN שליט״א *and* HARAV DAVID COHEN שליט״א, *treasurehouses of Torah knowledge and judgment have given unstintingly of their time and sagacity, reading all of the book and offering invaluable comment and advice.*

The ArtScroll staff has once more responded despite various, sometimes unfair, but unavoidable pressures: REB AVIE GOLD *as proof-reader and research-editor;* MRS. SHIRLEY KIFFEL, MRS. LEAH LOWINGER, SHIMON SHAMILZADEH *and* PAULA KATZ.

REB SHEAH BRANDER, *colleague and friend, has once more responded to a demanding task with skill and aplomb. The visual beauty of the book tells more than words of the caliber of his craftsmanship.*

We are grateful to REB YAAKOV ELMAN *who has done much research on* Jonah *and graciously pointed out sources and reference material.*

We express particular gratitude to MR. *and* MRS. ISRAEL COMET *of Beachwood, Ohio who helped make possible the publication of this book. People of warmth, vision, love of Torah, and dedication to its dissemination, they leave their mark on many a worthy Torah undertaking in America and Israel.*

Finally, אַחֲרוֹנוֹת אַחֲרוֹנוֹת חֲבִיבוֹת — *feelings of gratitude and indebtedness that cannot be put into words. Our wives,* CHANA SCHERMAN *and* ROCHEL ZLOTOWITZ *bore much of the brunt of this undertaking. The pressures were more severe than ever and they came at an inopportune time. Nevertheless, with good cheer and encouragement, they performed double duty at home in the interest of* הַרְבָּצַת תּוֹרָה. *May they be granted their fervent prayer: that our homes be wellsprings of Torah and our children be its bearers.*

Rabbi Nosson Scherman / Meir Zlotowitz
Rosh Chodesh Menachem Av, 5738
Brooklyn, New York

An Overview/

◆§Jonah
◆§Repentance, and
◆§Yom Kippur

An Overview/
Jonah, Repentance, and Yom Kippur

Prologue

לָמָה בָרַח יוֹנָה? דָּן דִּין בֵּינוֹ לְבֵין עַצְמוֹ: אָמַר אֲנִי יוֹדֵעַ שֶׁזֶה הַגּוֹי קְרוֹבֵי תְּשׁוּבָה הֵם. עַכְשָׁיו עוֹשִׂים תְּשׁוּבָה וְהקב״ה שׁוֹלֵחַ רוֹגְזוֹ עַל יִשְׂרָאֵל, וְלֹא דַי שֶׁיִּשְׂרָאֵל קוֹרְאִים אוֹתִי נָבִיא שֶׁקֶר אֶלָּא אַף עוֹבְדֵי עֲבוֹדָה זָרָה.

Why did Jonah flee? He passed judgment upon himself. He said, I know that this nation [the Ninevites] is close to repentance. Now they will repent and the Holy One, Blessed be He, will dispatch His anger against Israel. And as if it were not enough that Israel calls me a false prophet, even idolators [will do so] (Pirkei d'Rabbi Eliezer Ch. 10).

Jonah's story is read in full on Yom Kippur. *Surely its message is perfectly suited to this day of primeval uniqueness.*

The story of Jonah is deceptively simple, but upon even casual analysis, it presents mind-boggling difficulties. A prophet is dispatched to warn a populous city that it must change its ways or be destroyed — yet he refuses to go. He attempts to flee from the Omnipresent. Condemned to die, he is saved by a miracle. Finally he carries out his mission and brings about a mass repentance of almost unprecedented dimensions, yet he remonstrates with God that His mercy was unjustified. Jonah's story is read in full on *Yom Kippur.* Surely its message is perfectly suited to this day of primeval uniqueness and his story is one that bears the message of a repentance that only God could fathom. How?

שָׁאֲלוּ לְחָכְמָה חוֹטֵא מַהוּ עוֹנְשׁוֹ? אָמְרָה לָהֶם חַטָּאִים תְּרַדֵּף רָעָה. שָׁאֲלוּ לִנְבוּאָה חוֹטֵא מַהוּ עוֹנְשׁוֹ? אָמְרָה לָהֶם הַנֶּפֶשׁ הַחוֹטֵאת הִיא תָמוּת. שָׁאֲלוּ לַתּוֹרָה חוֹטֵא מַהוּ עוֹנְשׁוֹ? אָמְרָה יָבִיא אָשָׁם וְיִתְכַּפֵּר. שָׁאֲלוּ להקב״ה חוֹטֵא מַהוּ עוֹנְשׁוֹ? אָמַר יַעֲשֶׂה תְשׁוּבָה וְיִתְכַּפֵּר . . .

They asked Wisdom, 'What is the sinner's punishment?'

It told them: 'Sinners — let them be pursued by [their] evil' [Proverbs 13:21].

They asked Prophecy, 'What is the sinner's punishment?'

It told them: 'The soul that sins — it shall die!' [Ezekiel 18:20].

They asked Torah, 'What is the sinner's punishment?'

It told them: 'Let him bring a guilt-offering and gain atonement!'

They asked the Holy One, Blessed be He, 'What is the sinner's punishment?'

He told them: 'Let him repent and gain atonement!' (Midrash, Yerushalmi Makkos 2:6).

We know that God longs for repentance and that His most treasured prize is a broken heart.

The efficacy of repentance is above logic. We accept it as a matter of course because we are conditioned to know that it is the last hope of even the most hardened sinner; because we know that God longs for repentance and that His most treasured prize is a broken heart. But, as the *Midrash* makes plain, neither Wisdom, nor Prophecy, nor Torah accepted the possibility of repentance. To them, forgiveness was unachievable — Wisdom decreed that the sinner should be pursued by his evil, and Prophecy decreed that the wake of sin brings death. Torah declared that atonement could be achieved only by guilt-offerings. Why those three attributes should have been so uncompromising we shall ex-

But one fact remains undeniably plain — only God sanctioned repentance.

amine below, but one fact remains undeniably plain — only God sanctioned repentance. Without His mercy, the sinner's fate was bleak indeed. With His mercy, a moment of sincere repentance could wipe out a lifetime of sin, and even transform transgressions into virtues. Why?

> אָמַר ר׳ יַנַּאי מִתְּחִלַּת בְּרִיאָתוֹ שֶׁל עוֹלָם צָפָה הקב״ה מַעֲשֵׂיהֶם שֶׁל צַדִּיקִים וּמַעֲשֵׂיהֶם שֶׁל רְשָׁעִים, וְהָאָרֶץ הָיְתָה תֹהוּ, אֵלּוּ מַעֲשֵׂיהֶם שֶׁל רְשָׁעִים ... יְהִי אוֹר, אֵלּוּ מַעֲשֵׂיהֶם שֶׁל צַדִּיקִים ... יוֹם מַעֲשֵׂיהֶם שֶׁל צַדִּיקִים ... חֹשֶׁךְ, מַעֲשֵׂיהֶם שֶׁל רְשָׁעִים. יוֹם אֶחָד, שֶׁנָּתַן לָהֶם הקב״ה יוֹם אֶחָד. וְאֵיזֶה? זֶה יוֹם הַכִּפּוּרִים.
>
> *Rabbi Yannai said, from the beginning of the creation of the world, the Holy One, Blessed be He, looked at the deeds of the righteous and the deeds of the wicked. 'And the earth was empty'* [Genesis 1:2] *— these are the deeds of the wicked ... 'Let there be light'* [ibid. v. 3] *— these are the deeds of the righteous ... 'Day'* [ibid. v. 5] *— the deeds of the righteous ... 'Night'* [ibid.] *— the deeds of the wicked. 'One day'* [ibid] *— for the Holy One, Blessed be He, assigned one* [i.e., a unique] *day. Which? — the Day of Atonement (Bereishis Rabbah* 3:8).

The time for repentance is always, but *Yom Kippur*, the Day of Atonement is unique. From the beginning of creation, God foresaw that the world would be a confusing mixture of good and evil, of righteous and wicked. Indeed, it was His will that this be so, for man was created to surmount the challenge of this confusion, to choose light and reject darkness (see *Overview* to *Bereishis I).* Nevertheless, God created יוֹם אֶחָד, *one day*, a unique day, an indispensable day — a day which was necessary for man's ascension out of the darkness and into the light: *Yom Kippur*. Plainly, *Yom Kippur* provides

Plainly, Yom Kippur *provides man with an opportunity, a spiritual condition which he can duplicate at no other time.*

man with an opportunity, a spiritual condition, which he can duplicate at no other time. What is it?

Let us seek to understand the three — the man, the concept, and the day; Jonah, Repentance, and *Yom Kippur.* Let us attempt to probe their essence as revealed and illuminated by the Sages and the commentators.

⤙§Jonah

בֶּן צָרְפַת הָאַלְמָנָה הוּא יוֹנָה בֶּן אֲמִתַּי. הָיָה צַדִּיק גָּמוּר

The son of the widow of Tzorfas [the child whom Elijah brought back to life] was Jonah. He was a complete tzaddik (Midrash Shocher Tov 26:7).

שָׁקוּל כְּאֵלִיָּהוּ, אֱלִישָׁע מְשָׁחוֹ

Jonah was equal to Elijah, Elisha anointed him (Mishnas Rabbi Eliezer).

יוֹנָה תָּבַע כְּבוֹד הַבֵּן וְלֹא כְּבוֹד הָאָב

Jonah defended the honor of the child [Israel] rather than the honor of the Father [God] (Mechilta, Pesichta Bo).

יוֹנָה בֶּן אֲמִתַּי נָבִיא אֱמֶת הָיָה

Jonah ben Amittai was a true prophet (Yerushalmi Sanhedrin 11:8).

I. Jonah the Prophet

Destined for Greatness

THE Sages testify to Jonah's greatness; the very fact that he was a prophet and that God persevered in utilizing him for the mission to Nineveh despite his apparent recalcitrance is in itself testimony to his righteousness. But his very stature makes the questions about him all the more difficult. If he was so exalted, then how could he seem to sink so low? How could he refuse to obey the command of God? How could he attempt to flee from prophecy? Why was he averse to bringing about the repentance of the masses of Nineveh? Why was he displeased when the Ninevites heeded his warning and repented with an intensity that has remained a model down through the ages?

If he was so exalted, then how could he seem to sink so low?

It would seem that Jonah was destined for greatness from early youth. The prophet Elijah was dispatched to Tzorfas where, he was told, a widow would provide for him (I *Kings* 17:9). He went and found a woman so poverty stricken that she was convinced that both she and her young son would soon die of starvation. Elijah blessed her with a miraculously inexhaustible supply of food. Clearly, he had been sent to Tzorfas in order to preserve the lives of the widow and her son. Not long afterward, the child became ill and died. 'Have you come to me to make my sin apparent?' demanded the distraught mother. Elijah tenderly took the child and carried him up to the little attic provided him by the widow, laid him on the bed she had given him, and pleaded with God to revive him. The child came back to life and Elijah returned him to his grateful mother. She said:

Elijah had been sent to Tzorfas in order to preserve the lives of the widow and her son.

עַתָּה זֶה יָדַעְתִּי כִּי אִישׁ אֱלֹהִים אָתָּה וּדְבַר ה׳ בְּפִיךָ אֱמֶת

Now I know that you are a man of God and the word of HASHEM in your mouth is truth (ibid. 17:24).

Jonah's life was part of Elijah's mission. The *Talmud (Sanhedrin* 113a) says that Elijah was sent to Tzorfas only so he could bring to bear the power of resuscitation of the dead. Jonah became the living demonstration of the power of God through His prophet. He became the proof that Elijah was the prophet of truth, that the word of God was truth. Indeed, that concept became imbedded in his own name. He was *ben Amittai,* son of truth, man of truth (see *commentary* to 1:1).

Jonah became the living demonstration of the power of God through His. prophet.

He was ben Amittai, *son of truth, man of truth.*

The young Jonah became Elijah's disciple and, when Elijah ascended to heaven, Jonah became the disciple of Elisha.

The First Mission

One mission which Elijah had received prior to his ascension was to anoint Jehu as king of the Ten Tribes of Israel. Elisha appointed one of his disciples to fulfill that task and to charge Jehu with the responsibility of removing a blight from Israel by killing all the wicked survivors of the evil House of Ahab. A prophet was dispatched to carry out the historic task (II *Kings* 9:1-10); he was young, but he was to have a long and significant prophetic career ahead of him. The young prophet was Jonah *(Pirkei d'Rabbi Eliezer* 10; *Seder Olam* 19). After Jehu carried out his task of erasing the name of Ahab from Israel, another prophetic message came to him assuring him that because he had carried out God's will, he would be rewarded with a dynasty that would produce four kings after his own reign. That prophecy, too, was brought him by Jonah (II *Kings* 10:30, see *Rashi* and *Seder Olam*). Indeed, *Maharzu* (to *Bereishis Rabbah* 21:5) maintains that all the prophecies to the House of Jehu, which reigned for nearly a century, were given through Jonah.

All the prophecies to the House of Jehu, which reigned for nearly a century, were given through Jonah.

Jeroboam and Jerusalem

Jonah anointed Jehu in the year 3055 (705 B.C.E.). Sixty years later, Jehu's grandson, Jeroboam II became king of the Ten Tribes. Spiritually, the kingdom of the Ten Tribes was in a period of decline. It had suffered defeats by outside enemies and did not seem destined to endure for long as an independent state. But God was not yet ready to condemn His recalcitrant children. He wanted Israel to grow great and strong again — to give it the opportunity to recognize, if it would, that God had not forsaken it. Perhaps then, Israel would repent. So again Jonah was given a prophecy to the King of the Ten Tribes of Israel. The word of God was that the constricted, eroded boundaries of Israel would reach their greatest eminence under Jeroboam. So it happened:

God was not yet ready to condemn His recalcitrant children. He wanted Israel to grow great and strong again.

> *He [Jeroboam] restored the boundary of Israel from the approach to Chamas until the Dead Sea, according to the word of HASHEM, God of Israel, which He spoke through His servant Jonah son of Amittai the prophet, who was from Gas Chefer (II Kings 14:25).*

Jeroboam II, like his earlier namesake, was an evil king. His conquests proved to be only a last blaze of glory. The Ten Tribes were exiled only fifty-two years after the completion of his reign in 3153 (607

Jeroboam II, like his earlier namesake, was an evil king. His conquests proved to be only a last blaze of glory.

B.C.E.). His son Zechariahu reigned for only six months and then Jehu's dynasty came to an end. According to one reading of *Seder Olam,* Jonah died during Zechariahu's reign at the age of one hundred-twenty (see *Seder Zemanim n.* 3 to *Seder Olam* 18).

According to *Pirkei d'Rabbi Eliezer* (ch. 10) Jonah had another major prophecy to the Jewish people. He was sent to warn the inhabitants of Jerusalem that the Holy City would be destroyed because of their sins. The people repented and, following the rule that an evil prophecy can be annulled by repentance, the city was saved. This experience and its aftermath played a part in Jonah's later decision not to go to Nineveh as we shall see.

A Mission Refused

The date of Jonah's mission to Nineveh is not known. According to *Pirkei d'Rabbi Eliezer* it took place after his missions to Jeroboam and Jerusalem. At any rate, it almost certainly took place during the reign of Jeroboam, from 3114 - 3153 (646 - 607 B.C.E.) [But see *Yevamos* 98a and *Radal v.* 7 to *Pirkei d'Rabbi Eliezer* 10.]

Nineveh was the capital of Assyria, the Iraq of the present. It was not yet a great power — that would come later when Providence appointed Assyria to be the *rod of HASHEM's wrath (Isaiah* 10:5), the dominant country of the world, which, under Sennacherib, exiled the Ten Tribes and besieged Jerusalem. In Jonah's time, Nineveh was an important city with a large population. For a variety of reasons (see *commentary*), God wished to bring a spirit of repentance to Nineveh. As His emissary, He chose Jonah. But Jonah did not wish to go. Why?

God wished to bring a spirit of repentance to Nineveh. As His emissary, He chose Jonah. But Jonah did not wish to go. Why?

He had two reasons. The nations were 'near to repent'; they could be easily motivated to repent [according to *Michilta, Pesichta Bo, Yerushalmi Sanhedrin* 11:2 and *Tanchuma*: all nations; according to *PdRE,* only Nineveh]. They would heed Jonah's call and earn God's mercy, but if that were to happen, it would point the most accusing of fingers at sinful Israel. God had appointed a multitude of prophets to chastise Israel, yet it refused to heed their call. God's chosen people, His first-born, spurned His pleas for their repentance. How could anyone justify Israel's obduracy in the face of Nineveh's compliance? Were Jonah to go to Nineveh he would be the instrument of a terrible condemnation of Israel. Jonah had to choose between obeying God and defending the honor of Israel. In order to shield the child from the wrath of its Father, he chose not to go to Nineveh.

Jonah had to choose between obeying God and defending the honor of Israel.

Jonah had another reason for not wishing to go. When he had prophesied against Jerusalem and the people repented, the ignorant members of the populace had reviled him. 'False prophet!' they called him. He had foretold the destruction of the city, but the city still stood and prospered. As *Radal* makes clear, only ignorant people joined in the jeers; the scholars knew that repentance had changed the decree. To them Jonah was God's true prophet who had been the agent of salvation. But there had been a vocal outcry against him and Jonah had tasted the bitterness of vilification. Were he to go to Nineveh and were his warnings to result in a mass repentance as he was sure it would, the entire Assyrian nation would reverberate with the shout, 'Jonah is a false prophet!' That, Jonah wished to avoid, so he fled to the sea *(PdRE).* The Sages further say that when Jonah asked the sailors to throw him overboard, his intention was that he would rather die than cause harm to Israel.

The entire Assyrian nation would shout, 'Jonah is a false prophet!'

When Jonah asked the sailors to throw him overboard, his intention was that he would rather die than cause harm to Israel.

Thus, the Sages give us two reasons for Jonah's flight: his wish to avoid an indictment of Israel and his wish to avoid personal vilification. Both reasons require deeper understanding. Furthermore, how can it be that wicked Nineveh should be more receptive to repentance than righteous Israel? If the Ninevites and other nations were quicker to repent than Israel, then why does Israel enjoy its privileged position in the hierarchy of nations? And we must still explain how a prophet of Jonah's stature, one whom *Mishnas Rabbi Eliezer* ranks as the equal of Elijah, could presume to think that he could flee from God's authority.

II. A Reluctant Prophet

Jonah's Dedication

NOAM ELIMELECH (to *Shelach*) comments homiletically that the *Yonah*, dove, a bird which maintains an inviolable loyalty to its mate, is used in parables of the Sages to symbolize Israel's loyalty to God. God says of Israel אַחַת הִיא יוֹנָתִי, *unique is she, My constant dove (Shir HaShirim* 6:9). Jonah the prophet is so named because he, too, represents total loyalty to God. His flight to the sea was not an effort to deny that bond or break it. Rather it was an attempt by Jonah to lessen his own receptivity to the spiritual heights of prophecy: on the sea and away from *Eretz Yisrael*, the spirit of prophecy does not rest on man (see *commentary).*

Jonah the prophet represents total loyalty to God. His flight to the sea was not an effort to deny that bond or break it.

Against that backdrop we can best appreciate the self-sacrifice of Jonah's flight. Only a prophet can appreciate the spiritual bliss of prophecy. To be worthy of such a state is beyond the dreams of even great people; Jonah was there and he chose to give it up in order not to shame Israel by the comparison of its stubbornness with the obedience of Nineveh to the warning of God's prophet. It was not from God's authority that he fled; had he not recognized God's sovereignty, there would have been no need to flee. His own country, tragically, was filled with people who refused to acknowledge the word of God. *They* had no need to seek passage to Tarshish to evade the word of God; they flouted it in Samaria, in Judah, even in Jerusalem. Jonah fled because he was close, because he believed, because he was exalted. He fled not to diminish the Word of God, but to diminish his own receptivity to prophecy.

He fled not to diminish the Word of God, but to diminish his own receptivity to prophecy.

More — he knew full well that he risked the onus of a prophet who suppressed his prophecy and thereby becomes liable to death by the hand of heaven (*Sanhedrin* 89a, see *Commentary* to 1:3). Nevertheless, he was ready to forfeit his attainment and even his life — to commit an עֲבֵירָה לִשְׁמָהּ, *transgression for a noble cause* — for the sake of Israel.

Sanctification of the Name

In his zeal to sacrifice himself for the sake of Israel, he followed the example of Moses, the master of all prophets. After Israel fashioned and worshiped the Golden Calf, God's judgment decreed that the nation be destroyed and that Moses and his descendants take their place as the Chosen people. Moses acknowledged the guilt and he exacted punishment from the guilty parties. But then he turned to God and beseeched Him to forgive the sinful people — וְאִם אַיִן מְחֵנִי נָא מִסִּפְרְךָ אֲשֶׁר כָּתָבְתָּ, *but if* [*Israel can*]-*not* [*be forgiven*] *erase me from Your Book which You have written (Exodus* 32:32). So zealous was Moses in his love of Israel that he wished his name to be stricken from the Torah and from life if his people were to lose their chosen status. David, too, took responsibility upon himself when a plague struck his nation (*II Samuel* 24:17). Jonah followed their example. Rather than become the instrument of Israel's calumny, he was ready for any fate — exile, degradation, even death (*Mechilta* ibid.).

So zealous was Moses in his love of Israel that he wished to be stricken from the Torah and from life if his people were to lose their chosen status.

He had another object of devotion — God. True, according to *PdRE* he had been branded a false prophet once before, by the common folk of Jerusalem, when their repentance saved the city from destruction, and he had no wish to be so branded by the entire population of Nineveh. Yet if we take this reason simplistically as a distinguished man's wish to safeguard his reputation and his reluctance to submit to public derogation, then we fail to reckon with the stature of Jonah. This disciple of Elijah and Elisha had seen the lack of regard that sinners could have for the noblest of men. He had been chosen as the prophet of an era when idolatry and disregard for prophets were the order of day in *Eretz Yisrael*. Nevertheless he persevered. That ignorant people in

This disciple of Elijah and Elisha had been chosen as the prophet of an era when idolatry and disregard for prophets were the order of day. Nevertheless he persevered.

Jerusalem castigated him should hardly have affected him personally — after all, he knew why Jerusalem had been spared and so did the great and holy people who formed its leadership. Jonah's prophecy had saved the city because it prompted the people to repent! Are prophets of God so weak that they test public opinion before doing their duty?

Let us return once again to the prayers Moses employed to save Israel at the time of the Golden Calf and again when the spies brought back their slanderous reports about *Eretz Yisrael.*

> *Why should the Egyptians claim saying, 'With evil did he take them out, to kill them in the mountains?' (Exodus* 32:12).
>
> *Perhaps they will say in the land from which You took us, 'Because of HASHEM's inability to bring them to the Land ...' (Deuteronomy* 9:28).
>
> *The nations will say, '... because of HASHEM's inability to bring this people to the Land ...' (Numbers* 14:15-16).

Can it be that God was swayed by the argument that the Egyptians might misinterpret His motives?

Can it be that God was swayed by the argument that the Egyptians might misinterpret His motives? Surely every sinner could present a similar argument. Should not God have responded כָּל הָרוֹצֶה לִטְעוֹת יָבֹא וְיִטְעֶה, *whoever wishes to err, let him err (Bereishis Rabbah).*

Moses' prayer was truly a highly exalted one, that was saturated with love and dedication to God. It was an outgrowth of Moses' awareness that the highest purpose of creation is to sanctify God's Name. Israel's goal, as expressed in the *Shmoneh Esrai* of *Rosh HaShanah* and *Yom Kippur*, is that the fear of God come over *all* creatures, [וּבְכֵן תֵּן פַּחְדְּךָ.], that they *all,* without exception, come as a single, united group to serve God. One who is apathetic to another can listen dispassionately as the latter is vilified. One who loves another cannot bear even to hear him criticized. Love does not brook indifference. Moses' love of God caused him to be revolted at the very thought that even a single Egyptian would dare to

One who loves another cannot bear even to hear him criticized. Love does not brook indifference.

say that God was too weak to carry out His intended plan, especially if the Egyptians were to belittle the Exodus by saying that God lacked the power to complete the Exodus by bringing Israel into *Eretz Yisrael.*

No Room for Exceptions

Ramban lists the Exodus as prime proof of God's mastery of creation for it was an open demonstration of His power to manipulate nature to suit His Divine purpose. The Ten Commandments speak not of the God Who created heaven and earth, but of the God Who withdrew Israel from Egypt — because that act was undeniable proof that God was the God of Israel and the God Who was beholden to no force on earth.

No one then alive had witnessed creation, but millions had seen the events of the Exodus.

No one then alive had witnessed creation, but millions had seen the events of the Exodus *(Kuzari).* If that public display of God's Omnipotence was one purpose of the Exodus, then Moses could not countenance the denial that God had the power to carry out His will. To Moses, such a doubt would constitute חִילוּל הַשֵּׁם, *desecration of the Name.* Lowly people might shrug at heathen denials of God. A spirit of 'tolerance' may influence people to be apathetic to desecration of Shabbos, commercialization of *kashruth,* laxness of morals. But the lack of passion is less a testimony of the triviality of the offense than of the grossness of the respondent.

Lack of passion is less a testimony of the triviality of the offense than of the grossness of the respondent.

One who seeks total, universal sanctification of God's Name cannot abide the snide remarks of even an Egyptian — or an ignoramus or a Ninevite. Therefore, we pray עֲשֵׂה לְמַעַנְךָ וְלֹא לְמַעֲנֵנוּ, [*O God*] *act for Your sake, not for our sake.* We do not imply ח״ו that God is in need of our salvation. Rather the intent of the plea is that His will be done in order that we may perceive His greatness. For Israel is the nation charged with the specific responsibility of bringing God's Presence to earth by exhibiting His mastery and His holiness in every area of existence. If Israel were to be wiped from the face of the earth ח״ו, then Moses' own perception of Sanctification of the Name would be mortally diminished. *He* — Moses— could not fulfill his own mission of Sanc-

If Israel were to be wiped from the face of the earth ח״ו, then Moses' own perception of Sanctification of the Name would be mortally diminished.

tification if Israel ceased to exist. Similarly, Abraham in his prayers for Sodom insisted that the Judge of the entire earth could not smite the innocent together with the guilty. *His* conception of God as Judge would be offended if he could not comprehend the justification of *every* aspect of the punishment he was about to witness. This, then, was Moses' prayer in the desert. The Name *must* be sanctified— but it could not be sanctified in his own eyes if Israel's grievous sin were punished in such a way that Egypt would find it a ludicrous indication that God lacked the power to carry out His will *(Michtav MeEliyahu)*.

This, then, was Moses' prayer in the desert. The Name must *be sanctified.*

It mattered not at all to Jonah *personally* that some fools in Jerusalem called him a false prophet. He knew, and so did those whose opinions truly mattered, that Jerusalem still stood only because his prophecy had prevailed. Nor would his personal fortunes change if all of Nineveh did the same. Jonah was *ben Amittai*, a man of truth, and he was not flustered by the babbling of people too blind to recognize the truth. But the Desecration of the Name! That, Jonah could not bear with equanimity.

Jonah was ben Amittai, *a man of truth, and he was not flustered by the babbling of people too blind to recognize the truth.*

III. Near to Repentance

Model of Repentance

The easy, imminent repentance of the Ninevites would be like an amusement park mirror in which Israel would be reflected as a hideous figure.

TWO TRAGEDIES loomed on Jonah's horizon. The easy, imminent repentance of the Ninevites would be like an amusement park mirror in which Israel would be reflected as a hideous figure, and the Name would be desecrated by those who decry His prophets as charlatans. So much did the prospects grieve him that he preferred to flee from prophecy.

אָמַר אֲנִי יוֹדֵעַ שֶׁזֶה הַגּוֹי קְרוֹבֵי תְשׁוּבָה הֵן

[Jonah] said, 'I know that this nation [Nineveh] is close [easily influenced] to repentance' (PdRE).

Chapter 3 of *Jonah* clearly shows that the repentance was real. The Sages derive a major rule of repentance from the turnabout of Nineveh, so much so, that they invoke the example of Nineveh to exhort Israel to repentance. When rain failed to descend and *Eretz Yisrael* was threatened by drought, days of public prayer and fasting were proclaimed. The elders would tell the people:

> אַחֵינוּ לֹא נֶאֱמַר בְּאַנְשֵׁי נִינְוֵה וַיַּרְא אֱלֹהִים אֶת שַׂקָּם וְאֶת תַּעֲנִיתָם אֶלָּא וַיַּרְא הָאֱלֹהִים אֶת מַעֲשֵׂיהֶם כִּי שָׁבוּ מִדַּרְכָּם הָרָעָה
>
> *Our brothers, it is not said of the people of Nineveh 'And God saw their sackcloth and their fast.' Rather (Jonah 3:10) 'And God saw their deeds for they repented from their evil way' (Taanis 156).*

The repentance of the Ninevites became an eternal lesson for Israel. Yet the Sages also teach:

> תְּשׁוּבָה שֶׁל רְמִיוּת עָשׂוּ אַנְשֵׁי נִינְוֵה
>
> *A repentance of deception was carried out by the people of Nineveh (Yerushalmi Taanis 2:1).*

There is no contradiction here. The Ninevites repented with a vigor that saved their city and became a lasting model, but in *absolute* terms — in comparison with the repentance that would be demanded of Israel — it was indeed sorely lacking. Judged by the standards expected of Israel, it was truly deceptive because it was superficial. Skin-deep repentance would do for Nineveh, but not for Israel.

Skin-deep repentance would do for Nineveh, but not for Israel.

Alshich comments that the nations are closer to repentance than Israel because the Evil inclination does not seek to block them as it does Israel. Why should it? Theirs is not the cosmic spiritual mission of Israel. They will never rise to the heights expected of Israel; therefore, the champion of evil feels no need to impede them as he does Israel.

Response to Fear

Meshech Chochmah (to *Pinchas)* notes that there are two levels of behavior: external and internal. One may perfect his actions, return illegal gains and

God takes note of man's repentance. Is it external? Then God responds by removing external danger.

Their repentance did no more than scratch the human surface.

refrain from sin — these are no mean achievements. They are difficult and significant, but they do not necessarily indicate that the person who accomplishes them has purified and sanctified his mind, heart, and soul. God takes note of man's repentance. Is it external? Then God responds by removing external danger and annulling the Divine afflictions that had hovered over him in punishment for his prior evil. Is it internal? Then God responds by providing invisible means of merit. Obstacles will vanish from his path, opportunities will present themselves, holiness will light his way. The Ninevites repented by returning stolen goods that they had in hand (see 3:8); they did the clearly indicated good and refrained from obvious evil. But their repentance did no more than scratch the human surface. God acknowledged it by lifting the threat of destruction, but no more. They were rewarded, but only commensurate with the level of their repentance.

Jonah's prophecy did not contain a call for repentance. His prophecy was an announcement — no more.

Bais Elokim sees in their repentance no more than a response to the threat. They feared for their lives. They were told that an upheaval was only forty days off. They saw doom staring at them. They were informed that their evil had come before God, and they were concerned only that the picture of evil, overt greed, and oppressive violence be banished from God's sight. Their deeds had brought potential disaster; they wished merely to fend off the catastrophe, not sanctify themselves. Indeed, no deeper form of repentance is demanded or expected of heathens. Therefore, Jonah's prophecy did not contain a call for repentance. His prophecy was an announcement — no more — that the evil of Ninevite behavior was leading to the city's destruction. God did not call for *teshuvah* because the essential significance of the word (as it will be explained below) was beyond their heathen capacity.

Only Israel is commanded by the Torah to repent. And, although even minimal repentance is accepted and rewarded, it is hardly enough. The level of attainment expected of Israel is beyond the capacity of a Ninevite. The demands upon Israel are greater and therefore more difficult to achieve. Nineveh could reach the limit of its spiritual capacity and make Israel seem to be a laggard by comparison. The point could justly be raised: if Nineveh can climb hills, why can Israel not scale mountains? Truly, more *should* be expected of the children of Abraham, Isaac, and Jacob, the echoes of Moses and Samuel, the strings of David's harp. Perhaps Israel, too, could climb hills, but its sensitive spiritual antennae would recognize the inadequacy of that *teshuvah* and scorn it as the long-distance runner disdains the pedestrian's breathless dash across the street.

The point could justly be raised: if Nineveh can climb hills, why can Israel not scale mountains?

IV. By the Hand of Heaven

In Defense of Israel

WAS JONAH liable to the heavenly death penalty of the prophet who suppresses his prophecy? Clearly his offense was of that magnitude as the *Talmud* states unequivocally in *Sanhedrin* 89a (see *commentary* to 1:4). It may be that Jonah's violation was unintentional and, therefore, not punishable; it may be that he was indeed punished in ways not revealed to us; his ordeal at sea, in the whale and in the aftermath of Nineveh's repentance may have sufficed; or the fact that he was denied further prophecy (*Yevamos* 98a); or it may be that the heavenly scales weighed so many deeds which are unknown to us and whose significance only God can know, that Jonah's sin was obscured by other considerations (see *Rambam, Hilchos Teshuvah* 7:1).

In God's estimation love for and loyalty to Israel weigh heavily, indeed.

Perhaps we may venture another thought. In God's estimation love for and loyalty to Israel weigh heavily, indeed. When an angel was sent to Gideon to tell him that he had been selected as God's agent to lead Israel to victory over Midian, Gideon replied vehemently:

> *If HASHEM is with us, why has all this befallen us? And where are all the wonders of which our ancestors told us, saying: 'Has HASHEM not raised us up from Egypt?' And now HASHEM has forsaken and placed us in the hand of Midian! (Judges 6:13).*

Gideon's strength *was his angry response in defense of Israel.*

In response to these stern words to the *angel,* HASHEM Himself appeared to Gideon telling him '*Go with this strength of yours and save Israel!*' Which strength? *Rashi* quotes *Tanchuma* that Gideon's *strength* was his angry response in defense of Israel. Such was his love for Israel that he mounted a virtual attack on God for having abandoned Israel. But because his motive was love of his people, God rewarded him not only by giving him the privilege of saving the nation, but by replacing the angel and Himself speaking to Gideon.

The Book of Jonah *is filled with lessons that, if they fall short of the ultimate demand upon Israel, can at least begin it along its way.*

The story of Jonah and Nineveh has been ordained by the Sages as an essential part of the teaching of *teshuvah* and it has been incorporated into the *Yom Kippur* liturgy as the sun settles toward the horizon and the final prayers of the day are readied to penetrate the gates of heaven. The Book of *Jonah* is filled with lessons that, if they fall short of the ultimate demand upon Israel, can at least begin it along its way:

— God's Providence extends to all the earth; no one is immune from His Providence or removed from His mercy.

— No one can run away from God. When it is His wish, a ship's crew, a storm, a fish, even a leaf or a worm, can retrieve or bring about the return of whomever He wants from wherever he flees.

— Repentance is never too late. The decree had been given, but the Ninevites were able to save themselves.

— God's mercy knows no bounds.

— True repentance lies in honest deeds and consideration for others, not in a facade of insincere piety.

Let us turn now to an examination of *Teshuvah* in the hope that through a better understanding we may approach closer to the goal set forth for us.

◆§Repentance

I. God's Own Gift

The Precondition

'Turn over a new leaf.' 'Let bygones be bygones.' These are familiar sayings that reflect a common, but faulty, perception of sin and repentance.

'TURN OVER a new leaf.' 'Let bygones be bygones.' These are familiar sayings that reflect a common, but faulty, perception of sin and repentance. Past misdeeds may present problems to be overcome, but only the future is crucial. The function of remorse is to prepare the way for future improvement, for, obviously, no one 'can turn over a new leaf' in his personal story unless he is ready to cover up the old leaves. The past put out of mind, however, one can embark confidently on a new future. In this view, repentance from sin is far simpler to negotiate than a reversal of business fortunes. The entrepreneur saddled with debt or malfunctioning machinery might wish he could avoid bankruptcy by simply turning to new ledger sheets, confident that his customers, suppliers, and debtors would be as willing as he to let bygones be bygones. Repentance, however, might seem to consist simply of making the current resolution more enduring than the many that doubtless preceded it.

Repentance is a concept that had no credence in any system save God's.

The perception is pleasant, but inaccurate. Repentance is a concept that had no credence in any system save God's. It was rejected on the basis of Wisdom, Prophecy, and Torah — but God decreed that it have an honored place in his scheme of creation.

שִׁבְעָה דְבָרִים נִבְרְאוּ קוֹדֶם שֶׁנִּבְרָא הָעוֹלָם אֵלוּ הֵן תּוֹרָה, וּתְשׁוּבָה . . .

Seven things were created before the universe. They are: Torah, repentance... (Nedarim 39b).

Ran (ibid.) explains that they had to be created even before the universe because, without them, creation could not endure.

There is a further implication in this dictum. Repentance defies the rules of creation. According to the conditions under which the world came into being, remorse and rededication would not be sufficient to remove the spiritual blight that should inevitably bring suffering, even death, upon the transgressor. But imperfect man could not conceivably survive under a regimen that held out no hope of spiritual rehabilitation. So repentance had to be a precondition of creation — without it creation could not endure; therefore God did not begin His labor until the possibility of repentance was as firmly ingrained into the universe as the laws of physics.

Imperfect man could not conceivably survive under a regimen that held out no hope of spiritual rehabilitation.

Timelessness

Indeed, God's willingness to accept the penitent is a function of His Four-Letter Name, the Name that designates His merciful attribute. The Thirteen Attributes of Mercy begin with ה׳,ה׳, the repetition of God's Four-Letter Name. The Sages comment

ה׳ ה׳ אֲנִי הוּא קוֹדֶם שֶׁיֶּחֱטָא הָאָדָם וַאֲנִי הוּא לְאַחַר שֶׁיֶּחֱטָא הָאָדָם וְיַעֲשֶׂה תְשׁוּבָה.

HASHEM, HASHEM *(Exodus* 34:6) — *I am He* [*i.e., the God of Mercy*] *before a person sins, and I am He after a person sins and repents (Rosh Hashanah* 17b).

It is only God's mercy which makes it possible for the sinner to repent and gain renewed acceptance. All God's other Attributes of Mercy are possible only because He is prepared to accept the penitent and return him to his pristine state.

That this possibility is expressed by God's Four-Letter Name helps clarify why repentance is a concept that would be beyond the realm of possibility without God's Own intervention. That name is composed of the words הָיָה הֹוֶה וְיִהְיֶה, *He was, He is, and He will be.* It expresses God's timelessness, His eternity. For, indeed, time itself is part of creation; it is no less part of the physical creation than are forests and oceans. In the spiritual realm, there is no distinction between past, present, and future. We can place

In the spiritual realm, there is no distinction between past, present, and future.

no age on God; He is without beginning and without end. Of course, such a concept is inconceivable to the mortal mind. Whatever we see, one of our first questions is, 'How old is it?' Timelessness is a concept foreign to our existence; from the moment something comes into being, it moves continuously closer to its death and disintegration. We *know* that God is eternal because it is one of the principles of Jewish belief that He is but we cannot *understand* how such a thing can be.

We know that כִּי לֹא מַחְשְׁבוֹתַי מַחְשְׁבוֹתֵיכֶם וְלֹא דַרְכֵיכֶם דְּרָכָי נְאֻם ה׳, *For My thoughts are not your thoughts, and your ways are not My ways, the words of HASHEM (Isaiah* 55:8) — because the very essence of His Being is different in *kind* from that of the finite world of which we are part. Flesh and blood, muscle and sinew, gold and silver, flour and water — all these are the earthly forms with which we can perform the commandments and thereby create spiritual resources, but those spiritual results transcend the physical matter which was used to create them; spiritual riches simply cannot be reduced to physical components. A few vials of paint, some brushes, and a canvas in the hands of a painter may be transformed into a masterpiece. Wood, sinew, brass, and hide can be made into the instruments of orchestra. A pen, a bottle of ink, and a ream of paper can be turned into a literary classic. But is there a fool who would measure the value of a masterpiece in cubic centimeters of paint; of a priceless violin in grams of wood and animal gut; of a classic book in square inches of paper and droplets of ink? If this is true regarding the products of man, surely it is even more true concerning the spiritual values of God's Torah and its commandments.

A few vials of paint, some brushes, and a canvas in the hands of a painter may be transformed into a masterpiece. But is there a fool who would measure the value of a masterpiece in cubic centimeters of paint?

Time, too, is one of the tools with which we create spiritual accomplishment, but it is no more a spiritual essence than is money. A good deed is timeless; so is a bad deed. Yesterday's spiritual growth still exists today; yesterday's spiritual blemish continues to blight the soul of the sinner who brought it into ex-

A good deed is timeless; so is a bad deed. Yesterday's spiritual blemish continues to blight the soul.

istence. The penitent, therefore, does not become a saint simply because he resolves to sin no more, for the sins of last year are still with him. They are no less a part of him than they were the day he committed them. Memories can grow dim, limbs can wither — but these are symptoms of physical frailty. It takes more to heal ravages to the spirit. How, therefore, can repentance help?

Wisdom's answer

They asked Wisdom what is the sinner's punishment? It told them: 'Sinners — let them be pursued by [*their*] *evil' (Proverbs* 13:21).

The truly ultimate wages of sin are not inflicted externally. To sin against God is unlike a violation of human law. The lawbreaker's activity is deemed illegal because it is in violation of the judgment of his fellow human beings. He is apprehended by an officer of the law, tried before a court, judged by a jury of his peers, sentenced by a judge, punished by a penal system. The entire procedure is, of course, the *result* of his misdeed, but it is far removed from the deed itself. One cannot say that his crime put him in prison; rather the crime set off a chain of events resulting in a progression of human actions that ended with the incarceration. A sin is different. The word for sin, חֵטְא literally means a *lack*, a *diminution.* The act of sin *in itself* diminishes the sinner. It makes him a lesser human being. It engenders within him an indifference to evil, a tolerance for evil, an appetite for evil — and, eventually, a distaste for good.

The act of sin in itself diminishes the sinner. It makes him a lesser human being.

כֵּיוָן שֶׁעָבַר אָדָם עֲבֵירָה וְשָׁנָה בָּה נַעֲשֵׂית לוֹ כְּהֶתֵּר

If someone commits a transgression and repeats it, it becomes to him like a permitted act. [*Moed Katan* 27a]

Every human being has his own list of things he would never do; in his scale of values, they are so wrong as to be unthinkable. Let him violate his standard of conduct once, and he will be disappointed

Every human being has his own list of things he would never do; in his scale of values, they are so wrong as to be unthinkable.

with, or angry at himself; he will resolve firmly never to be so weak again. Let him sin a second time, and another human reaction is engaged — the defense mechanism. If he has done it twice, then it cannot be *so* evil. Plainly the deed is thinkable, doable, permissible.

Rabbi Israel Salanter added a profound insight into man's character: 'What if someone commits the same sin a *third* time? Then נַעֲשֵׂית לוֹ כְּמִצְוָה, it becomes like a *commandment* for him!'

Forced by his need to justify himself, man changes his values to include what he cannot restrain himself from doing. The diabetic with an uncontrollable appetite for sweets will rationalize that a life devoid of enjoyment is no life — and he will proceed to eat himself into the grave. The once-honest businessman who consistently gave in to temptation will convince himself that commerce is a jungle where all who enter accept the possibility that they will be defrauded. One who abuses his credentials as a servant of Torah bases his derelictions on the lofty goals they are intended to further. The sinner changes. His actions besmirch him. His spiritual essence becomes ravaged and diminished. Whether or not his deeds are punishable by a court, whether are not he is apprehended and brought to justice, his sins inflict their own punishment for they become a cancer eating away at their perpetrator until his inner purity is replaced by spiritual rot. The corrupted soul is incapable of spiritual delight just as the cancerous lung cannot inhale invigorating air. The pleasures of the World to Come do not entice the sinner for he has grown incapable of appreciating them. The tortures of Gehinnom are nothing but the natural consequence of his sin.

The corrupted soul is incapable of spiritual delight just as the cancerous lung cannot inhale invigorating air.

Can a one-legged man be a long-distance runner? — Can a spiritual cripple scale heights once more? Wisdom answers, 'No!'

Thus, Wisdom proclaims that the sinner has no salvation, for his evil has become part of him. It is his own evil that pursues him, not some external foe who seeks his destruction. His own חֲטָאִים, spiritual *diminution*, makes redemption impossible for him: can a one-legged man be a long-distance runner? —

can a spiritual cripple scale heights once more? Wisdom answers, 'No!'

Prophecy's Judgment

They asked Prophecy, 'What is a sinner's punishment?' It told them: 'The soul that sins — it shall die!' (Ezekiel 18:20).

Because he perceives the greatness of God with more clarity than even the wisest man, the prophet represents harsh judgment.

Because he perceives the greatness of God with more clarity than even the wisest man, the prophet represents harsh judgment. He recognizes that life and faculties are gifts that are meant to be used in the service of the King. If a child is given a hammer and nails to hang bookshelves, and instead uses them to punch holes in window panes, the hammer and nails will be taken away. Can the child win his point by insisting that he will break only a few small windows but scrupulously refrain from smashing expensive crystal? Surely not. He can no longer be entrusted with the tools that he misuses. Why, then, should the sinner be permitted to hold on to life and use it to flout the will of its Giver. Prophecy is outraged by the suggestion that the sinner can escape with only a slap on the wrist or a promise for the future. For sin is as timeless as spirituality—there is no yesterday, no tomorrow; the sin has been done and it burrows its way into the very soul of the sinner. Of one whose transgression is so grievous that his *soul* is cut off from the source of holiness, כָּרֵת, the Torah says, עֲוֹנָהּ בָּהּ, *its [the soul's] sin is 'in it.'* The impunity becomes *part* of him and it cannot be shed like yesterday's soiled suit of clothes. Prophecy answers, therefore, that there is no 'punishment' for the sinner in the sense that he can be freed of the corrosive effects of his deeds. He must die.

Prophecy answers, therefore,that there is no 'punishment' for the sinner. He must die.

Torah Recreates

They asked Torah what is the sinner's punishment. It told them: 'Let him bring a guilt-offering and gain atonement.'

Torah represents a different insight, a higher one than either Wisdom or Prophecy. The world was created in accordance with Torah — הקב״ה הָיָה מַבִּיט בַּתּוֹרָה וּבוֹרֵא אֶת הָעוֹלָם, *God looked into the*

Torah and created the universe (Bereishis Rabbah 1:2, see *Overview* to ArtScroll *Genesis I).* Torah preexisted the world and the universe was created to be the physical means by which the commandments could be realized and performed. As the plan from which a total vacuum was transformed into a vast universe, Torah contains the formula for lifting a sinner from his impurity and returning him again to his earlier state because it was the plan from which he was created. By sinning, the transgressor brought his spiritual nature down to the level of its physical cloak, his intellectual potential to his animal nature. But Torah cannot be contaminated; it remains spiritually and intellectually pure. Thus it retains the capacity to raise the sinner up from the morass. [As we shall see below, this mixture of the spiritual and the physical is an innate challenge of human existence, and *Yom Kippur* is unique in its capacity to separate them.]

Torah contains the formula for lifting a sinner from his impurity and returning him again to his earlier state because it was the plan from which he was created.

The means ordained by Torah to attain this end are the קָרְבָּנוֹת אָשָׁם, *guilt-offerings.* The קָרְבָּן is a divinely ordained means to become closer to God [קָרְבָּן is derived from קרב=close]. It is the culmination of repentance, because a person who offers a *korban*, is considered as if he offered himself to God, as if he negates his own being entirely to the will of his Maker. [A full discussion of offerings will be presented in the *Overview* to *Vayikra.*] That done, he can achieve total closeness once again despite the effects of his sin. But this means is not perfect, because the Torah ordains guilt-offerings for only a limited number of sins. What of the many sins for which there are no guilt-offerings? And what of the sinner in time of no Temples and no offerings?

The קָרְבָּן is a divinely ordained means to become closer to God.

The Highest Response

They asked the Holy One, Blessed be He, 'What is the sinner's punishment?' He told them, 'Let him repent and be forgiven', as it is written, טוֹב וְיָשָׁר ה׳ עַל כֵּן יוֹרֶה חַטָּאִים בַּדָּרֶךְ, *Good and upright is HASHEM, therefore, he guides sinners on the way (Psalms 25:8).*

Wisdom is right — evil does diminish and destroy. Prophecy is right — the sinner does forfeit his right to life. Torah is right — only offerings can bring the sinner back to his earlier state of purity. By all the principles of creation, there should be no way to remove the effects of all sins.

But there *is* a way. It had to pre-exist creation; otherwise the principles of creation could allow it no existence. So תְּשׁוּבָה, *Repentance,* came *before* creation. It is God's own device, his gift to man — perhaps the greatest of all gifts, for without it there would be no possibility for man to regain his footing after he stumbles. And the very fact of his humanity condemns him to stumble, for there is no man who does not fall short of the ideal. Nevertheless, the sinner can return and be cleansed of all taint. 'Let the sinner repent and be forgiven,' God tells us.

It is God's own device, his gift to man — perhaps the greatest of all gifts, for without it there would be no possibility for man to regain his footing after he stumbles.

Unassisted, repentance would not be sufficient to wipe away the past, that is the testimony of Wisdom, Prophecy, and Torah. Often a sinner looks at his past and despairs of ever cleaning it. Were he to be left to his own devices, he would be right. But he is not alone, because God assures him that his attempts at sincere repentance will not be futile.

He is not alone, because God assures him that his attempts at sincere repentance will not be futile.

שׁוּבוּ אֵלַי וְאָשׁוּבָה אֲלֵיכֶם אָמַר ה׳

Return to Me and I shall return to you, says HASHEM (Malachi 3:7).

True, God asks that we return to Him through repentance, but He says more: *I shall return to you.* God Himself returns to us; He meets us. He consummates our repentance. For man alone cannot affect a complete atonement. His sins would remain with him were it not for God's mercy. Even if he were strong enough to face temptation again yet not succumb, the sin he had once tasted left a stain, however slight, on his inborn purity. Had he never sinned, he might feel no temptation for the sin would have been foreign not only to his desire but to his experience.

Innocence once lost can never be totally regained — except for God's assurance that He meets the penitent, greets him, and implants within him a *new heart and a new spirit (Ezekiel* 36:26).*

*The above exposition of the *Midrash* is based primarily on *Maharal, Nesiv HaTeshuvah* and also on *Michtav MeEliyahu II.*

II. God's Eternal Presence

Always Within Me

THIS KNOWLEDGE that God is always with him and ready to help guide him back is a bulwark of the Jew's faith. In one of God's last prophecies to Moses, He foretold that Israel would slide downward after Moses' death and incur God's wrath. Oppression and suffering would befall the nation and Israel would react by saying:

הֲלֹא עַל כִּי אֵין אֱלֹהַי בְּקִרְבִּי מְצָאוּנִי הָרָעוֹת הָאֵלֶּה.

Is it not because my God is not within me that all these evils have found me? (Deuteronomy 31:17).

At the depths of its travail, Israel would find the reason for its suffering in the lack of God's presence. *Reb Simcha Bunam of P'shis'cha* taught that this statement — ostensibly the first stirring of repentance — is in itself a grievous sin. The Jew must remember that God is always within him; to the extent that Israel realizes this and allows the knowledge to exalt its everyday affairs, it need never fear. Indeed, the holiness of God resting upon Israel is its defense, for, when its enemies see that the *Name of HASHEM* is upon Israel, they fear it (see *Deuteronomy* 28:10). Let Israel know that His Presence rests upon it and let it conduct its affairs accordingly, and opposition evaporates because the physical war is but a reflection of the spiritual one.

The Jew must remember that God is always within him; to the extent that Israel realizes this and allows the knowledge to exalt its everyday affairs, it need never fear.

God's Tefillin

That *Name of HASHEM* which Israel's enemies perceive upon it, our Sages expound, is תְּפִלִּין שֶׁל רֹאשׁ, *tefillin of the head (Berachos* 6a). The Sages teach

What chapters of the Torah are contained in His Tefillin *the* Talmud *inquires?*

that Hashem, too, wears *tefillin,* as it were. 'What chapters of the Torah are contained in His *Tefillin?*' the *Talmud* inquires?

Who is like Your people Israel! — a unique nation on earth.

Rav Chiya bar Avin replies that God's *tefillin* contains the verse וּמִי כְּעַמְּךָ יִשְׂרָאֵל גּוֹי אֶחָד בָּאָרֶץ, *Who is like Your people Israel! — a unique nation on earth (I Chronicles* 17:21). The Sages go on to list a series of other verses that He inserts into His *tefillin;* all of them lauding the uniqueness, the greatness of Israel. Indeed, the Sages cite the parallel between our *tefillin* and His

> אָמַר לָהֶם הקב״ה לְיִשְׂרָאֵל אַתֶּם עֲשִׂיתוּנִי חֲטִיבָה אַחַת בָּעוֹלָם שֶׁנֶּאֱמַר שְׁמַע יִשְׂרָאֵל ה׳ אֱלֹהֵינוּ ה׳ אֶחָד וַאֲנִי אֶעֱשֶׂה אֶתְכֶם חֲטִיבָה אַחַת בָּעוֹלָם שֶׁנֶּאֱמַר וּמִי כְּעַמְּךָ יִשְׂרָאֵל גּוֹי אֶחָד בָּאָרֶץ *The Holy One, Blessed be He, said to Israel, 'You made Me a unique entity in the universe as it says, Hear Israel, HASHEM, our God, HASHEM is one (Deuteronomy* 6:4); *and I make you a unique entity in the universe as it says, Who is like Your people Israel, a unique nation on earth' (Berachos* 6a).

Tefillin *represent the inseparable nature of God and Israel through the agency of the Torah.*

As the commentators explain, *tefillin* represent the inseparable nature of God and Israel through the agency of the Torah. יִשְׂרָאֵל וְאוֹרַיְתָא וְקוּדְשָׁא בְּרִיךְ הוּא חַד הוּא, *Israel, the Torah, and the Holy One, Blessed be He, are one (Zohar).* By binding upon himself the *tefillin* which contain declarations of God's Oneness and Israel's dedication to His commandments, the Jew declares his own allegiance to God, and he proclaims that God is unique — all-knowing, all-powerful, all-merciful. In response, God, too, dons *tefillin,* as it were — not physical *tefillin,* of course, because He is incorporeal — by showing His own allegiance to His chosen people: *Who is like Your nation Israel...?!* The two go hand in hand: to the extent that Israel exalts God, He exalts Israel. When Israel's pride, bearing, and intellect reflect openly-expressed dedication to the message of תְּפִלִּין שֶׁל רֹאשׁ, *tefillin of the head* — that God is One

To the extent that Israel exalts God, He exalts Israel.

and that Israel's destiny is inextricably bound up with that conviction, then the nations stand in awe of Israel because God rests His majesty upon the nation. It may be the tiniest and most defenseless on earth, nevertheless it is all-conquering, because it is the scepter that symbolizes the King's Own presence.

Let the situation change, however; let Israel despairingly declare that אֵין אֱלֹהַי בְּקִרְבִּי, *God is not within me (Deuternomy* 31:17, see above), and it will find itself beset by woe and oppression, for by denying God's loving presence within itself, it sheds the armor that makes it impregnable to all onslaughts *(Sfas Emes).*

The fact of God's constancy is at the root of repentance. God stands ready to assist him — 'return to Me and I shall return to you.'

The fact of God's constancy is at the root of repentance. Simultaneously it shames the Jew into recognizing the baseness of his ways, while also reassuring him that God stands ready to receive him should he but take the first step back. It is abundantly true that the goal demanded of man is beyond his capacity to achieve *alone,* however he need only begin. God stands ready to assist him — *'return to Me and I shall return to you.'*

The Heavenly Magnet

This is the concept of סַיַּיעְתָּא דִשְׁמַיָּא, *Heavenly assistance,* which helps man surpass himself in the attainment of spiritual goals.

Rabbi Simcha Zisel Ziev of Kelm illustrated this idea with a parable:

Once there was a king who promised great rewards to anyone who could scale an enormous ladder of a hundred widely spaced rungs. People heard of the reward and rushed to come and claim it, but when they saw the ladder, they left without even attempting the climb. Clearly the task was impossible of achievement; the king must have been mocking his loyal subjects. One by one the candidates drifted away until only one remained. Did he think he could do it? No — but he was driven by a stubborn thought. The king was neither fool nor sadist. If he offered the challenge then it must be possible to climb that ladder. And if the king were convinced

The king was neither fool nor sadist. If he offered the challenge then it must be possible to climb that ladder.

that it could be done, then this one remaining person would make the attempt.

The others laughed at him, reviled him, taunted him. What a fool he was to attempt the impossible! He was doomed to climb a few rungs and then fall off, exhausted and humiliated. He began to climb. Five rungs. Six rungs. his strength was giving out. Seven rungs. His legs were like rubber. Eight rungs. His lungs were bursting. Nine rungs. Total exhaustion. He was ninety-one rungs short of success, but he could go on no longer. About to fall, he thought again of the king's challenge. It *must* be possible or the king would not have asked it! He summoned up all his strength and determination and struggled up one more rung. Then, just as he was about to collapse, he felt himself lifted, as if by a huge magnet, and placed atop the ladder. He had succeeded because, without knowing how it could be done, he had had faith in the king.

It must be possible or the king would not have asked it! Then, just as he was about to collapse, he felt himself lifted, as if by a huge magnet and placed atop the ladder.

Indeed, the royal wish was not that all hundred rungs be climbed, for that was impossible. What the king wanted was that the people make this attempt and dedicate themselves totally to reach the limit of their ability — more was not required; the king would do the rest.

God wants us to scale heights that no human can imagine; but He does not expect us to do it alone.

So it is in our spiritual quest. God wants us to scale heights that no human can imagine; but He does not expect us to do it alone. He asks only that we make the effort — a sincere, diligent, uncompromising effort. By making the attempt we earn His help—the help which makes success possible (as heard from *Harav Mordechai Gifter).*

Let Wisdom see blemish. Let Prophecy see destruction. Let Torah see partial atonement through offerings. God sees repentance. He sees His children approaching Him and He goes out to meet them. He supports their efforts and eases them:

פִּתְחוּ לִי פֶּתַח אֶחָד שֶׁל תְּשׁוּבָה כְּחוּדָּהּ שֶׁל מַחַט וַאֲנִי פּוֹתֵחַ לָכֶם פְּתָחִים שֶׁיִּהְיוּ עֲגָלוֹת וּקְרוֹנוֹת נִכְנָסוֹת.

Make Me a single opening of repentance

like the point of a needle. Then I will provide you with entrances that wagons and carriages can enter (Shir HaShirim Rabbah 5:3).

To which *Rabbi Mendel of Kotzk* commented that the opening of repentance need be only as tiny as the point of a needle, but it must be all the way through. The intention to attain greatness must be sincere. Then the ultimate achievement, thanks to God's help, is infinitely greater than any human effort could make possible.

III. Elements of Repentance

Judgment Agrees

REPENTANCE has been defined simply as

קְרִיבָה לַה׳ מֵרִיחוּק הַחֵטְא

An approach to HASHEM from the distance of sin (Bais Elokim, Shaar HaTeshuvah 2:1).

By sinning, a person perpetrates a two-fold evil: he causes himself harm through a deed that will result in his punishment and suffering, and he angers the Creator by ignoring His will. Of the two, the latter is the more grievous outcome. Even if there were a reason for God to withhold His punishment, and decide in His mercy not to punish the sinner at all, his deed and the arrogance underlying it have built a barrier between God and himself. The distance matters more than the retribution, for man's purpose in life is surely higher than a mere avoidance of pain. A disease-ridden patient is only minimally served if, instead of being treated for the illness, he is drugged liberally enough to kill the pain. Similarly, man's goal in life must be closeness to God and elevation toward holiness — not avoidance of the wages of transgressions.

Man's goal in life must be closeness to God and elevation toward holiness — not avoidance of the wages of transgressions.

This is not to say that the sinner should not fear the inevitable punishment — indeed, such fear can be the prelude to repentance just as physical pain is often the stimulant to a patient's quest for a cure. Without the experience or the anticipation of suffering, many a patient and many a sinner would have remained on the sidelines of physical and spiritual well-being. But just as the antibiotic is more *vital* than the aspirin, so the retracing of the steps away from God is more important than the avoidance of Divine anger. The ultimate goal of the sinner must be to regain the spiritual intimacy that was his before he made himself distant from God by flouting His will.

Just as the antibiotic is more vital *than the aspirin, so the retracing of the steps away from God is more important than the avoidance of Divine anger.*

In the above definition of repentance, the Name, HASHEM was chosen carefully. It is to HASHEM, God in His aspect of Mercy, that the sinner must draw close. For, as we have seen above, the efficacy of repentance is one of the truly great manifestations of God's mercy. Wisdom and Prophecy could not countenance it, Torah gave it limited sway, but God awaits the sinner's return. Indeed, according to Rabbi Meir, repentance had to precede creation *(Nedarim* 36b); according to *Pirkei d'Rabbi Eliezer (ch.* 43) it was a condition imposed during the six days of creation. In either case, repentance was a concept that underlay the existence of the universe for without it, creation could not endure.

Wisdom and prophecy could not countenance it. Torah gave it limited sway, but God awaits the sinner's return.

Nevertheless, the very fact that the concept of repentance was coupled with the beginning of creation proves that it has deeper overtones than simply undeserved mercy. Creation was accomplished with the Name Elohim, the Name that bespeaks Judgment. God's original intention was that man be judged fairly, but strictly, on the basis of his deeds. Only afterwards, in recognition of human frailty, did God add mercy to His guidance of the world, for man could not long prevail if he were to be so strictly held to account (see ArtScroll *Genesis* 2: 4). It follows that if repentance was there at the first stirrings of creation, then it was part of the *Elohim*-Judgment aspect of God's plan. Even then, the conditions giving sinful man the possibility of return to God had to exist — *Judgment* decreed that Mercy should make man acceptable even though he has opened only a needle's

It follows that if repentance was there at the first stirrings of creation, then it was part of the Elohim-*Judgment aspect of God's plan.*

hole in the great wall his sins have created. Mercy plucks him from the tenth rung of the ladder up to its zenith. But Judgment sets the ladder in place. Judgment allows the wall to be breached and destroyed. So it is that many of the Scriptural verses calling for repentance combine the Names of *HASHEM* and *Elohim, Mercy* and *Judgment:*

וְשַׁבְתָּ עַד ה׳ אֱלֹהֶיךָ

And you shall return to HASHEM, your God.

כִּי תָשׁוּב אֶל ה׳ אֱלֹהֶיךָ

When you return to HASHEM, your God (Deuteronomy 30:2,10)

שׁוּבָה יִשְׂרָאֵל עַד ה׳ אֱלֹהֶיךָ

Return, O Israel, up to HASHEM your God (Hosea 14:2)

Even Judgment ordains the possibility of repentance because the commands of the Torah are so many and their laws so complex that no one can help but fall short of perfection.

Even Judgment ordains the possibility of repentance because the commands of the Torah are so many and their laws so complex that no one can help but fall short of perfection. In accepting the Torah, Israel undertook an enormous challenge. The nation could no longer content itself with fidelity to the Seven Noachide Laws, with observing minimal standards of conduct. It had to be ready to scale the heavens, to ask of itself מָתַי יַגִּיעוּ מַעֲשַׂי לְמַעֲשֵׂי אַבְרָהָם יִצְחָק וְיַעֲקֹב, *When will my deeds approach those of Abraham, Isaac and Jacob?* Impossible demands? Perhaps, but nothing less would do. In pursuit of such goals a Jew could stumble, but even the strictest application of judgment required that he be given the opportunity to lift himself from the ground, brush off the mud, and continue on his lofty path *(Bais Elokim, ibid.,* 1,2. See also *ibid.* 13,14).

The Two Essentials

Rabbeinu Yonah lists twenty components of repentance, but of them, two are absolute essentials:

חֲרָטָה עַל הֶעָבַר וַעֲזִיבַת הַחֵטְא

Remorse over the past and giving up the sin [for the future] (Shaarei Teshuvah; see also Bais Elokim, Shaar HaTeshuvah 2:2).

The other eighteen factors intensify and elevate the repentance, but these are two which constitute it.

Sin consists of two factors: thought and deed. The sinner contemplates his transgression, then he commits it. By חֲרָטָה עַל הֶעָבָר, *remorse over the past*, he negates his past thoughts. Those plans are no longer his. He regrets them. He rejects them. He wishes he had never had them. They were foolish. Wrong. They no longer represent the kind of person he strives to be, the kind of person he is.

By חֲרָטָה עַל הֶעָבָר, remorse over the past, *he negates his past thoughts. Those plans are no longer his.*

By עֲזִיבַת הַחֵטְא, *giving up the sin*, he demonstrates the reality of his resolution. The opportunity to sin again returns. The conditions and temptations are there, but the penitent forswears them. By not committing the act he proves the validity of his resolution. Thus, he has purged both his thoughts and his deeds; the old desire is gone, the old act is not repeated.

By עֲזִיבַת הַחֵטְא, giving up the sin, *he demonstrates the reality of his resolution.*

The paths to repentance, however, vary from person to person. The non-habitual sinner, the person who has committed a particular sin once or twice because he let his passions run away with him, should begin with חֲרָטָה, *remorse*. Because he is not a habitual sinner, the crucial factor for him is not to devise means to avoid repetition of the deed. He does recognize the evil of his deed, but not enough. He must deepen his perception of the wrongness of his sin, then the avoidance of the sin in the future will flow naturally from that awareness.

The non-habitual sinner should begin with חֲרָטָה, remorse.

But for the habitual sinner, especially one whose misdeeds involve the satisfaction of lusts and appetites, mere remorse will avail little, because his passion will not allow him to forgo the sin the next time around. The glutton will not be helped by remorse if he is unable to resist the sort of food he is trying to avoid. This sort of sinner must first devise ways of עֲזִיבַת הַחֵטְא, *avoidance of sin*. Let him devise a personal system of reward and punishment, seek methods of behavior modification, avoid the place, the friend, the situation that arouse the desire he

But for the habitual sinner, especially one whose misdeeds involve the satisfaction of lusts and appetites, mere remorse will avail little.

seeks to suppress and eradicate. Only after conquering the tendency to sin can he begin to sensitize his attitudes to the level where he can begin to feel remorse *(Shaarei Teshuvah).*

Each individual penitent will have his own set of spiritual problems and his own set of responses.

Each individual penitent will have his own set of spiritual problems and his own set of responses. But every human being has the responsibility to examine his deeds, weed out the base ones, elevate the best ones, come to grips with the commandment to repent — for, like the commandments to observe the Sabbath and to refrain from eating non-kosher food, the precept of repentance is universal and applicable to everyone.*

Never Ending Repentance

In explaining the formulation of *Shmoneh Esrai,* the Sages base the order of the first three middle blessings (the section of weekday prayer that contains requests for the granting of needs) on the verse *(Isaiah* 6:10):

וּלְבָבוֹ יָבִין וָשָׁב וְרָפָא לוֹ

His heart shall understand and repent and it shall be healed for him.

Thus, the first request in the *Shmoneh Esrai* is for דַּעַת, *wisdom,* and בִּינָה, *understanding;* the next is that God return us to the path of His Torah and His service; the third is for forgiveness, spiritual healing. The order of the blessings and an examination of their content provide an insight into man's obligations as well as into the meaning of repentance. (The following is based upon *Iyunim BiTefillah* by *Harav Moshe Eisemann).*

The order of the blessings and an examination of their content provide an insight into man's obligations as well as into the meaning of repentance.

Man's first plea is for wisdom because wisdom is the very essence of his humanity and his mission on earth. Without his intelligence, man is but a two-legged animal, for it is man's intelligence, his

*In addition to remorse and avoidance of future sin, a prime requisite of *every* repentance is וידוי, *confession.* In fact, confession is the only aspect of repentance which is *specifically* ordained by the Torah. (see *Rambam, Hilchos Teshuvah).* However, the commentators agree that confession falls under the category of remorse, for the person who genuinely regrets what he has done will confess his misdeeds to God and beg his forgiveness.

imagination and his gift of intelligent speech which constitute the צֶלֶם אֱלֹהִים, *image of God,* in which he was created. As the Sages say of wisdom:

> דְדָא בֵּיה כּוּלֵּי בֵּיה דְדָא לֹא בֵּיה מַה בֵּיה?... דְדָא
> קָנִיתָ מַה חָסַרְתָּ דְדָא חָסַרְתָּ מַה קָנִיתָ?
> *If someone has this [wisdom] he has everything, if one lacks this, what has he? ... If you acquire this, what do you lack, and if you lack this, what have you acquired? (Nedarim 41a).*

The difference between Moses and Pharoah or between the Chofetz Chaim and Hitler are obvious. But how does one recognize the subtle differences between the holy and the almost-holy.

The wisdom requested in the first request-blessing of *Shemoneh Esrai* is particularly the kind that enables one to differentiate between the spiritual and the profane. The differences are not at all easily perceived. Everyone on his own individual level can distinguish between the extremes: the difference between Moses and Pharoah or between the Chofetz Chaim and Hitler are obvious. But how does one recognize the subtle differences between the holy and the almost-holy, the sort of choices a Jew is called upon to make constantly as part of his trek to his spiritual goal? For the fall of *decent* people is paved by failure to make subtle distinctions, by entrapment in gray areas where definitions are blurred; it is all too simple to choose the wrong alternative when one is convinced that he marches with angels.

The uniqueness of the soil is its potential to produce growth and plant life. No other creature formed from the earth has this potential as does man.

This ability to think and differentiate is the secret of man's potential for growth and greatness. Therefore, explains *Maharal,* although all land animals were fashioned from the earth, only man is called אָדָם, *Adam,* derived from *adamah,* earth, because he is uniquely similar to his source. The uniqueness of the soil is its potential to produce growth and plant life. No other creature formed from the earth has this potential as does man. Animals can reproduce their species, but none can match man's potential to create.

Then, having acquired wisdom, understanding, knowledge — the ability to differentiate — man pleads:

הֲשִׁיבֵנוּ אָבִינוּ לְתוֹרָתֶךָ וְקָרְבֵנוּ מַלְכֵּנוּ לַעֲבוֹדָתֶךָ
Return us, our Father, to Your Torah, and bring us near, our King, to Your service.

The most righteous of men recites the same blessing; for him too, there is a need to return.

Of what *return* do we speak, here? Surely the blessing was not composed only for the sinner whose concern is with repentance. The most righteous of men recites the same blessing; for him too, there is a need to return, to repent, to seek God's help in achieving his goal. A clue can be found in the text of הֲבִינֵנוּ, *Make Us Understand,* the concise digest of *Shmoneh Esrai* which the Sages composed for those who find it impossible to recite the full text. In place of the blessing of repentance, the Sages instituted the words:

וּמוֹל אֶת לְבָבֵנוּ לְיִרְאָה אֶת שְׁמֶךָ
Circumcise our heart to fear Your Name.

Ramban (Deuteronomy 30:6) explains the concept of 'Circumcision of the Heart' as the exalted service of God which Israel will attain after the coming of Messiah. *Ramban* says, 'the choice of good [over evil] will be natural, the heart will not desire what is not worthy; it will not desire it at all — that is the circumcision which is referred to here ... Then, man will return to what he was before the sin of Adam...'

Obviously, the aspiration embodied in this blessing goes far beyond the common perception of repentance. We think of sinners when we speak of repentance, but one who prays for assistance in attaining the level of Adam before his sin, of cutting through the overlay that deceives his heart into seeking less than perfection — he is hardly sinful, and impure. But he *does* pray for assistance toward his goal of repentance, because the true meaning of repentance is the return of God-given potential to the service of the One who gave it.

The true meaning of repentance is the return of God-given potential to the service of the One who gave it.

It is instructive that the prayer for repentance refers to God as *'Our Father'* who returns us to Torah. Our loyalty to Torah is an expression of dedication to God not merely as His servants, but as His *children.* By absorbing His values and wisdom as they are expressed in His Torah, we are His children, for it is the gift of Torah that enables us to liken ourselves to God just as a child is the product of his father.

The high aspirations of the previous two blessings give us a new insight into the third blessing as well.

In this light, the next blessing asks for forgiveness. The high aspirations of the previous two blessings give us a new insight into the third blessing as well. In the sense that it washes away the stains of sin and even of shortcoming, forgiveness that is requested in the third blessing is a prerequisite of the repentance that leads to the spiritual state of the dawn of creation and its climax, the state described in the first two blessings.

IV. Repentance — the Ultimate Definition

A New Life

AS WE HAVE seen, there are many gradations in *teshuvah*. What, then, is repentance?

> אָמַר רֵיש לָקִיש גְּדוֹלָה תְּשוּבָה שֶׁזְּדוֹנוֹת נַעֲשׂוֹת לוֹ כִּשְׁגָגוֹת ... אָמַר רֵיש לָקִיש שֶׁזְּדוֹנוֹת נַעֲשׂוֹת לוֹ כִּזָכֻיוֹת ... לֹא קַשְׁיָא, כָּאן מֵאַהֲבָה כָּאן מִיִּרְאָה
> *Reish Lakish said: Repentance is great for [as a result of it] intentional sins become transformed into unintentional sins ... Reish Lakish said: Repentance is great for [as a result of it] intentional sins become transformed into meritorious deeds ... This [apparent contradiction] is not difficult — in the first instance [the repentance comes] from love, in the second instance [it comes] from fear (Yoma 86b).*

While regret for sins of the past is an essential ingredient of repentance, there are varying levels of regret. One may realize that he has made mistakes. He may wish to become part of a righteous group he admires. He may fear the eventual punishment for his sins. He may acquire a sense of awe for the majesty of God Whose will he has not obeyed. These levels of remorse vary widely in their quality. As we have seen above, time neither dulls nor obscures spiritual deficiencies. Yesterday's sins remain today's realities. They can remain blemishes on the soul of the sinner despite a total turnabout in his deeds, they can be weakened, or they can become so elevated that they are reckoned as great and virtuous deeds. All depends on the existence of, and the quality of, the penitent's remorse. All levels of repentance are accepted, but not equally.

Yesterday's sins remain today's realities. They can be weakened, or they can become so elevated that they are reckoned as great and virtuous deeds.

One may, indeed, decide to let bygones be bygones and begin anew. Obviously there must be a measure of regret over the past, otherwise why should the penitent change his manner of living? But the emotional involvement of such a change need not be more than superficial. People change jobs, move to new homes, adopt new schedules, apply themselves to their studies or work — these are everyday occurrences that need not be accompanied by weeping or emotional regret over deficiencies of the past. They betoken no more than a new seriousness of attitude and resolve which is commendable. As repentance, too, it gains a significant degree of divine acceptance, but it cannot erase what was. The commentators refer to it as the repentance of a proselyte:

גֵּר שֶׁנִּתְגַּיֵּר כְּקָטָן שֶׁנּוֹלַד דָּמֵי
A proselyte is like a new-born child (Yevamos 22a).

Even if he has not succeeded in elevating his past, he has broken with it. He has begun a new and highly commendable life, but a blotch remains in the spiritual realm where the past continues to exist. What is this person who parts from his past but does not cleanse it? He is a צַדִּיק גָּמוּר, *a completely righteous person*, for, as the Talmud says in *Kiddushin* 49b, with a momentary impulse to repent, a totally evil man can become totally righteous. Surely a moment's repentance cannot be sufficient to rectify a lifetime of sin, but it *can* be enough to begin a *new* life, unrelated to the old one *(Michtav Me'Eliyahu).*

Repentance out of Awe

There is a higher level of repentance. It is reminiscent of the famous story of Rabbi Saadia Gaon who was asked by his disciples how he, a man of history greatness and piety, could engage in constant repentance. What sins had he committed for which he was repenting?

Rabbi Saadia told them that once, as a traveler, he had spent a day at an inn. The innkeeper, a pious Jew, was unaware that his guest was one of the most distinguished personages of the age, but he treated him courteously as he would any other guest. The next morning, the leading citizens of the town converged on the inn to greet Rabbi Saadia and benefit from his wisdom. When they had departed, the innkeeper approached Rabbi Saadia trembling and in tears, 'Please, Master, forgive me for not serving you properly.'

'But you treated me very well. Why do you apologize?'

'Had I only known yesterday who you were, I would have served you as befits a person of your stature.'

'I treated you as I treat all my guests. Had I only known yesterday who you were, I would have served you as befits a person of your stature!'

That, Rabbi Saadia told his students, illustrates the feelings that a Jew should constantly have. The innkeeper was in no way remiss. However, if he had known a day earlier what he found out a day later, he would have acted differently. In our service of God, we should feel similarly. Every day we should grow in our knowledge of Torah and in our awareness of God's greatness. Surely we realize when we are middle-aged that our service of God when we were teenagers was immature and unsophisticated. If only we had had the wisdom then that we have now, we would have acted differently. The same holds true when we examine our deeds of yesterday. If we have fulfilled our responsibilities properly, today's awareness of God's greatness should be greater than yesterday's. Should we not repent therefore for failing to serve God yesterday as we do today?

If we have fulfilled our responsibilities properly, today's awareness of God's greatness should be greater than yesterday's.

When one *does* serve God this way, his spiritual perceptions grow day by day with heightened recognition of God's grandeur. This is תְּשׁוּבָה מֵיִּרְאָה, *repentance motivated by fear.* At its grossest level, יִרְאָה means simply *fear, dread,* in the face of the suffering that will befall the sinner. He repents because he fears pain just as the driver will obey traffic laws because he fears a summons or a fine. At its most sublime level, יִרְאָה is not at all related to fear of punishment. It is *awe* and *reverence.* The penitent who attains this level of יִרְאָה is awestruck at God's greatness much as a peasant of old trembled in the presence of his king — not because of what the king could do to him, although an absolute monarch can surely work his will — but because he is overawed at the majesty of his ruler.

At its most sublime level, יִרְאָה, is not at all related to fear. It is awe *and* reverence.

Whether out of physical fear or spiritual reverence, this penitent gains a higher level of observance than he had previously known. Looking back at his earlier deficiencies, God recognizes that they were caused by a lack of knowledge. Had the erstwhile sinner been of the same mind then as he is now, he would never have sinned. The transgressor is chagrined at his earlier failures — had he only known!

The transgressor is chagrined at his earlier failures — had he only known!

In this form of repentance עֲוֹנוֹת נַעֲשׂוֹת כִּשְׁגָגוֹת, *intentional sins are transformed into unintentional sins.* A שׁוֹגֵג, *unintentional sin,* is one that is committed out of carelessness or lack of knowledge. The woodsman whose axe caused the death of a passerby did not know the victim was nearby, else he would not have swung his axe. Yesterday's sinner did not have today's perceptions. Otherwise he would have been as observant yesterday as he is today. He has not erased his earlier deeds, but in God's scale they are considered to be unintentional *(Michtav Me'Eliyahu).*

He has not erased his earlier deeds, but in God's scale they are considered to be unintentional.

There is yet a higher form of repentance, one in which even the most grievous sins become transformed into virtues. How is such a thing possible? We can understand forgiveness for sin; we can understand the penitent earning a clean slate, but how can an animal slaughtered before an abomination come to be reckoned as if it were an offering brought on the altar of God?

The answer lies in a deeper understanding of the word תְּשׁוּבָה. We translate it as *repentance,* but that is not a true translation; it is only as an outcome of *teshuvah* that the sinner repents his sin. When people think of *teshuvah,* they may think of remorse, atonement, fasting, affliction, purity, return of the sinner to the service of God. All of these are related to *teshuvah,* but none of them *is teshuvah. Rabbi Tzadok HaCohen* of *Lublin* explained that *teshuvah* means to 'bring back to God' the talent, ability, potential, strength, enthusiasm — in short, all of the human characteristics that properly belonged to God, but instead were used for sin, must be retrieved and presented to God. If someone had taken money from another person, he would make amends by retrieving the money and returning it to his victim. The sinner must do the same. He had expropriated life and strength given him by God; he took them for himself as if he were free to do with them as he pleased. More, by sinning he took God's gifts and used them to defy God.

If someone had taken money from another person, he would make amends by retrieving the money and returning it to his victim. The sinner must do the same.

Now when he realizes his folly he can gain a new recognition of God's greatness. How was he able to sin? Because God gave him the strength to do so! There is no corner of the universe free of His life-giving Providence. Even the lustful libertine, the priest of Molech, the brutal murderer, were enabled to commit their deeds only because God allowed them to. They used *His* life, *His* strength, *His* intelligence, *His* enthusiasm, *His* senses. In recognizing that even the defiant transgressor is playing out a role in God's scheme, the penitent takes all the ingredients that he thought he had stolen from God, and he presents them to God. His *teshuvah* is a return to God of the elements of his defiance of God, and by doing so the erstwhile sinner will have revealed God in every act where in his folly he thought he had displaced Him *(Tzidkas HaTzaddik).*

In recognizing that even the defiant transgressor is playing out a role in God's scheme, the penitent takes all the ingredients that he thought he had stolen from God, and he presents them to God.

The source of this esoteric concept may be found

in the writings of Rabbi Moshe Chaim Luzzatto. He writes that the ultimate purpose of creation is יחוד ה׳, the recognition of *God's total unity.* That, *Ramchal* defines as the recognition that every aspect of creation – even the most bestial evil, the most profane manifestations of apparent injustice, the sanguinity of the wicked and the suffering of the righteous – *even these* do not occur in defiance of God. Instead, everything, even the most incomprehensible and revolting, are somehow part of His master plan.

As the *Chazon Ish* replied to questions about the slaughter of the Six Million: 'We do not yet know the entire picture. It is as if we were to glimpse a passage of the Talmud without having seen *Rashi, Tosafos,* and the other commentaries. Would we have the right to say that the passage is difficult, contradictory, beyond comprehension? All we could say is that we have seen too little to understand, too little even to say that we don't understand as yet. History is no different. When the final chapter is written, we will surely understand everything because God does nothing without a merciful purpose. Now, we don't know. We have not been shown. But we must believe!'

So, too, says *Ramchal,* before the End of Days history will contain unprecedented challenges to faith. That period of spiritual crisis will be the prelude to the Final Redemption. All riddles will be solved and all the world will recognize that the hand of God was everywhere and in everything *(Daas Tevunos).*

Sin Contributes Too

Another insight is offered into the concept that even sins can become virtues for one who repents out of love for God. The penitent motivated by love for God recognizes the enormity of his sin more and more as he meditates upon the monstrosity of what he has done. He soiled the soul that God gave him, abused the life that God gave him, exploited the potential that God gave him — and for what? To defy

God! And now that he repents, who accepts his repentance? God! In the powerful metaphor of *Tomer Devorah*, it is as if God in all His Glory stoops to clean away the excrement of the sinner. How great is the remorse of the penitent! The more he sinned, the greater his remorse. And as he draws closer to God and gains ever greater recognition of God's mercy, his remorse increases. Thus, the repentant sinner negotiates spiritual heights greater than he had ever dreamt possible — all because of the effect on him of his earlier sins. Not only does he push away from himself the sinful life in which he had indulged, he utilizes that very life and the revulsion it causes within him to scale ever higher rungs of spirituality. Thus his sins truly become virtues, for they are the goads that drive him to greatness.

V. On Many Levels

From Near and Far

THUS, REPENTANCE exists on many levels. For the very greatest of penitents, it transforms everything into holiness. Indeed, the repentance of a single person can reach such heights that it can atone for his entire generation (*Yoma* 86b) because the sins of his generation can serve to increase his perception of God's mercy in allowing them to live, survive, and thrive in spite of their evil. Just as the penitent's own prior sins can lead him to greater heights of love, so, too, the sins of a corrupt generation can lead a righteous person to ever loftier levels of appreciation of God's mercy. When this happens, even the multitudes of sinners become ennobled for they become the tools which enable the *tzaddik's* service to achieve its greater holiness (*Michtav MeEliyahu*).

The sins of a corrupt generation can lead a righteous person to even loftier levels of appreciation of God's mercy.

No one is free from the obligation to raise himself to a greater level of service. Whether the sinner who must shake himself loose from the shackles of his passion or the totally righteous *tzaddik* who must seek new perceptions of God's presence in the least likely depths — all have a responsibility to look to their actions and set higher goals. For a penitent is not only one who sinned and repents, but one who negates himself entirely and seeks to be drawn only after God's will. Repentance is not dependent on sin; its function is to return the holy soul to its source and root *(Shem MiShmuel).*

Repentance is not dependent on sin; its function is to return the holy soul to its source and root.

שׁוּבָה יִשְׂרָאֵל עַד ה׳ אֱלֹהֶיךָ

Return, O Israel, up until HASHEM, your God (Hoshea 14:2).

This is one of the classic exhortations to repent; it introduces the *Haftarah* of *Shabbos Shuvah,* the Sabbath between *Rosh Hashanah* and *Yom Kippur.* It calls equally to sinner and *tzaddik:*

'Return, even if you are sunk in the lowest depth, because the possibility always exists that you can rise *up until HASHEM* Himself. No height is denied you for repentance can reverse all!

'And you, *tzaddik,* you, too, must return even though you have already so excelled that you have come *up until HASHEM.* Because you are flesh and blood, you are not perfect, but because you have within you the breath of God, a holy soul — you *can* raise yourself even higher. And, therefore, you must!' *(Sfas Emes).*

The prophet Hoshea (ch. 14) continues with his call to repentance. It is not difficult, he says. It requires no sacrifices by the thousands, no inhuman exertions. It requires but the realization that can be gained from an honest evaluation of the truth — armies have no power, human promises have no credence, idols of any sort have no validity. God does not resist the advances of even those who have not earned His indulgence. To the contrary, he seeks them, encourages them, helps them. For the sinner inured by sin, calloused by his indulgence in evil, God makes the path back from evil easier if he will but make the first step. How chagrined he will be to learn after it is too late that his evil inclination, standing as a barrier between him and repentance,

God does not resist the advances of even those who have not earned His indulgence. To the contrary, He seeks them, encourages them, helps them.

was no more than a hair's-breadth! *(Succah* 52b).

How easy would be the path back — if only they would take it! And if they refuse to take it, what excuse could they offer? Because:

> יְשָׁרִים דַּרְכֵי ה׳ וְצַדִּקִים יֵלְכוּ בָם וּפֹשְׁעִים יִכָּשְׁלוּ בָם
>
> *Upright are the ways of HASHEM, so righteous shall walk in them and transgressors shall stumble in them (Hoshea* 14:10).

God's ways are straight and simple, fair and just. What justification could evildoers have?

The very uprightness and fairness of God's ways which serve as guide for the righteous, will be the stumbling-block of the wicked when they are brought to judgment. If only they could argue that God's ways were difficult and involved, treacherous and forbidding — then they could claim that they should not be judged harshly for having failed to take them. But God's ways are straight and simple, fair and just. What justification could evildoers have? — none but their own wickedness and lust, their blindness and passion. The very uprightness of God's ways are the undoing of the wicked *(Drashos HaRan 6).*

Lesson for the Wicked

The Sages teach that Joseph taught the path of repentance to the wicked. An astounding statement! Joseph, the select of his brothers, the favored heir of Jacob; how could he be considered the model for the wicked?

Could any wicked sinner ever claim that he was more driven to sin than Joseph. Surely not. But Joseph resisted. He placed before himself not the image of his temptress, but the image of his father.

He was. Joseph was trapped by his master's wife and continuously enticed to sin. Finally he was alone with her and tempted beyond his endurance to resist *(Genesis 39:22 see Rashi).* His family was gone. He and she were alone in the house. She foresaw that they were destined for one another *(Midrash)* — and indeed she had glimpsed the truth for Joseph eventually married her daughter. Nothing was lacking in the drive to sin. Privacy, temptation, passion, rationalization. Could any wicked sinner ever claim that he was more driven to sin than Joseph. Surely not. But Joseph resisted. He placed before himself not the image of his temptress, but the image of his father. The reality of Jacob may have seemed to be something Joseph would never again see, but he never lost sight of the *image* of Jacob, the goal to live up to the title 'Son of Jacob' — so he refused to sin, whatever the consequences might be. Thereby Joseph became the model for sinners, because he taught sinners that the path toward evil need never be inexorable.

But God says Give me an opening the size of a needle's point, and I will give you an opening beyond your imagination.

One path is always open — the road to repentance. Wisdom says the sinner cannot escape his self-created evil. Prophecy says the life that sinned has no right to endure. Torah says only guilt-offerings can avail. But God says *Return to Me and I shall return to you.* Give me an opening the size of a needle's point, and I will give you an opening beyond your imagination. *Return O Israel* — for you can attain the unattainable. You can rise *up until HASHEM your God.*

☙ Yom Kippur

This section of the *Overview* is based primarily on the exposition of *Harav Mordechai Gifter* in *Pirkei Emunah* I.

I. The Challenge of Purity

To Differentiate

RABBI YANNAI *(Bereishis Rabbah* 3:8) says that at the start of creation, the Holy One, Blessed be He, foresaw the deeds of the righteous and the deeds of the wicked. Emptiness and night represented the deeds of the wicked; light and day represented the deeds of the righteous. At first, light and darkness reigned together in a confusion of forces, until God separated them and gave each its own domain. *Rabbi Yannai* concludes that God ordained a unique day for the benefit of creation — *Yom Kippur.*

The expression 'deeds of the wicked' refers not to their evil *deeds, but to their* good *deeds.*

Avnei Nezer explains that the expression 'deeds of the wicked' refers not to their *evil* deeds, but to their *good* deeds. The *Midrash* makes clear that the *mixture* light and darkness constituted an unacceptable alternative to light. For the confusion of forces that prevailed until God separated them, the fall of night which obscures shapes and clouds perceptions — these are symbolic of wickedness. For man must learn to differentiate. He must learn to identify the hair's-breadth which separates good from evil. Man, like His universe, is created with an unformed mass of potential; he must spend his lifetime sorting out gold from glitter, substance from illusion, good from evil. It is the work of eternities, but there is one day, a unique day, when the task is eased. *Yom Kippur.*

Man, like His universe, is created with an unformed mass of potential; he must spend his lifetime sorting out gold from glitter.

The challenge of man is not to become otherworldly, for so long as his body plays host to his soul, he is a creature of *this* world. Rather, his mission is to endow earthly existence with a clear-headedness that slices away confusion and adulteration of essentials. His bodily functions are not to cease — indeed, the Torah commands him to care for his body and safeguard his health; the human being who gives up his life in the quest to become an angel is a sinner, not a saint.

No, let him live the life of a human being, but endow his life with purity.

Purpose

What is טַהֲרָה, *purity?*

> Purity is the perfection of the heart and the thoughts ... A person should leave no room for his [Evil] Inclination in his deeds, rather all his deeds should be permeated with wisdom and reverence and not with sin and lust. This applies even to physical and material deeds ... even when he enjoys only the bare necessities, he must still purify his heart and his imagination so that even in the little that he takes for himself, he should intend no personal pleasure or gratification at all, but his intention should be for the good which emanates from the deed ... *(Mesillas Yesharim ch.* 16).

Purity, then, is purpose. Man was created by God for a spiritual purpose.

Purity, then, is purpose. Man was created by God for a spiritual purpose, and he is called upon to endow his entire life with the attitude that every deed, morsel, and thought must be directed toward that purpose. Obviously the task is not simple, and, as we have seen above in our discussion of the many levels of repentance, it is an unending task. The elements of the universe were all created on the first day, the rest of the six days of creation consisted of clarifying, separating, and forming *(Ramban).* The rest of history consists of man taking the universe with which he was presented, and further developing it. Whatever happened, is happening, and will happen until the final redemption at the End of Days, is a continuing outgrowth of the first moments of confusion when everything existed and nothing was formed, when all was a mixture of elements and the crucial task of separation had not yet begun.

So, too, is man. He is a confusion of forces that can ascend to the heavens if they are defined, nurtured, and purified. The potential of the universe is infinite; so is that of man, the miniature universe. As *Mesillas Yesharim* makes plain, the keys to this goal of purity are *wisdom and reverence:* wisdom to recognize, and reverence to direct. Because רֵאשִׁית חָכְמָה יִרְאַת ה׳, *the beginning of wisdom is the fear of God (Psalms* 111:10). Without fear of God, humanity is not short of dazzling intellectual prowess, the mental gymnastics that turn values into grotesque caricatures of truth and decency. With reverence, however, wisdom can function as the tool that fashions material man into a fountain of purity.

Without fear of God, humanity is not short of dazzling intellectual prowess, the mental gymnastics that turn values into grotesque caricatures of truth and decency.

To be a wellspring of purity on earth is the function of *Yom Kippur.* It requires a renewed quest for purity and it provides the spiritual conditions that make it possible. As *Rabbeinu Yonah* writes:

> It is a positive commandment of the Torah that man arouse his spirit to repent on *Yom Kippur* as it says ... *from all your sins, before HASHEM shall you be purified (Shaarei Teshuvah* 2:14)

Arouse the Spirit

Rabbeinu Yonah says that one is required to *'arouse his spirit* to repent.' The commandment to repent is not limited to *Yom Kippur.* Whenever one sins, he is obligated to repent. Even if one has not sinned, he is obligated to repent in the sense that he must not be content with whatever level of service he has been able to attain. He must strive continuously to elevate his perceptions and aspirations. But on *Yom Kippur, Rabbeinu Yonah* says, there is a particular obligation to *arouse* oneself. There is another key word in the above passage: *Rabbeinu Yonah* quotes the verse that *Yom Kippur* is particularly a time of purification.

But on Yom Kippur, Rabbeinu Yonah *says, there is a particular obligation to* arouse *oneself.*

One can repent all year long without attaining the

level of Purity; indeed, the sort of purity described by *Mesillas Yesharim* is far beyond the capacity of even a sincere penitent. It is a goal which demands untold years of concerted effort. The *aspiration* toward such purity should be a goal of all service and particularly of repentance, but one must beware of the dangerous delusion that simple abstinence and asceticism constitute purity. On *Yom Kippur*, however, the commandment of repentance is intensified. One must strive for a purer repentance than he may have been capable of during the rest of the year.

The aspiration *toward such purity should be a goal of all service and particularly of repentance.*

And, as always, when the Torah commands, God provides the means for fulfillment. *Daas Tevunos* postulates that when Israel was commanded to perform a particular precept or strive toward a particular goal, God provided it with the spiritual capacity for success (see *Overview* to ArtScroll *Akdamos).* The Jew who is commanded to seek purity on *Yom Kippur* is given the resources to find it; such is the uniqueness of *Yom Kippur* that the day brings with it the potential for purity.

The Jew who is commanded to seek purity on Yom Kippur *is given the resources to find it.*

Thus, even repentance from misdeeds is different qualitatively on *Yom Kippur* than it is on other days. Every sin consists of the deed and of the attitudes that underlie it. Just as man can more easily control his hands than his eyes, his actions than his imagination, so it is infinitely easier to avoid sinning in deed and to repent from sinful deeds than it is to avoid, and repent from, sinful thoughts *(Shaarei Teshuvah* 3:26). But *Yom Kippur,* the day of purity, calls for one to uproot those attitudes and thoughts — for such is the challenge of purity.

Even repentance from misdeeds is different qualitatively on Yom Kippur than it is on other days.

And on *Yom Kippur* one must *arouse* himself to achieve the goal of the day, a goal that is placed within reach by God's command to achieve it, for, as the *Midrash* teaches, after the confusion of good and bad, light and darkness, there is a unique day when the two can be parted and the truth shine through — *Yom Kippur.* How? What is there about *Yom Kippur* that proclaims purity?

A Day of Rest

Rambam in his discussion of the requirements of the day, provides us an insight:

> There is a further positive commandment on *Yom Kippur*. It is to *rest* on it from eating and drinking *(Shvisas Asor* 1:4). It is forbidden to bathe, to apply oil to the body], to wear shoes, or to cohabitate. It is a positive commandment to *rest* from all these just as it is commanded to *rest* from eating (ibid 1:5).

How noteworthy that *Rambam* does not speak of צוֹם, *fasting*, or עִינוּי, *affliction*. Instead he chooses to speak of resting from all of the indulgences that are prohibited on *Yom Kippur*. It is as if eating, drinking, and the other activities are ordeals from which one is freed on *Yom Kippur*. indeed, if we understand properly the depth of the *Yom Kippur* task, then we understand that it is truly a day of rest. The activities that are forbidden on *Yom Kippur* represent the indulgence of the animal part of the body-soul partnership that is man. Such indulgence stands in the way of the attainment of purity which calls for the supremacy of mind and soul. The purpose of fasting on *Yom Kippur* is not self-affliction. *Yom Kippur* is not like *Tisha B'Av*, a day of tragedy and mourning.

It is as if eating, drinking, and the other activities are ordeals from which one is freed on Yom Kippur.

Such indulgence stands in the way of the attainment of purity which calls for the supremacy of mind and soul.

If the fasting of *Yom Kippur* were intended as a form of suffering, then the Torah would not have ordained the fast if *Yom Kippur* fell on a Sabbath; one does not fast on the Sabbath. Sabbath is a day of joy not of suffering. If *Tisha B'Av* falls on a Sabbath, the fast is postponed to Sunday, because it is not permitted to interfere with the joy of Sabbath. But not *Yom Kippur*, for the fast of *Yom Kippur* is not an imposition, it is a 'rest' — man is freed from the shackles of his dependence on food and drink to satisfy his soul's flesh-and-blood host.

The fast of Yom Kippur *is a 'rest' — man is freed from the shackles of his dependence on food and drink.*

The essence of *Yom Kippur* is the transcendence of limitations. *Pirkei d'Rabbi Eliezer* (ch. 46) quotes the angel of sin, Sammael — Satan himself — as he comes before God on Yom Kippur:

> Sammael saw that sin was not found among them [Israel] on Yom Kippur. He said to God: 'You have a unique nation which is like the ministering angels in heaven. Just as the angels have bare feet, so the Jews have bare feet on *Yom Kippur.* Just as the angels neither eat nor drink, so the Jews neither eat nor drink on *Yom Kippur...'*

Yom Kippur *is not to be seen as a day of suffering but as a day when Jews become elevated to the status of the angels.*

It is abundantly clear from *PdRE* that *Yom Kippur* is not to be seen as a day of suffering but as a day when Jews become elevated to the status of the angels. Therefore, the halacha is that on *Yom Kippur* Jews recite aloud the praise of the angels: בָּרוּךְ שֵׁם כְּבוֹד מַלְכוּתוֹ לְעוֹלָם וָעֶד, *Blessed is the Name of His glorious Kingdom forever and ever.* All year long, it is said silently because it is the song of the angels, but on *Yom Kippur,* Jews *are* angels and they have the right to recite it openly.

Yom Kippur *is a day of mercy and the mercy is earned* בְּדִין, *by right.*

Yom Kippur, the day when Jews utilize this God-given capacity to transcend the limitations of their physical nature is called יוֹם רַחֲמִים בְּדִין, *a day of mercy by right (Ramban, Leviticus* 23:24). The commentators explain that *Yom Kippur* is a day of mercy — a day when even Sammael is forced to praise Israel before God — and the mercy is earned בְּדִין, *by right.* God confers mercy on people when they earn it (see above on *Teshuvah)* for it is His will that when people begin to repent, he grants atonement far beyond their ability to earn. A minimum sincere effort is rewarded greatly, provided the effort is made. Thus the mercy of *Yom Kippur* is won by right, for it is God's will that the service of the day should gain Israel entry into the world of angels.

Endowing the Physical

Because the service of the day is a Divinely granted means of gaining purity, even the preparation for the day assumes a unique nature. *Meiri (Essay on Teshuvah)* comments that the precept to eat on *Erev Yom Kippur* is designed to free the body on *Yom Kippur* so that it need not expend energy on

Even the eating and drinking are tantamount to the fasting and solemn service of Yom Kippur *itself.*

anything save the service of God. Thus because the enjoyment of food and drink on the day before *Yom Kippur* is a device to make possible the successful assault on a spiritual summit on *Yom Kippur,* even the eating and drinking are tantamount to the fasting and solemn service of *Yom Kippur* itself. As the Sages teach כָּל הָאוֹכֵל וְשׁוֹתֶה בַּתְּשִׁיעִי כְּאִלּוּ הִתְעַנֶּה בַּתְּשִׁיעִי וַעֲשִׂירִי, *Whoever eats and drinks on the ninth [day of Tishri, Erev Yom Kippur] is considered as if he had fasted on the ninth and the tenth (Yoma* 86a). The dedication of the ninth day elevates even the eating to the level of a spiritual experience.

Sfas Emes notes that the confession of *Yom Kippur* is included in the afternoon prayer of *Erev Yom Kippur* because, the Talmud explains, there is a slight possibility that one may choke on his *Erev Yom Kippur* meal and therefore be unable to confess on *Yom Kippur.* How, asks *Sfas Emes,* is this danger alleviated by the pre-*Yom Kippur* confession; since confession is part of the *Yom Kippur* service, what effect can it have if it is recited prematurely? Just as one who recites his morning prayers before dawn has not fulfilled his obligation, so, too, one who recites his *Yom Kippur* obligation a day early will not have fulfilled his obligation! From this halachah, *Sfas Emes* derives that the status of *Erev Yom Kippur* is actually equivalent to that of *Yom Kippur* itself, therefore, the *Yom Kippur* confession is quite appropriate on the Ninth of Tishri for it has the status of *Yom Kippur* itself. Thus, a day of feasting is equal to a day of fasting! Why? How? Because, as we have seen, purity — the core of the *Yom Kippur* service — is meant to carry over to every pursuit. Even food and drink become pure and holy when their purpose is pure and holy!

Purity — the core of the Yom Kippur *service — is meant to carry over to every pursuit. Even food and drink become pure and holy when their purpose is pure and holy!*

II. Jonah's Message

THE SAGES have united the *Book of Jonah* with Repentance and *Yom Kippur*. The prophet, the sailors, the Ninevites — all teach eternal lessons of repentance. From the repentance of Nineveh which was sincere by its own standards, to the dedication of Jonah whose greatness drove him to sacrifice spiritual growth and life itself for the sake of God's honor and Israel's — the *Book* is replete with teachings that go beyond time, nationality, and geography. The *Book of Jonah* does not tell us when the prophet lived, what part of *Eretz Yisrael* he was from, the nationality of the sailors, or the country where Nineveh was located. Whatever we know about these historical phenomena we piece together from other sources. The *Book* itself does not tell us, for these details matter but little. The story happened at a specific time in particular places, but its implications are universal. Repentance preceded creation of the earth; it is timeless — so, too, the story of Jonah is beyond the bounds of space and time. Its lesson is the timeless lesson of repentance.

The Book *is replete with teachings that go beyond time, nationality, and geography.*

Repentance is timeless — so, too, the story of Jonah is beyond the bounds of space and time. Its lesson is the timeless lesson of repentance.

The *Zohar* esoterically sees a parable in the story of Jonah. The prophet is the soul who is exiled into a body on earth. It is called *Yonah* from the root ינה, to *deceive,* to *cheat* as in the same root as לא תונו, *do not deceive (Lev.* 25:17). As *Rav S.R. Hirsch* explains, it refers to the unfair advantage taken of another's weakness. The soul comes to earth as a particle of God's holiness, but it allows itself to become deceived by the physical allures of earth. Its only hope is to come to its senses and descend into the purifying waters which shut out the earthly mirages that have blinded it to its true purpose.

Such is the universal and timeless message of Jonah. It is a message of sincerity and purity, read at a time when God sits on the throne of mercy, anxious

Such is the universal and timeless message of Jonah. It is a message of sincerity and purity, read at a time when God sits on the throne of mercy.

to bestow compassion upon His one, unique nation — if only they pierce their hearts with a needle's-point of repentance.

May He open wide His gates of mercy and may the angelic purity of Israel's *Yom Kippur* spill over to become the soothing waters of redemption.

— Rabbi Nosson Scherman

לעילוי נשמת
ראובן שלמה בן פרידעל פישמאן הי״ד
Reuven Shlomo Fishman
נקטף בדמי ימיו ע״י רוצחים שונאי ישראל
כ״ו אייר ה׳תשל״ח
נעשה קדוש בחייו, ונקרא קדוש במותו
בא ללמוד ונמצא מלמד
נעשה מופת לחבריו —
שקדן, למדן, עובד ה׳
המקום ינחם קרוביו ואוהביו
ת. נ. צ. ב. ה.

ספר יונה

א א־ב

א וַיְהִי֙ דְּבַר יהוה אֶל־יוֹנָ֥ה בֶן־אֲמִתַּ֖י
ב לֵאמֹֽר׃ ק֠וּם לֵ֧ךְ אֶל־נִֽינְוֵ֛ה הָעִ֥יר הַגְּדוֹלָ֖ה

I.

1. The call to Jonah.

וַיְהִי דְּבַר ה׳ — [*And*] *the Word of* HASHEM *came* [lit. *was.*]

A prefatory formula used often in Scriptures to introduce an impending prophetic revelation.

The word דבר, *word* or *speech,* in this context expresses one of the highest of the ten forms of prophecy listed by the Sages (*Bereishis Rabbah* 44:6).

From the use of the same expression וַיְהִי דְּבַר ה׳ to introduce the prophecies to Elijah *(I Kings* 21:17,21); to Isaiah (38:1); and often to Jeremiah (1:14; 11:2 and elsewhere) we find that this formula precedes *direct commands to action,* as was the case here with Jonah *(Da'as Soferim).*

According to *Yerushalmi Sukkah* 5:1, this prophecy came to Jonah while he was attending the שִׂמְחַת בֵּית הַשּׁוֹאֵבָה, festival of the water-drawing during *Sukkos* at the Temple in Jerusalem.

יוֹנָה בֶּן־אֲמִתַּי — *Jonah son of Amittai.*

Information about the man is meager. Jonah is identified with the prophet *Jonah son of Amittai from Gas Chefer* mentioned in *II Kings* 14:25. He prophesied during the reign of King Jeroboam son of Joash [*Jeroboam II* — 3114-3153 from Creation (646-607 B.C.E.)] regarding the restoration to Israel of territory which had been previously lost to Aram. According to *Pirkei d'Rabbi Eliezer,* he also prophesied that Jerusalem would be destroyed as a result of the sins of its people. This latter prophecy was annulled, however, because the people repented [see further].

Rabbi Yochanan in *Yerushalmi Sukkah* 5:1 infers that Jonah was of the tribe of Zevulun since, according to *Joshua* 19:13, Gas Chefer was located in the territory of Zevulun. Rabbi Levi, however, deduces that Jonah was a member of the tribe of Asher. [This latter opinion follows the tradition preserved in *Pirkei d'Rabbi Eliezer* Chapter 33, which identifies Jonah as the child whom Elijah resuscitated (see *I Kings* 17) in gratitude to the boy's mother, the widow from Tzorfas in whose attic he boarded. Tzorfas was near Zidon which was in Asher's territory (see *Judges* 1:31); hence Rabbi Levi deduces that Jonah was from Asher.] Subsequently, Rav Levi expounded that Jonah's *father* was from Zevulun and his *mother* from Asher [see also *Bereishis Rabbah* 98:11.]

The Sages (see *Seder Olam* 19) identify Jonah as the prophet sent by Elisha to anoint Yehu (*II Kings* 9:1; see *comm.* there, and *Overview).*

According to a tradition cited by *Abarbanel,* Jonah attained a very

[Please note: *The source for every comment has been carefully documented. Whenever* M.Z. *has added an explanatory comment of his own it is framed in square brackets.*]

I
1-2

AND *the Word of HASHEM came to Jonah son of Amittai saying:* 2 *'Arise! Go to Nineveh, that*

advanced age; more than 120 years.

בֶּן אֲמִתַּי – *Son of Amittai.*

The *Midrash* [*Vayikra Rabbah* 6:6] records a view that wherever a prophet's father's name is specified as well as his own, it indicates that he is a prophet, son of a prophet. The Rabbis hold, however, that whether or not the father's name is mentioned, it should be assumed that his father was a prophet too.[1]

לֵאמֹר – *Saying.*

The word לֵאמֹר [*saying*], lit. *to say,* implies that the prophet should relay the subsequent message to others (*Aderes Eliyahu* to *Genesis* 2:16).

Therefore, as *Alshich* notes, the absence in the next verse of a *specific message which Jonah was to transmit* is noteworthy [see *comm.* to next verse.] *Alshich* accordingly concludes that an *implied* message to Israel was implicit in the very wording of God's subsequent command that Jonah go to Nineveh and simply *cry out against her.* This word of God now came to Jonah לֵאמֹר, i.e., in order to convey to Israel by implication, God's anger over Israel's consistent obdurate refusal to repent despite many exhortations by numerous prophets. This obstinacy was in startling contrast to the mighty and influential Ninevites who would not be haughty and would abandon their evil ways after only *one* prophetic warning.

2. קוּם – *Arise!*

– A call to action *(Radak).*

נִינְוֵה הָעִיר הַגְּדוֹלָה – *Nineveh, that* [lit. *the*] *great city.*

Nineveh was the principal city of Assyria, Israel's bitterest enemy, and is mentioned often in Scripture. It lay on the eastern bank of the Tigris. It was the city of Senacherib (*II Kings* 19:36), and as we see below (4:11) its population exceeded one hundred and twenty thousand.

According to *Genesis* 10:11 (as explained by *Rashi* there), Nineveh was built by Asshur; while according to *Ramban* Asshur in that verse refers to Assyria and the subject there is *Nimrod* who built Nineveh.

Although it is clear that the reference to *great city* in *Genesis* 10:12 refers to Nineveh from its parallel description here (see *Yoma* 10a), *Chizkuni* suggests that Nineveh and Calah merged into one great metropolis forming *one great city.*

In any event, the commentators note that Nineveh's size is noted here in anticipation of 4:11, and to emphasize that although the Ninevites were from such a large metro-

1. There is a *Midrashic* view that בֶּן אֲמִתַּי [lit. *son of truthfulness*] refers to Jonah's stature as a prophet. He was known as a בֶּן אֲמִתַּי, *person of truth,* because his prophecy concerning the restoration of Israel's borders under Jeroboam *from the entering of Hamath unto the sea of the plain* [*II Kings* 14:25] was explicitly fulfilled.

After his prophecy regarding the destruction of Jerusalem was not fulfilled because the people repented, however, he came to be distrusted by *ignorant segments of the populace.* They called him a false prophet because they did not comprehend that God changes an evil decree in response to repentance [see *Yoma* 73b and *Overview*] *(Radal).*

א ג וּקְרָ֣א עָלֶ֑יהָ כִּֽי־עָלְתָ֥ה רָעָתָ֖ם לְפָנָֽי׃ וַיָּ֤קָם
ג יוֹנָה֙ לִבְרֹ֣חַ תַּרְשִׁ֔ישָׁה מִלִּפְנֵ֖י יְהוָ֑ה וַיֵּ֨רֶד

polis, they were not haughty, but would be receptive to the prophet's exhortation.

It would further appear that Nineveh was notorious for its wickedness and it was singled out because due to its size it exercised a profound influence on the entire Assyrian empire *(Radal).*

וּקְרָא עָלֶיהָ — *And cry out against her* [lit. *and call upon her.*]

Rashi comments: Cry out My call [i.e., the message I will give you. Its exact substance was not yet conveyed.]

[Cf. *Midrash* cited in footnote, end of 3:2.]

Radak suggests that from the later account in 3:4 that in effect Jonah proclaimed Nineveh's impending destruction within forty days, we may surmise that he was now bidden to deliver the same call.

According to *Ibn Ezra*, Jonah was not now to proclaim Nineveh's impending destruction. The essence of the call was to be, as the rest of the verse makes clear: כִּי עָלְתָה רָעָתָם לְפָנָי, *that their wickedness has ascended before Me.*

Alshich [as noted above] suggests that the charge קְרָא עָלֶיהָ, *cry out against her,* implies that Jonah merely utter a *brief reproof*; that *in itself* would prove sufficient to bring the Ninevites to repentance and thereby serve as a message to errant Israel that it should follow suit.

Metzudos interprets similarly that *cry out against her* denotes reproving and warning them in the manner of the prophets, but that the exact content of the call was not yet given him.

Malbim, too, interprets that at this first mission Jonah was not yet commanded to foretell their *punishment* — for that decree had not yet been sealed. Rather, he was to exhort them to repent [see further.]

[The root עַל, lit. *upon,* often has the connotation in Scripture of *against* (or *concerning*), as reflected in the Translation. Comp. e.g., *Deut.* 20:19: לְהִלָּחֵם עָלֶיהָ, *war against her; Esth.* 8:8: כִּתְבוּ עַל, *write against.* Cf. also *comm.* to וּקְרָא אֵלֶיהָ in 3:2.]

כִּי עָלְתָה רָעָתָם לְפָנָי — *For their wickedness has ascended before Me* [i.e., has come to My notice.]

I.e., the wickedness they perpetrate has ascended to the heavenly spheres, standing as it were before Me and accusing them *(Metzudos).*

It is the wickedness they committed against Israel [as further evidenced by the fact that they were the people who would one day] exile the Ten Tribes *(Mahari Kara).*

In a more esoteric manner, *Minchah Gedolah* interprets this wickedness as the harmful influences of רוּחַ הַמַּשְׁחִית, *spirit of destruction,* which is generated by evil deeds, which now 'ascended' to God. God later unleashed this evil Force in the guise of the stormy wind which threatened only Jonah's vessel and no others.

⌁§ Why was God concerned with the sinfulness of the Ninevites?

Why did He send His prophet to forewarn non-Jews of the consequences of their wickedness?

Many reasons are offered. We cite several, briefly:

Nineveh merited God's compassion since it had only recently become sinful

I *great city, and cry out against her, for their*
3 *wickedness has ascended before Me.'* 3 *But Jonah*
arose to flee to Tarshish from before HASHEM*'s*

as evidenced by its appellation in 3:3 as *a city great to God.* Furthermore, the fact that the Ninevites did not destroy any places of idolatry as part of their repentance proves that they wre innocent of that cardinal sin, and that their wickedness was limited to moral and social sins. God therefore took compassion upon them and gave them an opportunity to repent *(Ibn Ezra).*

Radak explains that the sin of the Ninevites lay especially in the area of חָמָס, *robbery* and *oppression* (see 3:8). Thus it paralleled the evil of the Generation of the Deluge [see *Genesis* 6:11,13] and the Sodomites, which were destroyed because of their similar descent to חָמָס. As a general rule, God intervenes directly in the affairs of the nations only when they resort to this form of behavior because it is destructive of the social order and, therefore, contrary to His wish that man live and thrive in a society. Therefore, in order to preserve His creation, God intervenes, something He would not do had the sinfulness involved only idolatry or immorality.

Malbim [following *Abarbanel* who differs from *Ibn Ezra* above, inasmuch as they maintain that the Ninevites *were* idolatrous] understands God's intervention in the light of Assyria's future role in Jewish history. God intended Assyria to be שֵׁבֶט אַפּוֹ, *rod of His anger* [see *Isaiah* 10:5] to punish Israel by destroying the Northern Kingdom and exiling the Ten Tribes. Had Assyria remained as wicked as it was in Jonah's time, simple justice would not have permitted that it be God's tool to punish Israel which, wicked though Israel may have become, was still more righteous than the thieving, violent Assyrians. Therefore, God dispatched Jonah to cause Nineveh, the Assyrian capital, to repent, and thus become worthy of its future mission.

[It is to be emphasized that implicit in all these reasons is the underlying concept that Jonah's mission to the Ninevites was primarily to set an example for Israel of the efficacy of true repentance. Certainly, its *long-term* effect was mainly on the Jews and not the gentiles, since *Jonah* has remained a lesson of repentance for Israel. The Ninevites were only the *immediate* beneficiaries (see *Overview).*]

3. Jonah's recalcitrance.

וַיָּקָם יוֹנָה לִבְרֹחַ תַּרְשִׁישָׁה — *But Jonah arose to flee to Tarshish.*

— I.e., the sea of Tarshish, outside of *Eretz Yisrael (Rashi).*

[*Rav Saadiah Gaon* identifies it with Tarsis, while others (cited by *Ibn Ezra),* identify it with the city of Tunis; or Tartessus in ancient Spain beyond the Rock of Gibraltar. *Keses HaSofer* to *Genesis* 10:4 disagrees with the latter view on the basis of the description of Tarshish in *Ezekiel* 27:12 which positions it amid the countries of Asia Minor. That would apparently refer to Tarzia in the Balkans, although this is not certain. In any event, Jonah's intended destination was *outside* the Land of Israel in a direction opposite that of Nineveh, i.e., Nineveh was to the northeast while Jonah fled westward.]

[*Rashi*'s comment follows *Targum* who usually renders the word תַּרְשִׁישׁ throughout Scripture as *sea. Onkelos* similarly renders the word *Tarshish* in *Exodus* 28:20 where it refers to one of the stones in the priestly breastplate as כְּרוּם יָמָא, the color of the sea. According to this view of תַּרְשִׁישׁ as a term for 'sea,' it is clear why so many cities were called Tarshish; it would be logical for coastal cities dependent on sea traffic to take such a name.]

[As will be noted below, Jonah fled seaward because prophecy is not given at sea. Therefore *Rashi* interprets the phrase as: 'the *sea* of *Tarshish*,' since the city *itself* was not necessarily his destination; he only intended to stay afloat at sea and evade thereby the prophetic call *(Harav David Feinstein)*.]

☙ Why did Jonah flee God's command?

[Jonah perceived the redemptive purpose of his mission inasmuch as his call to them was not merely as a prediction of Nineveh's overthrow, but as an implicit call to repentance. Then, once they repented God would be disposed to forgive them (see 4:2).] He rationalized: The gentiles are near to repentance*: If I address them and they indeed repent, then I will in effect be condemning Israel by contrast, for they consistently remained obdurate in the face of prophetic admonitions (*Rashi* citing *Mechilta Bo*).[1]

*[For a discussion of why Israel should have been more reluctant to repent than Nineveh, see *Overview*.]

Thus, according to the Sages [*Pirkei d'Rabbi Eliezer* Chapter 10 as explained by *Radal*] Jonah was motivated by two concerns: A) — If he were to carry out his mission the Ninevites would repent and be spared, but God would pour out His wrath against Israel for not having similarly repented in the face of repeated divine calls [as *Rashi* explains above]; and B) — If the Ninevites were to survive, they would accuse him of prophesying falsely with the result that the Name of Heaven would be profaned through him. [As is the way of wicked scoffers: they would not attribute the annulment of the decree to their repentance. Instead, they would complacently say that Jonah's prophecy was unfounded to begin with, or that God lacked the power to punish them. They would not comprehend that God would change an evil decree once it was issued even after repentance *(Radal)*.]

Following *Malbim* [end of *v.* 2], Jonah prophetically perceived that evil would eventually befall Israel as a result of his mission. The Ninevites would indeed repent and they would accordingly become worthy of their later role as the 'rod of God's anger' in becoming God's instrument in later punishing Israel. Jonah therefore devised whatever plan he could — and chose even to have himself cast into the sea [*v.* 12] — to avoid being an agent in bringing harm upon Israel.

Malbim continues that this, as *Abarbanel* points out, is the meaning of the *Mechilta* [discussed in the *Overview*]: — *Jonah protected the honor of the child* [*i.e., Israel*] *rather than the honor of the Father* [*HASHEM*] *and risked his own life to save Israel.*

Rabbeinu Bachya contends that Jonah was motivated by humility. He patterned himself after Moses, reasoning 'If Moses was reluctant to accept God's call to redeem the righteous Jews from Egypt because he considered himself unequal to the task (*Exodus* Chapter 3); then surely I, who am being sent to wicked people, should seek to avoid my mission by fleeing to a place where God will not reveal Himself to me.' For his excessive humility, he was not punished. However, he was punished for not wishing to admonish the Ninevites when commanded to do

1. Jonah chose a destination outside of *Eretz Yisrael.* He said: 'I will flee to the Sea since the Shechinah does not rest [i.e., reveal itself to prophets *(Metzudos)*] outside of the Land.'

The Holy One, Blessed be He, said to him: 'By your life! I have agents like you to dispatch and fetch you.' [This agent was the storm God later sent over the sea *(Mechilta Bo)*.]

This is comparable to a servant of a priest who fled from his master and entered a cemetery [where he knew that his master, as a priest, could not defile himself by following him]. So the master said to him: 'By your life, I have other servants like you [i.e., non-priests] whom I can dispatch to retrieve you!' (*Rashi* citing *Mechilta Bo*).

[On Jonah's reason for selecting the *sea,* see *comm.* further s.v. מִלִּפְנֵי ה׳.]

so, because righteous people bear the responsibility to chastise even evildoers.

מִלִּפְנֵי ה׳ — *From before HASHEM's Presence.*

I.e., from before the Glory of HASHEM [כְּבוֹד ה׳] *(Radak).*

— Jonah intended to flee from the land of Israel, all of which is considered לִפְנֵי ה׳, *before HASHEM.*[1]

As *Pirkei d'Rabbi Eliezer* [henceforth referred to as *PdRE*] explains, Jonah sought a destination where God's glory is not proclaimed. Jonah said: 'If I ascend above the heavens, it is said [*Psalms* 113:4]: עַל הַשָּׁמַיִם כְּבוֹדוֹ, *above the heavens is His glory*; if upon the earth, it is said of that, too [*Isaiah* 6:3]: מְלֹא כָל הָאָרֶץ כְּבוֹדוֹ, *the whole earth is full of His Glory.* Rather, I will escape to the sea, to a place where His Glory is not proclaimed. [Note the wording: where His *glory* is not proclaimed (i.e., where Scripture does not *specifically* mention that His כָּבוֹד, *Glory,* is present), for Jonah did not err by thinking that God's *dominion* does not extend over the seas, ח״ו. Rather, he reasoned that God does not reveal Himself to His prophets in the sea since the sea is esoterically not conducive to the revelation of prophecy *(Radal).*]

There is a difference between מִפְּנֵי ה׳ [lit. *from HASHEM's Presence*] i.e., from His knowledge and Providence from which obviously no one can flee, and מִלִּפְנֵי ה׳, *from being before HASHEM's Presence,* which implies from before the *Shechinah* [the Source of prophetic revelation.] That degree of holiness is present only in *Eretz Yisrael;* Jonah therefore chose to leave the Land to avoid receiving a second command regarding this matter. He selected a sea route rather than a desert route because prophetic revelations sometimes occur outside the Land as they did in the case of Ezekiel, and in the case of Elijah who saw a vision on Mt. Horeb when he fled from Jezebel [*I Kings* 19:9] On board ship however, he hoped to avoid another prophetic call, either because he imagined that seafarers are anxious about their safety until they reach land [and prophecy alights only on a person of calm spirit], or that he would lack the requisite for prophetic communication if he were on a crowded boat surrounded by heathens *(Abarbanel; Malbim).*

Thus, *Radak* explains, it was not from the *presence* of God that the prophet — who was full of wisdom and knowledge [which are among the prerequisites of prophecy] — had presumed to flee, for as David said [*Psalms* 139:7] *Where can I flee from Your Presence?* — Rather due to the various motivations of love of Israel, and justifications set forth above, Jonah desired to flee *from*

1. As the Sages comment: Know that the *Shechinah* is not revealed outside of the Land, as it says, *But Jonah arose to flee to Tarshish from before HASHEM's Presence.* Did he actually hope to flee from before HASHEM? — It is said *(Psalms* 139:7-10): אָנָה אֵלֵךְ מֵרוּחֶךָ וְאָנָה מִפָּנֶיךָ אֶבְרָח. אִם אֶסַּק שָׁמַיִם שָׁם אָתָּה וְאַצִּיעָה שְּׁאוֹל הִנֶּךָּ. אֶשָּׂא כַנְפֵי שָׁחַר אֶשְׁכְּנָה בְּאַחֲרִית יָם. גַּם שָׁם יָדְךָ תַנְחֵנִי וְתֹאחֲזֵנִי יְמִינֶךָ, *Where can I go from Your spirit, and where can I flee from Your Presence? If I rise up to the heaven, You are there; if I make my bed in the Lower Depth, You are there. If I take the wings of morning and dwell in the most distant sea, there, too, Your hand will guide me, and Your right hand shall grasp me.*

And it is written [Zechariah 4:10] עֵינֵי ה׳ הֵמָּה מְשׁוֹטְטִים בְּכָל הָאָרֶץ, *The eyes of HASHEM hover throughout the earth.*

Rather, Jonah's intention [as emphasized in the *commentary*] was to flee *Eretz Yisrael* to a place where the *Shechinah* does not reveal itself *(Mechilta).*

א
ג

יָפוֹ וַיִּמְצָא אָנִיָּה| בָּאָה תַרְשִׁישׁ וַיִּתֵּן
שְׂכָרָהּ וַיֵּרֶד בָּהּ לָבוֹא עִמָּהֶם תַּרְשִׁישָׁה

that which was before God, i.e., *from* the prophetic contact with Him which he thought was possible only in the Holy Land. [See footnote.]

Ibn Ezra compares this expression to *Genesis 4:16:* וַיֵּצֵא קַיִן מִלִּפְנֵי ה׳ [lit. *And Cain departed from before the Presence of* HASHEM] which the Sages interpret figuratively [that he departed *spiritually,* as it were, turning his back on God's wishes (see *Gur Aryeh ad loc.*)] This interpretation is dictated by the fact that actual departure from God's presence is impossible as evidenced by Cain's own question there in 4:14: *Can I be hidden from Your Presence?* Here, too, Jonah is not described as trying to flee from God's Presence, but from standing before Him in His service.

וַיֵּרֶד יָפוֹ — *He went down to Jaffo.*
The ancient port-city *(Metzudos).*

Jonah lived in Gas Chefer in the portion of Zevulun [see *v.* 9] and the closest port city was Acco, not Jaffo. Nevertheless (as noted in *comm.* to *v.* 1), the Divine call came to him at the שִׂמְחַת בֵּית הַשּׁוֹאֵבָה, *Festival of the Water-drawing* [*during the Sukkos festival*], in the Temple in Jerusalem *(Yerushalmi Sukkah* 5:1). He therefore fled to Jaffo, which was the closest port to Jerusalem (*Radal* to *PdRE* 10:13 [3]).

וַיִּמְצָא אָנִיָּה בָּאָה תַרְשִׁישׁ — *And* [*he*] *found a Tarshish-bound ship* [lit. *ship coming Tarshish*].

The word *Tarshish* lacks a preposition indicating whether the ship was going *to* or *from* the city. Our translation follows *Targum* who renders *Tarshish-bound ship* [Although, since *Targum* translates *Tarshish* as *sea,* his rendering is actually *sea-bound*].

This rendering is further supported by *Radak* who comments that the word בָּאָה [*coming*] has its accent on the second syllable making it present tense, the meaning being: *The ship was coming* [in the sense of *arriving*] *to Tarshish,* i.e., it was ready to sail and arrive in Tarshish.

[It was the vessel that regularly ferried pasengers (present tense בָּאָה, *always coming)* between Tarshish and Jaffo *(Ohel David).*]

Pirkei d'Rabbi Eliezer offers the following:

Jonah went down to Jaffo, but found no ship in port; the last ship had sailed two days previously. In order to test Jonah, God caused a storm on the sea which forced a Tarshish-bound ship to return to port. Jonah rejoiced since he considered this Divine approval for his action.

[The above *Midrash* is further supported by the phrase 'he *found* a ship' which implies that although no ships were docked in port at that time, in this instance a ship had been 'prepared' for him in order to test him.]

Malbim explains that the very wording of the verse which describes the ship as בָּאָה תַּרְשִׁישׁ [lit. *coming Tarshish*] rather than more explicit הוֹלֶכֶת לְתַרְשִׁישׁ, *voyaging*

I 3 *Presence. He went down to Jaffo and found a Tarshish-bound ship; he paid its fare, and boarded it to travel with them to Tarshish from before HASHEM's Presence.*

toward Tarshish, implies [as does the *Midrash* cited above] that the ship *was just returning from Tarshish. Malbim* continues that this very fact lends support to the Talmudic interpretation cited below that Jonah was so anxious to embark that he paid the fares for the entire passenger load. For, ordinarily a ship that had just arrived in port would not set sail again until a lapse of at least several days while it assembled a sufficient number of passengers to fill up all its berths.

וַיִּתֵּן שְׂכָרָהּ – *[And] he paid* [lit. *gave*] *its fare.*

[This verse mentions that he paid the fare even before it mentions that he boarded, and the noun שְׂכָרָהּ implies that he paid *its* (lit. *her*) fare rather than simply '*the* fare' or '*his* fare']:

– He paid the fare even *before* boarding the ship which is noteworthy since passengers on a vessel do not customarily pay their fare before disembarking; furthermore [not only did he pay his *own* fare, but שְׂכָרָהּ implies that] he paid the fare for the *entire passenger-load* of the ship *(Rashi; Mahari Kara;* comp. *Nedarim* 38a). [1]

Jonah paid for the entire passenger load [apparently even for the empty berths] because he was in such a hurry to depart that he did not want them to wait for additional passengers and cargo *(Radak).*

In the literal sense of the verse, however, *Ibn Ezra* and *Radak* agree that שְׂכָרָהּ [lit. *her fare*] could mean that Jonah paid only *his portion of the fare due her* [i.e., the ship.]

וַיֵּרֶד בָּהּ לָבוֹא עִמָּהֶם – *And boarded it* [lit. *and descended into it*] *to travel* [lit. *come*] *with them.*

I.e., with the others on the ship *(Metzudos).*

Radak explains that because the sea shore is lower than the surrounding terrain the Hebrew idiom for entering the sea is 'descending into the sea' as in the expression יוֹרְדֵי הַיָּם בָּאֳנִיּוֹת, *those who descend into the sea on ships (Psalms* 107:23). *Radak* also cites his father's explanation that this idiom is used because the ship itself is low in the water, and one *descends* into it *(Radak).*

מִלִּפְנֵי ה' – *From before HASHEM's Presence.*

[This is repeated; perhaps to accentuate the seriousness of his actions, and to emphasize that it was his intention to flee only מִלִּפְנֵי ה', *from before God's* prophetic call as explained above.]

1. The *Talmud* [*Nedarim* 38a] derives from this verse [which portrays Jonah as having the means to pay the fare of the entire ship] that wealth is one of the necessary qualifications for prophecy: 'The Holy One, Blessed be He, causes His Divine Presence to rest only upon one who is strong, wealthy, wise, and humble.'

[Wealth, according to the *Rosh* was included among these qualifications — although, as evidenced by the fact that many of the Sages were poor, poverty is not a character flaw — since wealth endows its possessor with the sense of independence, thus making him better able to proclaim the Word of God.]

ד מִלִּפְנֵי יהוָה: וַיהוה הֵטִיל רֽוּחַ־גְּדוֹלָה
אֶל־הַיָּם וַיְהִי סַעַר־גָּדוֹל בַּיָּם וְהָאֳנִיָּה
ה חִשְּׁבָה לְהִשָּׁבֵר: וַיִּירְאוּ הַמַּלָּחִים וַיִּזְעֲקוּ

☙ Was Jonah guilty of suppressing a prophecy?

In *Sanhedrin* 89a, the halachah is formulated that הַכּוֹבֵשׁ אֶת נְבוּאָתוֹ ... מִיתָתוֹ בִּידֵי שָׁמַיִם, *one who suppresses his prophecy...is liable to the death penalty at the hands of heaven.* To this, the *Talmud* elaborates הַכּוֹבֵשׁ אֶת נְבוּאָתוֹ – כְּגוֹן יוֹנָה בֶּן אֲמִתַּי, *one who suppresses his prophecy: for example, Jonah son of Amittai (ibid.).*

It would thus seem clear that Jonah incurred this penalty, for refusing to carry out his mission to Nineveh.

It may be that he was spared from this ultimate punishment because his refusal was motivated by an intense love for Israel (see above). In the execution of heavenly justice, all considerations are weighed. As a result, it may be that God forgave Jonah's sin of suppressing a prophecy because his intention was not to flout God's word, but to avoid the inevitable degradation that would befall Israel if the Ninevites were to repent promptly *(Harav David Feinstein)* [See *Overview.*]

– *Malbim*, however, consistent with his interpretation [based on *Abarbanel*] in *v.* 2 [s.v. וּקְרָא עָלֶיהָ], holds that during this first call God had not given Jonah a specific prophetic message to relate to the Ninevites. Had he been given such a specific message, he would *indeed* have been guilty of suppressing his prophecy. Rather, Jonah considered himself to be in violation of only a positive מִצְוָה, *command* to reprove the Ninevites rather than of suppressing *prophecy.* He embarked for Tarshish lest God give him a second command, commissioning him to deliver *a specific prophecy*, the suppression of which would incur the death penalty.

[It may be conjectured that, as *Sanhedrin* 89a states clearly, Jonah was indeed guilty of suppressing his prophecy but, because he thought that *general reproof* did not constitute a prophecy (see *Malbim* above), his sin was unintentional and, therefore, he did not incur the penalty of death at the hands of heaven.]

4. וַה׳ – *Then* [lit. *and*] HASHEM.

God is here identified by the name HASHEM which reflects His מִדַּת הָרַחֲמִים, *Attribute of Mercy* [rather than אֱלֹהִים which reflects His מִדַּת הַדִּין, Attribute of *Strict Justice;* (see *comm.* to ArtScroll *Genesis* 1:11 s.v. אֱלֹהִים, and 2:4 s.v. ה׳ אֱלֹהִים)]. Because Jonah acted sincerely out of legitimate concern for Israel's welfare, rather than for his own welfare, he merited that all of God's actions toward him should be manifestations of Heavenly mercy *(Daas Soferim)* [and because it is God's Attribute to draw men to repentance].

[As the *Mechilta* notes, Jonah acted for Israel's benefit, intending to give his life for the sake of Israel.]

The prefix ו, *and*, in וַה׳, *And HASHEM* implies a רִבּוּי, *exegetical amplification*, which adds something to the predicate noun, meaning: *HASHEM together with His celestial court (Tanchuma, Vayera.* [see *comm.* to Artscroll *Bereishis* 19:24 וַה׳ הִמְטִיר, and 21:1 וַה׳ פָּקַד]).

וַה׳ הֵטִיל רוּחַ־גְּדוֹלָה אֶל הַיָּם – *Then* [lit. *and*] *HASHEM cast a mighty wind toward the sea.*

[The verse picturesquely portrays God as taking a wind out of His treasury, as it were, and casting it over the seas.] *Cast* is idiomatic.

[4] *Then HASHEM cast a mighty wind toward the
sea, and it became such a mighty tempest in the sea
that the ship threatened to be broken up.* [5] *The
sailors became frightened and cried out each to his*

The idea is that God originated the wind on shore and directed it toward the sea so as to prevent the vessel's safe return to land *(Ibn Ezra).*

Malbim notes that this wind is specifically attributed to God: It was not a *natural storm* since it was unseasonal, but one which was clearly the result of Divine Providence, for as the Sages interpreted, [see below] only Jonah's vessel was affected by it.

Rav M. Hirsch notes that the use of וַה׳ הֵטִיל instead of the usual conversive וַיָּטֶל ה׳ denotes the pluperfect: HASHEM *had* cast [see *Rashi* to *Genesis* 4:1 וְהָאָדָם יָדַע, Adam *had* known]. He accordingly explains the verse as וַה׳ הֵטִיל רוּחַ גְּדוֹלָה אֶל הַיָּם, *HASHEM had sent a stray wind out to sea,* וַיְהִי סַעַר גָּדוֹל בַּיָּם, *and* [i.e., when the ship reached the open sea] *it became a violent storm in the sea.*

וַיְהִי סַעַר־גָּדוֹל בַּיָּם — *And it became* [*such*] *a mighty tempest in the sea* [i.e., the wind *developed* into a mighty tempest at sea.]

[Or render: *And there was a mighty tempest in the sea*].

The word סַעַר, *tempest,* refers to the turbulent waves caused by the violent storm *(Metzudos).*

וְהָאֳנִיָּה חִשְּׁבָה לְהִשָּׁבֵר — *That* [lit. *and*] *the ship threatened* [following *R' M. Hirsch;* lit. *was thought*] *to be broken up.*

It appeared as if it would imminently be broken *(Rashi).*

The inanimate ship is represented poetically as fearing for its own safety; compare such expressions as [*Ezekiel* 14:13] אֶרֶץ כִּי תֶחֱטָא לִי, *when a land sins against Me (Ibn Ezra).* The meaning in our verse is that the *occupants* of the ship thought her to be in imminent danger of breaking up from the force of the crashing waves and turbulent storm *(Mahari Kara; Radak).* [See *Tosafos Nazir* 10a s.v. פָּרָה, that whoever saw the ship would think that it was about to be broken up.]

The *Midrash* [*Bereishis Rabbah* 24:4] derives from the definite article הָ, *the* ship, that it was *only Jonah's ship* that appeared in danger of becoming shipwrecked. Other ships in the area, however, sailed by in tranquility. [See *Radak, v.* 7, below.]

The *Midrash* (ibid.) goes on to compare this wind to the similarly localized wind that destroyed only Job's house [*Job* 1:19], and to the third mighty wind mentioned in Scriptures, that which struck in the days of Elijah. Of the three, only Elijah's was world-wide [*I Kings* 19:11.] (cf. also *Vayikra Rabbah* 15:1).

5. וַיִּירְאוּ הַמַּלָּחִים — [*And*] *the sailors* [or: *mariners*] *became frightened.* — [Over the impending destruction of their vessel].

[*Rashi* in *Exodus* 30:35 renders the word מְמֻלָּח there as *stirred together,* and goes on to suggest that sailors are called

א אִישׁ אֶל־אֱלֹהָיו וַיָּטִלוּ אֶת־הַכֵּלִים אֲשֶׁר
ה בָּאֳנִיָּה אֶל־הַיָּם לְהָקֵל מֵעֲלֵיהֶם וְיוֹנָה
יָרַד אֶל־יַרְכְּתֵי הַסְּפִינָה וַיִּשְׁכַּב וַיֵּרָדַם׃

Malachim since they *stir up* the water with their oars when propelling their ship like one who whips up a bowl of beaten eggs.]

Ramban there maintains, however, that mariners are called *Malachim* [from the word מֶלַח, *salt*] because they know the 'taste' of the sea as if they could feel if it is 'salty' or 'sweet,' i.e., they know whether the sea will be violent or calm for voyage. He goes on to maintain that the term *Malachim* does not apply to *oarsmen* as *Rashi* suggests, but it is applied to navigators who are familiar with the sea.

וַיִּזְעֲקוּ אִישׁ אֶל אֱלֹהָיו — *And cried out, each* [man] *to his own god.*

The first thing men do when on the brink of disaster is to pray *(Abarbanel).*

And as the *Talmud* notes: 'Sailors are generally pious' *(Kiddushin* 82a). [See *Psalms* 107:23 cited in *v.* 11 below.]

Rashi citing *PdRE* notes that the crew was drawn from each of the Seventy Nations [representing the universal family of man; see ArtScroll *Bereishis* I, p.309].

PdRE continues . . . Each one had his deity in his hand and each one proclaimed: 'The god who shall reply and deliver us from this trouble shall be [deemed the true] God!' [cf. Elijah's appearance on Mt. Carmel, I *Kings* 18:24 *(Radal).*]

But, as *PdRE* concludes: their calls to their gods were to no avail.

וַיָּטִלוּ אֶת הַכֵּלִים אֲשֶׁר בָּאֳנִיָּה לְהָקֵל מֵעֲלֵיהֶם — [*And*] *they cast the ship's wares* [lit, *the utensils that were in the ship*] *overboard* [lit. *to the sea*], *to lighten it for* [lit. *from upon*] *them.*

So that the ship might be lighter and thus (floating higher on the water) be better able to escape the storm *(Metzudos).*

The Hebrew for *wares* [כֵּלִים, lit. *utensils*], is ambiguous, since it could refer either to the cargo, the furniture, or any of the weighty items on board. *Radal* [*PdRE* 10;31] records a tradition that, perceiving the ineffectiveness of their prayers, the sailors flung their *idols*, euphemistically referred to here as *utensils*, overboard.

Obviously the wares which were jettisoned were בָּאֳנִיָּה, *on the ship*—where else would they get wares? According to *Radal*, that the wares refer to idols, we may infer that only those idols which were *aboard* were cast away as useless since they were unable to quell the storm. The *institution of idolatry*, however, was not yet rejected by the sailors until *v.* 16 *(Reb Avraham Gold).*

וְיוֹנָה יָרַד אֶל יַרְכְּתֵי הַסְּפִינָה — *But* [*lit.* and] *Jonah had descended to* [one of] *the ship's holds* [lit. plural: *the innermost parts of the ship.*]

— Again the Hebrew construction, וְיוֹנָה יָרַד (as in *v.* 4 וַה׳ הֵטִיל) is in pluperfect: Jonah *had* gone below right from the beginning, when he first boarded the ship. Thus he was already asleep when the storm began. Otherwise, his going to sleep while all the others

I *own god; they cast the ship's wares overboard to*
5 *lighten it for them. But Jonah had descended to one*
of the ship's holds and had lain down and fallen fast
asleep.

started praying to their gods would have been a derisive action *(Rav M. Hirsch).*

Mahari Kara comments, however, that Jonah who, in his innermost heart, knew that he had sinned against God, realized that God would not accept his prayer. He descended to the ship's hold and lay down to sleep, unconcerned, as it were, about the ship's fate.

Abarbanel, in a similar vein, notes that the flow of the narrative implies that while the others indulged in praying to their individual gods, Jonah descended below and did not pray because he was ashamed to beseech Hashem. Instead, he went to sleep expecting to die.

[The translation which takes the prepositional prefix ו of וְיוֹנָה in the conversive: '*but* Jonah had descended', emphasizes the contrast between the gentiles fervently praying to their gods, and Jonah going below.]

Jonah had two intentions in going below deck:

A — He was apprehensive that when the ship sank and he would be thrown into the sea, God might command the waves to carry him back to shore (as indeed once happened to Rabbi Akivah [*Yevamos* 121a]). There Jonah would presumably be the recipient of a new command regarding Nineveh.

In order to avoid this, Jonah wanted to drown. To assure that he would not survive the sinking, he descended to the nethermost parts of the ship which are סָפוּן, *hidden.* To allude to this intent, our verse refers to the ship as סְפִינָה, in contrast to *v.* 3 where it is called אֳנִיָּה.

B — Since Jonah realized that the raging tempest was really on his account, he understood that if he were to drown quickly, the storm would subside. He, therefore, descended deep into the ship's hull where the waters would rush in first. Then the others would be spared since the storm would drown him first and end with his death *(Malbim).*

— [Apparently, such an action could not be termed suicide since he did not actually *jump into* the water.]

The phrase אֶל יַרְכְּתֵי הַסְּפִינָה, lit. *to the innermost parts of the ship,* is clearly elliptic, as it does not mean to suggest that he descended to *all* the innermost parts of the ship. Rather, this construction is similar to *Judges* 12:7 where Yiftach's burial is said to have been בְּעָרֵי גִּלְעָד, *in the cities of Gilead* where clearly *one of the cities* is meant. Here, too, the words *one of* are implied: he descended to *one of the ship's holds,* as in our Translation [following *Radak; Ibn Ezra.*]

וַיִּשְׁכַּב וַיֵּרָדַם — *And [he] had lain down and [he had] fallen fast asleep.*

— From the anguish of his soul *(PdRE).*

—Or according to *R' Bachya*: Jonah went below and slumbered in confident and faithful testimony to his certitude that his actions were

ו וַיִּקְרַב אֵלָיו רַב הַחֹבֵל וַיֹּאמֶר לוֹ מַה־לְּךָ
נִרְדָּם קוּם קְרָא אֶל־אֱלֹהֶיךָ אוּלַי
יִתְעַשֵּׁת הָאֱלֹהִים לָנוּ וְלֹא נֹאבֵד:
ז וַיֹּאמְרוּ אִישׁ אֶל־רֵעֵהוּ לְכוּ וְנַפִּילָה

justified, and that he could be confident of God's help.

Radal defends the *PdRE* interpretation that Jonah's ability to sleep under these circumstances was due to his utter anguish rather that *R' Bachya's* interpretation that he was sure that God would save him because he had fled for the sake of Heaven. *Radal* cites the similar circumstance when Elijah, in *I Kings* 19:4-5, requested for himself that he might die ... and he *lay and slept under a broom tree,* where the sleep there, too, was inspired by agony rather than confidence.

Rav M. Hirsch explains that the word וַיֵּרָדַם [which connotes very deep sleep] suggests that Jonah was so fast asleep that even the storm did not wake him up.

6. וַיִּקְרַב אֵלָיו רַב הַחֹבֵל – [*And*] *the captain approached* [*unto*] *him.*

The captain saw all those on board praying to their gods, while Jonah, in contrast, had gone to sleep. So the captain immediately approached him *(Mahari Kara).*

It must also be remembered that Jonah had *paid the fare for the entire ship* [*v.* 3]. Hence, it was only proper for the captain to seek out the patron who had chartered the vessel *(Harav David Cohen).*

The significance of *approaching him* was that the captain wished to awaken him and speak to him *privately* and reprove him for sleeping while others prayed as if he were indifferent about his own safety or did not believe in a God Who saves (*Radal* note. 33).

The translation רַב הַחֹבֵל as denoting *helmsman* or *captain* follows all commentators. רַב means *officer* or *one in charge;* חֹבֵל from the verb חבל, *tying,* and noun חֶבֶל, *rope,* refers to *a naval crew,* since it is their duty to steer a ship and to tie the sails etc. Cf. *Ezekiel* 27:8: הֵמָּה חֹבְלָיִךְ, *they are your pilots* [cf. *Radak; Ibn Ezra.*]

מַה לְּךָ נִרְדָּם – *How can you sleep so soundly?* [lit. *what is to you, O enslumbered?*]

The translation follows *Rashi*: How can you remain slumbering? This is no time for sleep!

– We are standing here between life and death and you are slumbering and sleeping? *(PdRE).*

– Don't you realize we are all in mortal danger? *(Metzudos).*

– Why don't you pray like the others? *(Mahari Kara).*

קוּם קְרָא אֶל אֱלֹהֶיךָ – *Up!* [lit. *rise!*] *Call to your God.*

I.e., pray to Him *(Targum).*

[According to *PdRE* as explained by *Radal,* the captain assumed that Jonah put such trust in his God that he felt no need to pray. Otherwise, how could he sleep at such a time? Therefore, implicit in the captain's question of *why* he slept, was the further question of his national origin. Jonah responded that he was a Hebrew, with total belief in HASHEM. That this exchange occurs later in *v.* 9 is no contradiction: *there* it was part of his discussion with the *crew*]:

To quote *PdRE:*

The captain said to him: 'Of what

I
6-7

[6] *The captain approached him, and told him: 'How can you sleep so soundly? Up! Call to your God. Perhaps God will pay us mind and we will not perish.'*

[7] *Then they said one to another: 'Come, let us cast*

people are you?' Jonah answered, 'I am a Hebrew.' The captain then said, 'We have heard that the God of the Hebrews is great. Arise, call upon your God!' [see continuation below.]

אוּלַי יִתְעַשֵּׁת הָאֱלֹהִים לָנוּ וְלֹא נֹאבֵד — *Perhaps God will pay us mind and we will not perish.*

[The Name אֱלֹהִים here is preceded in Hebrew by the definite article הָ, *the.* Possibly the intent is: 'Perhaps the God in Whom *you* believe will pay us mind, etc.', or perhaps, following *PdRE* above, they already recognized Him as the Supreme God.]

[Our translation of the rare verb יִתְעַשֵּׁת follows most commentators *(Rashi; Mahari Kara; Ibn Ezra; Radak)* who relate it to the root עשת in the word עֶשְׁתֹּנֹתָיו, *thoughts* in *Psalms* 146:4.]*

Thus, as *Mahari Kara* explains it, 'if you pray fervently to the Holy One, Blessed be He, perhaps He will turn His thoughts to our plight and show us mercy so we will not perish.'

Radak while also relating the verb to עשת, *thought*, perceives the nuance to connote *be appeased* [thus accounting also for the *hispa'el*-reflexive form of the verb]; *Targum* renders similarly: *will* [*allow Himself to*] *be merciful.*

Or, as *R' M. Hirsch* suggests: 'Call to *your* God, perhaps that God *will change His mind in our favor* so that we do not perish.'

Continuing *PdRE* [see above]: '...Perhaps He will work [thus interpreting יַעֲשֶׂה=יִתְעַשֵּׁת, *work (Radal)*] *miracles for us as He did for your ancestors at the Sea of Reeds.*'

— Your ability to sleep during such a dangerous time indicates a confident faith in your own righteousness. You might be confident that your God will save *you*; pray to him that He save *us* as well (*Minchah Gedolah;* [see on next verse s.v. לְכוּ]).

7. **וַיֹּאמְרוּ אִישׁ אֶל רֵעֵהוּ** — *Then they said one to another* [lit. *man to his comrade.*]

It is the *crew* which is now speaking *(Metzudos).*

[We are not told whether or not Jonah prayed. According to *Mahari Kara v.* 5 s.v. וְיוֹנָה יָרַד, it would seem that he did *not* pray, because the reason he went to sleep was that he considered it futile to pray since he was the culprit. In any event, this verse now shifts to the crew-members. Seeing that their prayers to their own deities were in vain, and seeing that the storm was not subsiding, they concluded that the

*Cf. *Rashi* to *Exod.* 32:12 where he explains וְהִנָּחֵם [relent] as הִתְעַשֵּׁת מַחֲשָׁבָה אַחֶרֶת, *consider a different thought* [i.e., change Your mind, so to speak *(Mizrachi)*]. See also *Rashi* further 3:10 s.v. וְנִחַם.

א גּוֹרָלוֹת וְנֵדְעָה בְּשֶׁלְּמִי הָרָעָה הַזֹּאת לָנוּ
ח וַיַּפִּלוּ גּוֹרָלוֹת וַיִּפֹּל הַגּוֹרָל עַל־יוֹנָה׃
ח וַיֹּאמְרוּ אֵלָיו הַגִּידָה־נָּא לָנוּ בַּאֲשֶׁר לְמִי־
הָרָעָה הַזֹּאת לָנוּ מַה־מְּלַאכְתְּךָ וּמֵאַיִן

storm was of a retributive nature and decided to cast lots.]

According to *PdRE*, it was at *this* point that Jonah advised them that the storm was on his account and that they should cast him into the sea. But the men would not consent to do so; instead they cast lots among themselves and the lot fell upon Jonah.

In the Book of Jonah his confession appears later, in *v.* 12, after the casting of the lots. The apparent discrepancy may be explained as follows: either because Biblical narratives are not necessarily in chronological sequence (אֵין מוּקְדָּם וּמְאוּחָר בַּתּוֹרָה) [but cf. *Pesachim* 4a], or because the implication is that their *plan* to cast lots occurred even *before* he confessed he was the cause of their misfortune. Scripture preferred to state the matter of the lots together with his revelation, for, by the time they were able to cast lots, the captain had already spoken to Jonah and had learned that he was a distinguished personage. They spoke to him before casting the lots and, although he accepted responsibility for their plight, they refused to accede to his request that they throw him overboard. Instead, they cast lots to determine whether his disobedience was truly the cause of the storm *(Radal).*

לְכוּ וְנַפִּילָה גוֹרָלוֹת — *Come, let us cast lots* [the rendering reflects the idiom; lit. *go and we will cast lots.*]

[*Lots* is in plural. See below.]

Why should they have suspected that the cause for this storm was to be found on board their own ship? Were there not other ships sailing the seas? Does the crew of every ship caught in a storm cast lots to establish guilt? But, as noted in *Pirkei d'Rabbi Eliezer*, the tempest was directed only against Jonah's ship. The crew could see other ships to their right and left plying to and fro peacefully through the tranquility of the sea (*Radak;* also *Rashi; Ibn Ezra;* et al).

According to *Minchah Gedolah*, the captain had considered Jonah's ability to sleep during the storm as a sign of his righteousness and confidence in his God Who would save him. [See end of previous verse.] The crew, however, contended that the reverse might be true: they were guiltless and Jonah might be the culprit. They therefore decided to cast lots to establish the guilt.

וְנֵדְעָה — *That we may determine* [lit. *and we will know.*]

[They relied on the result of a lot since the casting of lots in Scripture was generally considered to reflect Divine sanction (see, for example, *Rashi* to *Joshua* 7:17).]

[For the halachic implications of whether one may rely on the casting of lots in similar circumstances, consult the sources cited in Rav Reuven Margoliot's notes on *Sefer Chasidim, Mossad Harav Kook* ed., paragraphs 679 and 701.]

בְּשֶׁלְּמִי הָרָעָה הַזֹּאת לָנוּ — *On whose account* [lit. *in belonging to whom*] *this calamity* [*lit. evil*] *is upon us.* — I.e., בְּמַעֲשָׂיו שֶׁל מִי, *because of the deeds of whom,* לָנוּ, *among us* [has this calamity befallen us] *(Rashi).*

Ibn Ezra renders: because of whom.

I lots that we may determine on whose account this
8 calamity is upon us.' So they cast lots and the lot fell
on Jonah.

[8] *They said to him: 'Tell us, now: in regard to whom has this calamity befallen us? What is your*

וַיַּפִּלוּ גוֹרָלוֹת — *So* [lit. *and*] *they cast lots.*

Lots is plural. They did not act hastily, but with great restraint and cunning. They were apprehensive that the result of a *single* casting of lots would be inconclusive since the lot would have to fall on *someone* even if he were not guilty. They cast lots *numerous times,* so that if *it consistently fell on the same person* it would prove that the finding was accurate *(Akeidas Yitzchak* 63; *Abarbanel; Metzudos).*

וַיִּפֹּל הַגּוֹרָל עַל יוֹנָה — *And the lot fell on Jonah.*

I.e., each and every one *of the numerous castings of lots* consistently fell on Jonah *(Metzudos).*

...And this caused them to believe without a doubt, the accuracy of the result *(Akeidas Yitzchak).*

8. הַגִּידָה־נָּא לָנוּ — *Tell us, now.*

I.e., since the lots consistently fell on you, please inform us ... *(Metzudos).*

[Cf. similar expression used by Eliezer in questioning Rebecca at the well in *Genesis* 24:23: הַגִּידִי נָא לִי. *Haamek Davar* there explains: *give a fully detailed account.* It is implied by the verb הגד, *tell,* which denotes a *comprehensively detailed account* (in contrast with אמר, *say,* which has a more superficial connotation).]

בַּאֲשֶׁר לְמִי הָרָעָה הַזֹּאת לָנוּ — *In regard to whom has this calamity* [lit. *evil*] *befallen us?*

The translation reflects the ambiguity of the Hebrew. We follow *Rashi* who comments that the phrase implies: *because* of [*sins*] *against whom* i.e. against whom have you sinned with the result that this calamity has befallen us? *(Rashi).*

Cf. *Targum* who renders: בְּדִיל מָה, *for what reason ...?*

— Perhaps we can appease Him by making restitution *(Sforno).*

[*Radak* takes בַּאֲשֶׁר לְמִי to mean: *on account of whom* (synonymous with בְּשֶׁלְּמִי in *v.* 7). However, since the outcome of the lots has already identified Jonah as being the one on whose account the evil has befallen them, *Radak* interprets this in apposition to the implied subject *you.* They addressed Jonah as the responsible culprit]:

— 'Tell us, then, *you on whose account this calamity has befallen us'* [as evidenced by the outcome of the lots]: What is your trade, etc.?

According to *Malbim,* the fact that the lots fell upon someone indicated either that the person himself was guilty, or that he knew the reason for the calamity. They therefore approached him now with a double question: (a) to whom did you sin to bring about such calamity? [comp. *Rashi* above]; or (b) if you are not to blame, who among us is? The fact that the lot fell upon you means you must know.

א תָּבוֹא מָה אַרְצֶךָ וְאֵי־מִזֶּה עַם אָתָּה:
ט ט וַיֹּאמֶר אֲלֵיהֶם עִבְרִי אָנֹכִי וְאֶת יהוה
אֱלֹהֵי הַשָּׁמַיִם אֲנִי יָרֵא אֲשֶׁר־עָשָׂה אֶת

Then they asked him the questions that follow.

[It is also possible that the sailors were not prepared to condemn Jonah on the evidence of the lot alone (cf. *PdRE)* They sought a confession from him as did Joshua from Achan (see *comm.* to *Joshua* 7:19); or they wished to learn more details in order to help him repent and make amends. See *v.* 11.]

מַה מְּלַאכְתְּךָ — *What is your trade?* [lit. *work; occupation.*]

— Perhaps you have been remiss in the performance of your occupation [and this calamity is the punishment *(Mahari Kara)*] *(Rashi).*

— Perhaps you engage in an immoral or criminal occupation as a result of which you are guilty *(Radak)*;... and restitution is impossible since many victims were wronged *(Metzudos).*

וּמֵאַיִן תָּבוֹא — [*And*] *from where do you come?*

I.e., what is your home-town? *(Mahari Kara).*

— Perhaps a decree of punishment has been proclaimed against the people of that place [and you are being punished] although you are not there now? *(Rashi).*

— Perhaps you are fleeing because of some crime you committed there? *(Radak)*;

...And the distance is too great to return and make proper restitution *(Metzudos).*

מָה אַרְצֶךָ — *What is your land?*

— You might respond to the previous question by stating that the folks of your home-town are righteous, but perhaps the people of your native land are wicked [and you are now being punished on *their* account]? *(Mahari Kara; Radak).*

וְאֵי־מִזֶּה עַם אָתָּה — *And of what people are you?*

Even if you answer all of the foregoing in the negative, perhaps the people of your race in general have sinned — even if those of your native land are righteous, and we are all now being punished as a result? *(Rashi; Mahari Kara).*

Are they a people which is hateful to God because of its sinfulness? The phrase וְאֵי־מִזֶּה is equal to וּמֵאֵיזֶה, *and from which (Radak).*

Metzudos: The implication of this question [presumably since every people had its own national idolatry] is: who is your God, and how have you acted sinfully against Him?

9. I am an Ivri!

עִבְרִי אָנֹכִי — *I am an Ivri* [usually translated: *Hebrew*].

[This was the title used for Jews especially when they were referred to in contrast to gentiles. Joseph so identified himself (*Gen.* 40:15), and God used the designation of *God of the Ivrim* in His command to Moses to visit Pharaoh (*Exod.* 3:18). After the Exile of the Ten Tribes when the Tribe of Yehudah remained the principal branch of the nation, the term *Yehudi* for *Jew* came into general use.]

I *trade? And from where do you come? What is your*
9 *land? And of what people are you?'*
⁹ He said to them: 'I am an Ivri and HASHEM, the
God of the Heavens, do I fear, Who made the sea and

The title *Ivri* has been discussed in the *comm.* to ArtScroll *Bereishis* 14:13 where Abraham is referred as *the Ivri.*

To restate it briefly, *Rashi* there interprets the term to refer to those who originated from the 'other side' [עֵבֶר] of the River [Euphrates.]

The above follows the view of the Sages in the *Midrash.* Rav Yehudah said that the name *Ivri* in that verse signifies that the whole world was on one side [עֵבֶר], while Abraham was on the other side [i.e., he alone of all mankind stood apart and served the true God while all the others practiced idolatry.] According to Rav Nechemiah in the *Midrash,* עִבְרִי, *Ivri,* referred to Abraham as a descendant of עֵבֶר, *Eber.* [See *Gen.* 10:25; 11:16-26.]

It is the latter view in the *Midrash,* relating the title *Ivri* to the descendants of *Eber,* that is adopted by most of the commentators who seek the literal sense of Scripture:

Radak (Gen. 14:13) adds that although all of Eber's descendants traced their lineage to him, Abraham and his descendants are unique in being entitled *Ivrim,* for they alone remained loyal to the language of Eber [=Hebrew; see *Maharazu* to the *Midrash* cited above] while Eber's other descendants spoke Aramaic. They are therefore referred to as Arameans, as for example *Laban the Aramean* [*Gen.* 25:20], while Abraham's line through Jacob was called *Ivrim.*

Mizrachi to *Gen.* 39:14 asserts that the term *Ivri* was used only for someone who was *both* a descendant of Eber and who also originated form the other side of the river. Isaac is considered an *Ivri,* but Ishmael is not [because Ishmael's Egyptian mother Hagar, was not descended from Eber], although Ishmael, too, descended from the Abrahamitic line.

According to *Sforno* and *Tur (Gen.* 14:13) *Ivri refers to one who was a believer in the religion of Eber,* the great-grandson of Shem. [So *Ibn Ezra* to *our* verse.]

Sforno to our verse adds that the implication of Jonah's all encompassing answer was that he was an *Ivri,* a disciple of Eber. That is, he belonged to a people who have neither a trade, nor are they tied to a particular place of residence, but who wander from city to city to study and teach, and thus are not considered part of the general populace [and accordingly they would not be punished for the sins of those among whom they stayed.]

Radak comments similarly that the statement *I am an Ivri,* gave them now an answer to their latter two questions regarding his land and people [=*Eretz Yisrael* and the Jews.]

וְאֶת ה' אֱלֹהֵי הַשָּׁמַיִם אֲנִי יָרֵא – *And HASHEM, the God of the Heavens, do I fear.*

With this acknowledgment, Jonah responded by implication to their first question: Be assured that,

א
י־יא

י הַיָּם וְאֶת־הַיַּבָּשָׁה: וַיִּֽירְאוּ הָאֲנָשִׁים
יִרְאָה גְדוֹלָה וַיֹּאמְרוּ אֵלָיו מַה־זֹּאת
עָשִׂיתָ כִּי־יָדְעוּ הָאֲנָשִׁים כִּי־מִלִּפְנֵי יהוה
יא הוּא בֹרֵחַ כִּי הִגִּיד לָהֶם: וַיֹּאמְרוּ אֵלָיו

as a true believer in HASHEM, my trade is an honest one. I engage in no criminal activities. The term *'God' of the heavens* depicts Him as their Leader and Judge *(Radak).*

— And it is to Him that I sinned *(Metzudos).*

[The term יִרְאַת ה׳, *fear of God,* signifies an all-encompassing unconditional trust in God with reverent and humble obedience to His Torah and every *Mitzvah.* The crew, however, drew from this an implication that Jonah was literally *afraid* of God from Whom he was accordingly now fleeing (see *R' Bachya* cited end of *v.* 10 s.v. כִּי הִגִּיד לָהֶם). This is also the opinion of *Abarbanel.*]

אֲשֶׁר עָשָׂה אֶת הַיָּם וְאֶת הַיַּבָּשָׁה — *Who made the sea and the dry land.*

— And as the Supreme Ruler it is *He* Who caused this storm; *He* will quiet the storm when He desires it, and bring us back to dry land. Jonah used the term עָשָׂה, *made,* which means *bringing to a state of completion* [see *Rashi* and *Ramban* to *Gen.* 1:7], instead of the term בָּרָא, *created,* because although land and sea were created [בָּרָא] on the first day, they were not [עָשָׂה] fashioned by Him in their final form for man's use until He confined the waters on the third day of Creation [see *Gen.* 1:9] *(Radak).*

— Just as He made the dry land, He also made the seas, and His rule extends everywhere. The implication is that Jonah now made it a point to acknowledge publicly that it was futile for him even to entertain the notion of escaping God's influence by taking to the sea, for even there the Hand of God would seek him out and force him to complete his prophetic mission to Nineveh *(Metzudos).*

I.e., he now made it manifestly clear that they should not misinterpret his having taken to the sea as an indication that he did not thereby accept God's sovereignty over the seas. To the contrary! Hashem made the seas too! It was only His prophetic call which limits itself to the environs of *Eretz Yisrael,* that Jonah had intended to evade *(Alshich).*

Malbim suggest that it is apparent that just as Jonah specifically answered their latter four questions, he must also have specifically responded to their first question as well and related to them the full circumstances of his being a prophet, and his reason for fleeing from HASHEM's call.

10. וַיִּירְאוּ הָאֲנָשִׁים יִרְאָה גְדוֹלָה — *The men were seized* [lit. *frightened*] *with great fear.*

[The fear was motivated by Jonah's description of HASHEM's might, as well as the knowledge that it was against *Him* that Jonah had sinned, and that accordingly it was *His* anger which was now being

I the dry land.'
10 10 *The men were seized with great fear and they*
asked him: 'What is this that you have done?' For the
men knew that it was from before HASHEM'*s*
Presence that he was fleeing, for he had so told them.

manifested by the storm imperiling their lives (cf. *Metzudos).*]

— The *fear* in v. 5 was one of mortal danger; the *fear* here was of a higher form: *fear* (i.e. awe) *of God (Malbim).* [Perhaps that is why they are here described not as *sailors*, but as אֲנָשִׁים, *men,* which Scripture employs as a term of distinction.]

מַה־זֹּאת עָשִׂיתָ — *What is this that you have done?*

— Why have you acted this way — to run from a Ruler such as He? *(Rashi).*

— How could you have expected to escape His presence in the sea? (*Mahari Kara* [see *Amos* 3:9]).

— If your God is the God of the whole universe, Who is as much the God of the sea as of the land, for God's sake what is this then that you have done! *(R' M. Hirsch).*

This is not a simple query, but an exclamation of amazement: How could you have done such a thing, to rebel against God's Word and flee from the place of prophecy?! Comp. Laban's incredulous exclamation to Jacob in *Genesis* 31:26: *What have you done, that you have deceived me! (Metzudos).*

[An even closer parallel is God's rhetorical question to Eve in *Genesis* 3:13 מַה זֹּאת עָשִׂית, *What is this that you have done?* which *R' Meyuchas* explains as: How could you have done such a dastardly act?]

כִּי יָדְעוּ הָאֲנָשִׁים כִּי מִלִּפְנֵי ה׳ הוּא בֹרֵחַ — *For the men knew that it was from before* HASHEM'*s Presence that he was fleeing.*

[The verse again emphasizes that even the crew was aware by this time that it was not מִפְּנֵי ה׳, *away from* HASHEM, that Jonah presumed to flee, but, as explained in *v.* 3, he was attempting to flee *from* HASHEM'*s prophetic call* as implicit in the phrase מִלִּפְנֵי ה׳, literally: *away from* (serving *before* HASHEM.]

כִּי הִגִּיד לָהֶם — *For he had* [so] *told them.*

Although we are not told specifically of this revelation, *Radak* concludes after Jonah told them that he feared HASHEM, an exchange took place wherein Jonah revealed that he was a prophet who was evading a commission to go to Nineveh. *Ibn Ezra* also maintains that Jonah revealed his secret to them. [See *comm.* to *v.* 7 where it is noted that according to *PdRE* Jonah revealed his guilt to them even before they had cast the lots.]

[According to *R' Bachya,* an explicit confession did not take place. Rather the verse means that the crew *perceived it by implication*]:

The crew understood Jonah's expression *I fear the God of the heavens* to mean that he *feared* God's retribution. From this they discerned that it was against Him

א יב

מַה־נַּעֲשֶׂה לָּךְ וְיִשְׁתֹּק הַיָּם מֵעָלֵינוּ כִּי
יב הַיָּם הוֹלֵךְ וְסֹעֵר׃ וַיֹּאמֶר אֲלֵיהֶם שָׂאוּנִי
וַהֲטִילֻנִי אֶל־הַיָּם וְיִשְׁתֹּק הַיָּם מֵעֲלֵיכֶם

that he had sinned, and from Whom he was now in flight. This is the intent of our verse which states that Jonah had *'told'* them, although this conversation is nowhere explicitly recorded *(R'Bachya).*

Abarbanel however, holds that implicit in Jonah's expression *I fear the God of the heavens,* was an *actual confession* verbalized by Jonah that he was literally *afraid* of God's punishment, because he was fleeing from Him. Otherwise, there was nothing for him to *fear.*

According to *Metzudos:* From the previously recorded dialogue, the crew surmised that he was fleeing from HASHEM's prophecy as if he had told them so explicitly.

11. מַה נַּעֲשֶׂה לָּךְ וְיִשְׁתֹּק הַיָּם מֵעָלֵינוּ — *What must* [*lit. shall*] *we do to you that* [lit. *and*] *the sea subside from upon us?* [i.e. that its waves cease from breaking over us *(R' M. Hirsch)*]

— Advise us what our course of action should be *(Ibn Ezra).*

Having heard Jonah describe himself as a prophet of Hashem, they reverently refrained from harming him for who shall lay a hand upon the anointed of Hashem and be acquitted? Or, since the storm now threatening them all was in retribution for his fleeing Hashem's service, they were sorely afraid that they would all perish even before they had a chance to execute judgment, so they asked his immediate guidance *(Almosnino).*

[Apparently they felt that as a prophet, and as the cause of the storm, he would know the remedy.]

According to *Malbim,* they were asking him whether he was ready to repent and resume his mission to Nineveh.

They were ready to accompany him there or return him to *Eretz Yisrael,* back to God's jurisdiction, so to speak *(Abarbanel).*

[In general, sailors — *'they who go down to the sea in ships, who ply their trade in the* great *waters' (Psalms* 107:23; see footnote on next page — are depicted in Scripture as righteous people because they recognize the Hand of God everywhere for their work places them in constant peril. As the Psalmist (*ibid.)* continues: *'they saw the deeds of* HASHEM *and His wonders in the deep.'*(See *Mishnah, Kiddushin* 82a).]

The expression וְיִשְׁתֹּק הַיָּם, *that the sea subside,* is reminiscent of *Psalm* 170:30: וַיִּשְׂמְחוּ כִּי יִשְׁתֹּקוּ, *they were glad when they were quiet (Ibn Ezra; Radak).*[1]

כִּי הַיָּם הוֹלֵךְ וְסֹעֵר — *For the sea grows stormier* [lit. *is going and storming.*]

[The punctuation of the Translation follows those commentators who include this last clause *within the direct quotation of the sailors' question,* rather than as an informative observation recorded by Scripture.]

— 'We have no hope that the storm will subside [of its own accord without a symbolic act on our

[11] *They said to him: 'What must we do to you that the sea subside from upon us? — for the sea grows stormier.'*

[12] *He said to them: 'Pick me up and heave me into the sea and the sea will calm down for you, for I*

part] as evidenced by the fact that the sea is growing increasingly stormy' *(Radak).*

— The storm is increasing in intensity and there is no more time to procrastinate and consider the matter. Therefore *you* tell us what we should do to you, and so shall it be *(Metzudos).*

12. Jonah's suggestion.

שָׂאוּנִי וַהֲטִילֻנִי אֶל הַיָּם — *Pick me up and heave me into the sea.*

— So strong was Jonah's desire to die rather than [become the instrument of] Nineveh's repentance. But he would never have suggested this solution had he not previously overheard that they were planning to throw him overboard *(Ibn Ezra).*[2]

It was thus Jonah's absolute love for Israel that motivated him to make the supreme gesture of offer-

1. Since the description of the storm, its effects and the righteous sailors' response is so reminiscent of *Psalms* 107:23-32, we cite it in full:

[23] They who go down to the sea in ships,
who ply their trade in the great waters;
[24] They saw the deed of HASHEM
and His wonders in the deep.
[25] He spoke and set up a stormy wind
and it lifted its waves.
[26] They ascended to the heavens, plunged to the depths;
their souls were melted in misery.
[27] They went round and staggered like a drunkard,
and all their wisdom was unavailing.
[28] Then they cried to HASHEM in their distress;
and from their trouble He rescued them.
[29] He halted the storm to a stillness,
the waves were silenced.
[30] They were glad when they were quiet,
and He guided them to their desired haven.
[31] They thanked HASHEM for His kindness,
and His wonders for mankind.
[32] They exalted Him in the congregation of the people,
and in the assembly of the elders they praised Him.

2. According to *Mechilta, Bo,* however, Jonah's intention *from the very beginning* was to perish in the sea, as it says, *Pick me up and heave me into the sea.*

So do you find that our ancestral leaders and prophets offered their lives on behalf of Israel.

—Moses, as it is written [*Exodus* 32:32]: *'Yet now, if You will forgive their sin,* [and if not, please *blot me out of Your Book which You have written'*] . . . such being tantamount to Your taking my life;

— David, of whom it is written [II *Sam.* 24:17]: *'Lo I have sinned ... but these sheep, what have they done? Let Your hand, I pray You, be against me and my father's house.'*

— Thus we see[the great love our ancestors had for Israel] — for we find that the patriarchs offered their lives on behalf of Israel. [See *Overview.*]

א
יג־יד

כִּ֣י יוֹדֵ֣עַ אָ֔נִי כִּ֣י בְשֶׁלִּ֔י הַסַּ֧עַר הַגָּד֛וֹל הַזֶּ֖ה
יג עֲלֵיכֶֽם׃ וַיַּחְתְּר֣וּ הָאֲנָשִׁ֗ים לְהָשִׁ֛יב אֶל־
הַיַּבָּשָׁ֖ה וְלֹ֣א יָכֹ֑לוּ כִּ֣י הַיָּ֔ם הוֹלֵ֥ךְ וְסֹעֵ֖ר
יד עֲלֵיהֶֽם׃ וַיִּקְרְא֨וּ אֶל־יהוה וַיֹּאמְר֗וּ אָנָּ֤ה
יהוה אַל־נָ֣א נֹאבְדָ֗ה בְּנֶ֙פֶשׁ֙ הָאִ֣ישׁ הַזֶּ֔ה

ing his life for them [see *comm.* to *v.* 2 and 3 and Overview]. According to *Aburbanel,* this gesture was Jonah's saving grace.

Note that Jonah did not throw *himself* overboard. He decided that since there were gentiles aboard it would be preferable for *them* to throw him overboard [as this would smack less of suicide] (*Sefer Chassidim* 679). [See *Ohel David; Shem HaGedolim* s.v. *R'Yehudah ben HaRosh*].

It may be that Jonah wished to be thrown overboard so that he would die by drowning, a form of asphyxiation, since he was guilty of suppressing his prophecy, an offense for which one is liable to death at the hands of heaven (*Sanhedrin* 89a). According to *Sukkah* 53b, the form of death for withholding knowledge is asphyxiation. Since Jonah had been placed in a situation where drowning was imminent, he understood it to be a fitting punishment for his transgression *(R' Reuven Margoliot, comm.* to *Sefer Chasidim, ibid.).*

כִּי יוֹדֵעַ אָנִי כִּי בְשֶׁלִּי — *For I know that* [*it is*] *because of me* [lit. *because of that which is mine*].

— I.e., because of my sin *(Radak).*

— Have no fear that you will be punished as accomplices. The storm is directed toward *me alone,* not you; once you cast me into the sea you can be assured that the storm will subside and calm will return *(Malbim).*

13. But the sailors were reluctant to sacrifice Jonah ...

וַיַּחְתְּרוּ הָאֲנָשִׁים — *Nevertheless* [lit *and;* the conjunctive being rendered here as the conversive] *the men rowed hard.*

The verb literally refers to boring, or digging; here it is interpreted figuratively as *rowing hard,* since this is akin to 'digging into the water' with the oars and forcing one's way through the wall of waves *(Radak; Ibn Ezra).*

— They toiled like one who digs a tunnel *(Rashi)*; and vigorously rowed against the force of the storm *(Mahari Kara).*

[*Harav David Feinstein* notes that 'tunneling' often indicates a desire to do something stealthily, like the thief who burrows into a house to escape detection. Thus, the sailors tried to row back to shore as if 'tunneling' in an attempt to deceive God.]

Michlol Yofi offers a novel interpretation of this phrase: they *thought hard,* seeking ideas and plans to enable them to bring the ship back to shore.

Ibn Ezra interprets this verse as parenthetic, and in the past perfect: 'Now the men *had* rowed hard to return to shore but could not ... '

לְהָשִׁיב אֶל הַיַּבָּשָׁה — *To return to the shore* [lit. *the dry land*].

[Afraid to harm the prophet (as noted above)] their plan was to return to land and there put Jonah

know that it is because of me that this terrible storm
is upon you.' 13 *Nevertheless the men rowed hard to*
return to the shore, but they could not, because the
sea was growing stormier upon them.
14 *Then they called out to HASHEM, and said: 'O,*
please, HASHEM, let us not perish on account of this

off the ship after which they would continue their journey *(Metzudos).*

— Their purpose was to return him to the jurisdiction of his God *(Abarbanel)* as an alternative to heeding Jonah's suggestion of casting him overboard *(Alshich;* cf. *Malbim).*

According to *Daas Soferim,* however, the sailors' reluctance to throw Jonah overboard was based on a practical consideration. Having been informed that God's wrath resulted from Jonah's refusal to fulfill God's mission to Nineveh, the sailors reasoned that the Divine fury would only be increased — and turned against them — if they caused Jonah to drown, since, in effect, the mission would then definitely go unfulfilled. If they were to do that, they would be thwarting God's will and thus be subjected to punishment themselves.

וְלֹא יָכְלוּ כִּי הַיָּם הוֹלֵךְ וְסֹעֵר עֲלֵיהֶם — *But they could not, because the sea was growing stormier* [lit. *was going and storming*] *upon them.*

I.e., because the tempestuous waves were breaking upon them from the direction of the shore, forcing the ship away from the coast and ever further out to sea *(Metzudos).*

14. וַיִּקְרְאוּ אֶל ה׳ — *Then* [lit. *and*] *they called out to HASHEM* [i.e., *in prayer (Targum).*]

— They all began to believe in the Ineffable Name [HASHEM] so they proceeded to call upon Him *(Ibn Ezra).*

[Apparently they were thereby signifying their acceptance of Hashem, Whose might Jonah had described to them in *v.* 9, and Who had sent this storm. Originally they had cried out to their own gods *(v.* 5) for salvation, but seeing that their prayers were ineffective, and that it was Jonah's God, the God of the Heavens, etc., Who was responsible for the storm, they now directed their prayers to Him. They knew that they would be hurling him to certain death, and they feared that God would hold them responsible for his death. They therefore felt that a final, conciliatory prayer was in order before Jonah was thrown overboard.]

According to *PdRE* they uttered this prayer while standing with Jonah at the side of the ship.

אַל־נָא נֹאבְדָה בְּנֶפֶשׁ הָאִישׁ הַזֶּה — *Let us not perish on account of* [lit. *in*] *this man's soul.*

— I.e., [do not condemn us] for the sin of being about to take his life *(Rashi);* by throwing him overboard *(Metzudos).*

According to *Alshich,* before they cast him overboard they in-

א
טו־טז

וְאַל־תִּתֵּן עָלֵינוּ דָּם נָקִיא כִּי־אַתָּה יהוה
טו כַּאֲשֶׁר חָפַצְתָּ עָשִׂיתָ׃ וַיִּשְׂאוּ אֶת־יוֹנָה
וַיְטִלֻהוּ אֶל־הַיָּם וַיַּעֲמֹד הַיָּם מִזַּעְפּוֹ׃
טז וַיִּירְאוּ הָאֲנָשִׁים יִרְאָה גְדוֹלָה אֶת־יהוה

voked Hashem to rationalize their intentions by claiming that it would be improper to spare the man. Their reasoning was: אַל נָא נֹאבְדָה בְּנֶפֶשׁ הָאִישׁ הַזֶּה, *'let us not perish on account of this man,* for although he is a more distinguished personage than we, is it proper that we should forfeit our lives along with his? What possible benefit could there be from our dying along with him?' (*Malbim* interprets similarly).

וְאַל תִּתֵּן עָלֵינוּ דָּם נָקִיא — *And do not reckon it to us* [lit. *and do not place upon us*] *as* [*shedding*] *innocent* [lit. *clean*] *blood.*

The translation follows *Mahari Kara.*

[Lit. the phrase, *do not place upon us* ... implies: 'do not place the *onus* of innocent blood upon us,' i.e., our action should not be considered willful murder.]

For even though he is guilty of death by the hands of Heaven for suppressing his prophecy, nevertheless if we were to take his life without sufficient cause, we would be guilty. — Therefore we ask You not to consider us as murderers (*Malbim;* see *footnote* below).

[The sailors were emphasizing that although Jonah was not innocent in God's judgment, he was innocent *vis-a-vis* them for he had done nothing to merit death at *their* hands.]

כִּי אַתָּה ה׳ כַּאֲשֶׁר חָפַצְתָּ עָשִׂיתָ — *For You,* HASHEM, [or: *for You are* HASHEM]; as You wished so have You done.

— You have brought about this storm on his account *(Ibn Ezra).*

— And it is You who apparently wills it that we throw him overboard; do not blame us *(R' Eliezer of Beaugency).*

— Everything is subject to Your will. Had You wanted him to die some other way, nothing could have impeded You. It is Your decree that he die at our hands *(Metzudos).*

He has already been condemned by You, or else You would never have brought such a tempest upon us! Since our ship is the only one affected by this storm, it is quite evident that You wish him to be cast into the sea to calm it, *and it is as if You Yourself have done it! (Alshich; Malbim).*[1]

15. Jonah is cast overboard.

וַיִּשְׂאוּ אֶת יוֹנָה וַיְטִלֻהוּ אֶל הַיָּם — *And they lifted Jonah up and heaved him into the sea.*

1. See *Ramban* to *Gen.* 15:4 (cited briefly in ArtScroll *Bereishis II* p. 529) where in a fundamental dissertation *Ramban* discusses the philosophical implication of the guilt for the murder of someone whose death had already been predetermined on Rosh Hashanah. Because the murderer acted out of his own motives and was unaware of the decree, he cannot plead that he was merely carrying out God's decree. This is in contrast to one who heard the decree from a prophet and fulfills it because *he sincerely wishes to fulfill God's will* in which case,

I
15-16

man's soul and do not reckon it to us as innocent
blood, for You, HASHEM, as You wished so have You
done.' 15 *And they lifted Jonah up and heaved him*
into the sea, and the sea stopped its raging. 16 *Then*
the men feared HASHEM greatly and they offered a

[*Pirkei d'Rabbi Eliezer* describes the crew's continual reluctance — up to the very last moment — to cast Jonah into the sea. They did not do it in one step, but in gradual stages]:

First they took him and cast him into the sea up to his knees, and the storm abated. But when they lifted him out of the water [in an effort to save him rather than allow him to drown] the sea raged again. The next time they lowered him up to his navel and the storm abated, but again, when they lifted him out of the water onto the deck, the sea resumed its raging. The third time, they cast him up to his neck and the very same thing happened. [They considered this three-fold repetition to be a חֲזָקָה, an assertion of Jonah's guilt *(Radal)*]. Then *they lifted Jonah up and heaved him into the sea, and the sea stopped its rage.*

וַיַּעֲמֹד הַיָּם מִזַּעְפּוֹ — *And the sea stopped its* [lit. *from its*] *raging.*

— *Rage* is used here metaphorically to depict the forcefulness of the waves as if the sea were angry *(Metzudos).*

16. The conversion of the crew.

וַיִּירְאוּ הָאֲנָשִׁים יִרְאָה גְדוֹלָה אֶת ה׳ — *Then* [lit. *and*] *the men feared HASHEM greatly* [lit. *a great fear.*][1]

Awed at having witnessed this display of God's Providence and Omnipotence (Metzudos).

They underwent conversion in God's Name *(Mahari Kara).*

As *R' M. Hirsch* explains: The immediate calming of the raging

Ramban notes, he is guiltless and is even considered meritorious, as was Jehu, who killed the family of Ahab in obedience of the prophecy of Jonah (see *II Kings* 10:30). If however, one murders out of *personal vindictiveness, or hopes of gain,* then, though God's plan was accomplished through him, he is guilty. This is expressly stated with respect to Senacherib (see *Isaiah* 10:5-6). Pharaoh, too, deserved punishment because he acted overzealously out of *personal* vindictiveness in enslaving the Israelites.

This is also the case with Nebuchadnezzar. Although the prophets unanimously called upon him and his people to destroy Jerusalem [see, e.g., *Jeremiah* 25:9; *32:28* -29], and though the Chaldeans were aware that this was the command of God, nevertheless they were punished because Nebuchadnezzar had his own personal glory in mind [see *Isaiah* 14:13, 14; 47:8], and because he overzealously perpetrated evil against Israel beyond the requirements of the decree [see *Isaiah* 47:6.]

[Although they were gentiles and their act does not concern us *halachically,* it would be interesting to establish in which category the sailors belong: since they took every precaution before finally throwing Jonah entirely overboard (as *PdRE* notes, see next verse), can their action be considered a meritorious fulfillment of God's wish without vindiction? Or, since their primary aim in throwing Jonah overboard was to spare their own lives, were they guilty because their motive was tainted by self-interest?

See *Rama, Yoreh De'ah* 157:1 for the possibly analogous case of a demand that the specific guilty party be surrendered to his pursuer. The halachic status of lots in determining guilt would also come into play.]

ב א וַיִּזְבְּחוּ־זֶבַח לַיהוָה וַיִּדְּרוּ נְדָרִים׃ וַיְמַן
א יהוה דָּג גָּדוֹל לִבְלֹעַ אֶת־יוֹנָה וַיְהִי יוֹנָה

sea was the most conclusive proof of the nearness of HASHEM. This verse shows the deep impression which this visible evidence of the power of His hand made on those heathen men, for it elevated them to heartfelt recognition of Him.

וַיִּזְבְּחוּ זֶבַח לַה' — *And they offered a sacrifice to HASHEM.*

Could they have offered a sacrifice on board a ship? — The correct interpretation is as *Targum* renders: *they undertook to offer a sacrifice (Radak)* i.e., after they returned to shore *(Ibn Ezra).*

— *Pirkei d'Rabbi Eliezer* asks: Did they offer a sacrifice? Is it not a fact that sacrifices [i.e. שְׁלָמִים, *peace-offerings,* which are usually referred to by the generic term זְבָחִים, *sacrifices (Radal;* see *Menachos* 73b)], are not accepted from gentiles? — Rather this sacrifice refers to the blood of the covenant of circumcision [see *Sh'mos Rabbah* to 17:3,5 which interprets כֹּרְתֵי בְרִיתִי עֲלֵי זָבַח, *those that have made a covenant with Me by sacrifice (Psalms* 50:5), to refer to the covenant of circumcision *(Radal).*]

Accordingly *PdRE* notes that the sailors cast away their gods, returned to Jaffo and went up to Jerusalem and underwent circumcision. This is the interpretation of *offering sacrifices* in our verse.

[Those commentators who take *sacrifice* in the literal sense, would either explain that the *sacrifices* of our verse were עולות, *burnt-offerings,* which, following R' Akiva in *Menachos* 83b, may be accepted from gentiles. Although the term זְבָחִים can refer specifically to *peace-offerings,* it is also used as a generic term זֶבַח, *sacrifice,* which embraces all forms of sacrifices except for עופות, *fowl,* and מְנָחוֹת, *meal-offerings* (see *Zevachim* 109a). Or, possibly, that they did not offer their sacrifice in the Temple in Jerusalem, and the verse is merely informing us that when the gentile sailors got ashore, they offered sacrifices of their own in the Name of HASHEM, and undertook certain vows.]

וַיִּדְּרוּ נְדָרִים — *And* [*they*] *took* [lit. *vowed*] *vows:*

—To convert to Judaism *(Rashi).*

—To give alms to the poor *(Radak).*

They vowed to bring their wives and households to the true worship of Hashem. They fulfilled their vows and became true proselytes, and it is regarding proselytes such as these that we mention in our *Shemoneh Esrai* prayers: ... and upon the righteous proselytes (וְעַל גֵּרֵי הַצֶּדֶק) and over us may Your compassion be aroused.' *(Pirkei d'Rabbi Eliezer).*

II.

1. The great fish.

וַיְמַן ה' — *Then* [lit *and*] *HASHEM designated* [lit. *apportioned.*]

Radak explains that the word is to be understood in a sense similar to the word מִנָּה, *provided,* in *Daniel* 1:10. God had readied the fish for *sacrifice to HASHEM and took vows.*

II
1 *Then HASHEM designated a large fish to swallow Jonah, and Jonah remained in the fish's belly*

the moment Jonah was cast into the sea. Accordingly, it was a miracle that the fish swallowed him just then, and he did not drown. According to Rav Tarfon in *PdRE,* that fish had been specially designated [i.e. prepared for this special task (*Radal*)] from the six days of Creation to swallow up Jonah. Accordingly, the phrase is rendered in the pluperfect: *HASHEM had [already] designated.*

[Thus, the existence of the fish must be considered an essential pre-condition to the functioning of creation, like the other miracles listed in *Avos* 5:6 that were also predetermined in the final moments of active creation.]

Tosafos Yom Tov to *Avos* 5:6 notes that the inevitability of such miracles as the fish which plucked Jonah from the sea, is no contradiction to the doctrine of free will, for הַכֹּל צָפוּי וְהָרְשׁוּת נְתוּנָה, *all is foreseen* [by God] *yet permission is given* [to man to do as he wishes] (ibid 3:15). God's foreknowledge of man's eventual free-willed choice [in this case Jonah's free-willed decision to flee God's command and his ultimate casting overboard] does not foreclose man's freedom to choose despite the inability of human intelligence to grasp how this can be so if God has prior knowledge of what will be chosen. God's Intelligence is of a different order from ours and, as such, is unfathomable.

דָּג גָּדוֹל — *A large fish.*

[The *species* of this 'large fish' is not mentioned. The popular notion that it was a *whale* is baseless, since the text defines it only as a 'large fish.' It has been observed that both the sperm-whale and certain larger species of sharks would be capable of swallowing a man whole. But the identity of the species of the fish is unimportant and the attempt to identify it distracts us from the essential thread of our narrative. It suffices to mention that the verse emphasizes that this fish was prepared by God to act as His agent. That it was a *large* fish rather than a tiny one (although since it was a miracle God could theoretically just as well have designated a *small* fish for the purpose) was because even when resorting to miracles, God always employs an economy of means and therefore causes miracles to happen as close as possible to the natural order, leaving only the balance to heaven.]

[It may be noted that the multitudes of people who crowded into the Temple courtyard always had enough space to prostrate themselves on the Day of Atonement and confess their sins without being overheard — this despite the fact that they had theretofore been crowded (*Avos* 5:8). Thus, God provides space where needed even in a small enclosure. The same could have happened whatever the species which swallowed Jonah. See *Ramban* to *Gen.* 6:19).]

According to *R' Bachya,* גָּדוֹל, *great,* in this case does not refer to

ב בְּמְעֵי הַדָּג שְׁלֹשָׁה יָמִים וּשְׁלֹשָׁה לֵילוֹת:
ב ב וַיִּתְפַּלֵּל יוֹנָה אֶל־יְהוָה אֱלֹהָיו מִמְּעֵי

the fish's *size*, but to the fact that he was *great in years* having been designated since the Six days of Creation for the specific mission of swallowing this righteous man.

לִבְלֹעַ אֶת־יוֹנָה – *To swallow Jonah.*

I.e. as soon as Jonah was thrown from the ship. Thereby Jonah was saved from drowning *(Radak).*

The phrase tells us the specific purpose for which God had designated the fish: *HASHEM designated ... to swallow Jonah.* Therefore, the infinitive לִבְלֹעַ, *to swallow*, is used to emphasize that swallowing Jonah was the fish's sole reason for having been created and that the verse should not be interpreted to mean that God *now* prepared a fish which swallowed Jonah. This, in contrast to 4:7 where the verse says that God prepared a worm ... *which attacked the kikayon*, (not *to attack*) since that worm, unlike the fish, was not designated for that purpose since the six days of creation *(R' Bachya).*

— He was designated to swallow him *whole* without harming him at all *(Malbim).*

וַיְהִי יוֹנָה בִּמְעֵי הַדָּג – *And Jonah remained* [lit. *was*] *in the fish's belly.*

[The verse does not specifically mention that the fish *swallowed* Jonah. Since the beginning of the verse tells us that *swallowing* Jonah at that very moment was the fish's sole reason for having been created, and since this phrase speaks of Jonah as being inside the fish, then it is clearly implicit that the fish swallowed him.]

שְׁלֹשָׁה יָמִים וּשְׁלֹשָׁה לֵילוֹת – *Three days and three nights.*

One usually cannot survive in a fish's belly even for an hour! That he was able to survive for three days was in itself nothing less than a miracle *(Ibn Ezra).*[1]

Man needs oxygen to survive. The miracle was that God allowed him to survive like an embryo in its mother's womb *(Malbim).*

It was, furthermore, an additional miracle that he retained the presence of mind to pray therein *(Radak, v.* 2).

[The number three is significant. The *Midrash (Bereishis Rabbah* 61:1) enumerates many instances of important

1. *Rav Tarfon* said . . . Jonah entered the fish's mouth as if he were entering a synagogue where he stood [in order to be able to pray comfortably for God's mercy *(Radal)*]. The two eyes of the fish were like windows allowing light to come to Jonah.

Rabbi Meir said that a pearl was suspended inside the fish providing Jonah with illumination as bright as the noontime sun, enabling him to see all that was in the ocean-depths.

The fish told Jonah that he was to be eaten by the Leviathan that day. Jonah asked to be taken to him. He said to the Leviathan 'Because of you have I descended to see your dwelling place [in order to know where to find you *(Radal)*] for I will raise you and slaughter you for the banquet of the righteous in the Time to Come. [*Radal* offers an esoteric, allegorical interpretation to the above.] The Leviathan fled, whereupon Jonah asked the fish to show him all the wonders of the deep.

The fish showed Jonah the ocean current, the Sea of Reeds through which Israel passed

II three days and three nights.
2 [2] Jonah prayed to HASHEM, his God, from the

events in the history of Jewish salvation which occurred on the third day. Among them: Joseph freed his brothers on the third day (*Gen.* 23:18), and the Torah was received on the third day (*Exodus* 19:16).]

— God does not allow His righteous to remain in dire straights for more than three days (*Bereishis Rabba* 91:9).

2. Jonah's Prayer.

וַיִּתְפַּלֵּל יוֹנָה אֶל־ה׳ אֱלֹהָיו — [*And*] *Jonah prayed to HASHEM, his God.*

[The dual designation here of God as *HASHEM* and as *Elohim* reflects the manifestation of His Dual Attributes of Mercy and Justice (see *Comm.* to *Gen.* 2:4, 5). Jonah now prayed with a recognition of both manifestations of God. The Attribute of Justice had been shown by the tempest and by Jonah's three-day imprisonment in the fish. By saying אֱלֹהָיו, *'his'* God, the verse implies that Jonah acknowledged that he deserved strict judgment. Simultaneously, however, he used ה׳, the Four-Letter Name *HASHEM*, signifying mercy, to express his gratitude that HASHEM in His Mercy had prepared the fish to save him.]

The reference to *his* God indicates that Jonah felt a particular closeness to *his* God, Who had both pursued and rescued him. His prayer was an expression of thanks and faith (*Ramban, HaEmunah v'HaBitachon ch.* 15).

Ibn Ezra rejects the view of those who maintain that Jonah had recited the following prayer *after* he reached land, as a psalm of *thanksgiving*, rather than from the innards of the fish as an *appeal for help*. The use of the past tense in such phrases as *v.* 7: וַתַּעַל מִשַּׁחַת חַיַּי, *You brought my life up from the pit;* and *v.* 8: וַתָּבוֹא אֵלֶיךָ תְּפִלָּתִי, *my prayer came to You,* were adduced as evidence for the former view. *Ibn Ezra* rejects this proof since a prophet's every prayer is said in a spirit of prophecy, as are many such prophetic statements recorded in Scripture. Hence the 'prophetic past' tense is properly used since the prediction is confidently viewed as if it had already transpired. Furthermore the narrative itself clearly depicts the fish as ejecting Jonah only *after* the prayer was completed.

upon leaving Egypt [see *Comm.* to *v.* 6], the foundations of the earth, the lowest *sheol,* and *gehinnom.* He showed him the foundations upon which the Temple rests and the אֶבֶן שְׁתִיָּה, *foundation stone,* upon which the Holy Ark — and the entire world — rests.

The fish told Jonah that he was then under the Temple and that any prayers would be answered. Jonah asked the fish to stop; he stood and said the prayer of our chapter. His prayer was not answered, however, until he promised to fufill his vow (*v.* 10) to slaughter the Leviathan for the benefit of the righteous in the Time to Come. [It would thus seem that Jonah's repentance was of such profound significance that the culmination of the redemption, the festive סְעוּדַת לִוְיָתָן, *Banquet of Leviathan,* would be brought about by him. (See *Overview*).]

Immediately God signalled to the fish and it placed him on dry land (*PdRE).*

ב הַדָּגָה׃ ג וַיֹּאמֶר קָרָאתִי מִצָּרָה לִי אֶל־
ג יהוה וַיַּעֲנֵנִי מִבֶּטֶן שְׁאוֹל שִׁוַּעְתִּי שָׁמַעְתָּ

מִמְּעֵי הַדָּגָה — *From the fish's belly.* In *v.* 1, the fish is referred to as a דָּג [masculine gender] while here the feminine gender, דָּגָה, is used.

Rashi, following a *Midrash,* comments that originally Jonah was swallowed by a male fish whose insides were relatively spacious [see footnote end of *v.* 1]. Therefore [since Jonah was relatively comfortable], he gave no thought to praying. God then signalled to the fish, and it spit Jonah into the mouth of a pregnant female fish. There, together with her multitude of eggs, Jonah was cramped, and, motivated by his dire situation, he prayed.

Alshich cites this *Midrash* but attributes Jonah's failure to pray during his three days in the first fish to a pious, unprotesting acceptance of the penalty of death. He knew he was guilty and he thought that God was keeping him alive those few extra days in the fish in order to impress upon him His might and rule in defiance of the laws of nature. Perceiving God to be angry at him, he maintained humble silence. In reality, however, God wanted to evoke his prayer and repentance, and so He caused Jonah to be transferred to the constricted belly of a pregnant female fish. Jonah then realized that God's intention was not to further punish him, but to keep him alive and evoke repentance, whereupon he prayed.

[A *Midrashic* interpretation similar to that quoted by *Rashi* appears also in *Nedarim* 51b with the difference that דָּג is explained there as referring to *large* fish, while דָּגָה in common usage refers to *small* fish. In our case Jonah was spewed forth by a large fish and swallowed by a smaller one (the exegetical result being the same as *Rashi* here: it was only in the discomfort of the smaller fish that Jonah prayed).]

[*Maharsha* ibid., raises a question however, that according to the foregoing Midrashic interpretations, why is the fish who finally spewed forth Jonah to the dry land further in *v.* 11 referred to again as דָּג (male or large)? Is this to suggest that the דָּגָה returned Jonah to the דָּג who in turn ejected him to dry land? (This is indeed the interpretation offered by *Metzudos* in *v.* 11!) He concludes that the matter needs more investigation.]

A somewhat different interpretation is cited in *Zohar* II:47b — which by implication solves *Maharsha's* difficulty of why in *v.* 11 the term דָּג is used again. According to this *Zohar,* the fish which swallowed Jonah proved to be a great boon to him for once inside it he was safe from all other fish, and he also beheld wondrous things there [see footnote.] If he was so comfortable, why does it say in *v.* 3 that he called out of his *affliction?* — Because, as R' Elazar explained, when God saw Jonah enjoying himself, He said, 'Was it for this that I brought you here?' God then immediately killed the fish. Jonah found himself in dire straits because other fish were assembling and gnawing at its carcass. It was then that Jonah prayed *from the belly of the lower world* [*v.* 3.], that is, from the belly of the דָּגָה, the dead fish.

...God then responded to his prayer and brought the fish [דָּגָה] back to life, after which it came up on shore now, [referred to again as a דָּג] , and before the eyes of all, it spewed up Jonah.

R' Bachya also cites the *Zohar* and explains that the term דָּגָה is used in *v.* 2 to connote a dead fish, since that is the term used in *Exodus* 7:21 to refer to the fish that had died in the plague of Blood.

Radak [following one view in *Nedarim* 51b] comments that in פְּשׁוּטוֹ שֶׁל מִקְרָא, *the literal sense of the narrative,* there is no distinction between דָּג and דָּגָה, as evidenced by the fact that דָּגָה is used in the generic sense referring to the species as a whole in *Exodus* 7:21: *and the fish* (דָּגָה) — *that was in the river died.*

II
3

fish's belly, [3] *and said:*
"I called, in my distress, to HASHEM,
and He answered me;
From the belly of the lower-world I cried out —

According to *Radak* מִמְּעֵי, *'from' the belly,* is not synonymous with בִּמְעֵי, *'in' the belly.* It is rather an idiomatic way of saying that Jonah prayed *from* [i.e. due to] his troubled situation [arising from his stay in] *the fish.*

3. [This prayer was recited while Jonah was still imprisoned in the fish. The past-tense is known as the 'prophetic past.' It testifies to the confidence with which the prophet utters his prayer (see *Ibn Ezra, v.* 2).]

קָרָאתִי מִצָּרָה לִי — *I called, in my distress* [lit. *from trouble to me;* or: *from a narrow confine*], *to HASHEM and He answered me.*

The term קָרָאתִי, *I called,* refers to *prayer (Targum).* In *Devarim Rabbah, Vaeschanan* 1, קְרִיאָה is listed as one of the designations for prayer.

וַיַּעֲנֵנִי — *And He answered me.*

The past tense of the verb implies confidence in the *future.* [Although the word יַעֲנֵנִי is in future tense, the prefix ו, *vav,* reverses the tense from future to past. In such a use, the prepositional prefix ו is known grammatically as a ו הַהִיפּוּךְ, *vav* conversive, rather than a ו הַחִיבּוּר, *vav* conjunctive.] Since Jonah survived the ordeal for so long [when death should have immediately followed his ingestion into the fish] he was confident that this was an indication that God had answered his prayer and that he would live [since God does not wrought miracles for naught] *(Radak; Metzudos).*[1]

[This part of the verse echoes *Psalm* 120:1: קָרָאתִי אֶל ה׳ בַּצָּרָתָה לִּי וַיַּעֲנֵנִי, *I called to HASHEM in my distress and He answered me.* It is deeply significant that portions of the idioms and phrases of Jonah's prayer find their parallel in *Psalms.* This indicated the familiarity of *Psalms* to the Israelites of that period. The outpourings from the heart of King David struck responsive chords in every Jew in distress. (See *Overview* to ArtScroll *Tehillim).*]

I called to Him only מִצָּרָה לִי, when I was *in my distress,* and I was not deserving of an answer

1. Since after being twice swallowed up, once by the sea and then by the fish, he did not die of suffocation, but remained alive for three days in the belly of the fish, Jonah was convinced that it was his life, not his death, that was desired by God, and the creature that had swallowed him was sent by God to be the means of his salvation. That is why he did not pray to be saved, but instead recited a prayer of thanks for he was convinced that he was already saved. In the very fact that he was still alive and his mind was still clear, he recognized the most striking proof of the rescuing proximity of God. It represented his guarantee that God had forgiven him for his previous folly and would preserve him for future activity. The closeness, the lack of light and air of his prison, no longer held terror for him; the narrower it was, the less air and light it had, the more powerfully convincing was the consciousness of God's closeness to him, and the greater the happiness in that conviction *(Rav M. Hirsch).*

ד קוֹלִי: וַתַּשְׁלִיכֵנִי מְצוּלָה בִּלְבַב יַמִּים
וְנָהָר יְסֹבְבֵנִי כָּל־מִשְׁבָּרֶיךָ וְגַלֶּיךָ עָלַי
ה עָבָרוּ: וַאֲנִי אָמַרְתִּי נִגְרַשְׁתִּי מִנֶּגֶד עֵינֶיךָ

because I had fled from before Him [and accordingly brought the distress upon myself]. Nevertheless He did not withhold His response: וַיַּעֲנֵנִי, *He answered me! (Sefer HaIkkarim* 4:15).

Almosnino, rather than interpreting וַיַּעֲנֵנִי, *and He answered me* as a *fait-accompli*, prefers to read it as a prayer [וְיַעֲנֵנִי, *and He 'will' answer me* (treating the ו as a ו הַחִיבּוּר, *conjunctive prefix).*] He renders: *I called out to HASHEM that He answer me*, and put an end to my distress, whether by freeing me or permitting me to die.[1]

מִבֶּטֶן שְׁאוֹל שִׁוַּעְתִּי שָׁמַעְתָּ קוֹלִי — *From the belly of the lower-world I cried out, — You heard my voice.*

I.e., I am confident that You heard my voice *(Metzudos).*

The word שְׁאוֹל, *lower-world*, refers to the depths of the earth, the opposite of the heavens which are the heights *(Ibn Ezra).* Metaphorically it refers to the depths of the grave, the place of death *(Metzudos).* According to the *Zohar* [*III* 285] *She'ol* was one of the levels of Gehinnom. It is often used figuratively to indicate spiritual distress (for example *Psalms* 18:5).

In our verse, *Rashi* explains *She'ol* as a figurative reference to the constricted belly of the fish which was like a grave to Jonah.

שַׁוְעָה, denoting prayer emanating from a grieving heart, is one of the ten classes of prayer enumerated in *Sifri Va'eschanan.*

Harechasim LeBik'ah to *Genesis* 18:2 differentiates between צְעָקָה and זְעָקָה both of which are anguished outcries by the victims of crimes committed by man against his fellow man, and the term שַׁוְעָה which is used to describe only outcries *to God.*

Note the transition from third-person (וַיַּעֲנֵנִי, *He* answered me) to second-person (שָׁמַעְתָּ קוֹלִי, *You* heard my voice). Such transition is common in *Psalms* and in blessings where God is addressed both directly and obliquely in the same benediction. However Jonah's prayer is in contrast to the standard text of blessings which we *begin* in second person, indicating that prayer is so exalted that it enables mortal man to turn directly to God; *then we change* to third-person because we have no true understanding of God's manifestations. Jonah, however, because he had fled from God's presence, was ashamed to

1. *Abarbanel*, while he agrees with *Ibn Ezra* [*v.* 2] that Jonah's prayer took place from within the fish, disagrees that it is necessary to interpret the past tense as 'prophetic past' which alludes to future salvation. Rather, he suggests that the prayer recalls past events in the life of Jonah who is identified with the child whom Elijah brought back to life (following *PdRE* cited in *v.* 1 and *Overview).*

Accordingly, he interprets *v.* 3 as recalling Jonah's youth when he was near death's door: *I called to HASHEM in my distress and he answered me; from the belly of the lower-world* — i.e., from the very door of my grave since I was about to be buried — *I cried out and You heard my voice*, and caused the miracle of Elijah bringing me back to life.

Verse 4 refers to his current plight in having been cast overboard.

You heard my voice.
4 *You cast me into the depth,*
in the heart of the seas,
The river whirled around me,
Your breakers and waves all swept over me.
5 *Then I thought: 'I was driven from Your sight,'*

begin his prayer with the familiar second person, and therefore began in the less personal. It was only after he began to pray that the barrier was lowered and he became close enough to change to the direct form of address *(Harav Nosson Scherman).*

4. וַתַּשְׁלִיכֵנִי מְצוּלָה בִּלְבַב יַמִּים — *You cast me* [*into (Targum)*] *the depth, in the heart of the seas.*

[The word *into* is not in the Hebrew but it is implied.]

I.e., into the most turbulent part of the sea. This part of the sea is figuratively referred to as *heart* since the heart is the most active part of the body *(Metzudos).*

This recalls the sailors' casting of Jonah from the ship into the sea *(Malbim).* [He specifically acknowledges that it was God who caused him to be so cast.]

The plural *seas* is idiomatic since the incident took place in the midst of the Mediterranean Sea. However, *Yefes* [*ben Ali*] interprets that this occurred at the confluence of the sea of Suf with the sea of Jaffo *(Ibn Ezra).*

וְנָהָר יְסֹבְבֵנִי — *The river whirled around me* [lit. *engulfed me; encircled me.*]

Rav M. Hirsch renders: *the river whirled me around.*]

I.e., the *river* which is the tributary to the sea, for, as *Ibn Ezra* interpreted it, this occurred at the junction where the waters of the sea and the river meet *(Radak).*

כָּל מִשְׁבָּרֶיךָ וְגַלֶּיךָ עָלַי עָבָרוּ — *Your breakers and waves all swept over me.*

As I was in the belly of the fish deep beneath the sea *(Metzudos).*

— I did not ride over the waves (as did Rabbi Akiva — see *Yevamos* 121a) but the *waves all swept over me (Malbim).*

Note again the verse in *Psalms* 42:8, obviously drawn upon by Jonah: כָּל מִשְׁבָּרֶיךָ וְגַלֶּיךָ עָלַי עָבָרוּ.

5. וַאֲנִי אָמַרְתִּי — *Then* [lit. *and*] *I thought* [lit. *said*].

I.e., this was my thought as I was being hurled to my death into the sea *(Rashi).*

[The verb אמר, *say,* often means *think* in Scripture.]

נִגְרַשְׁתִּי מִנֶּגֶד עֵינֶיךָ — *I was driven from Your sight* [lit. *from against Your eyes.*]

I.e., [when I was hurled into the sea] going to my death, I was overcome with fear and] thought that I was being driven away from Your eyes *(Rashi),* that is, away from Your concern and Providence over me. I reached the point of thinking that You had kept aloof from me [and that I would meet certain

ב
ו־ז

אַךְ אוֹסִיף לְהַבִּיט אֶל־הֵיכַל קׇדְשֶׁךָ׃
ו אֲפָפוּנִי מַיִם עַד־נֶפֶשׁ תְּהוֹם יְסֹבְבֵנִי סוּף
ז חָבוּשׁ לְרֹאשִׁי׃ לְקִצְבֵי הָרִים יָרַדְתִּי
הָאָרֶץ בְּרִחֶיהָ בַעֲדִי לְעוֹלָם וַתַּעַל

death] *(Radak). Rambam* in *Moreh Nevuchim* 1:44 comments that the mention of God's 'eye' is anthropomorphic and refers in a figurative sense, to Providence. See *Deut.* 11:12: *The eyes, i.e. Providence, of* HASHEM *your God are always upon it* [i.e. *Eretz Yisrael*].

I had already believed that I was banished [נִגְרַשְׁתִּי] forever, that I would never again come before Your Presence *(Rav M. Hirsch).*

Alshich suggests that Jonah was afraid that as a result of having defiantly fled *Eretz Yisrael,* he was now banished from ever again returning to God's sight, i.e., the Holy Land *which God's eyes are always upon* [*Deuteronomy* 11:12].

Cf. again a parallel in *Psalms* 31:23: וַאֲנִי אָמַרְתִּי בְחׇפְזִי נִגְרַזְתִּי מִנֶּגֶד עֵינֶיךָ, *but I said in my panic, 'I am cut off from Your sight!'*

אַךְ — *But.*

— That is, but now that I realize that You performed the miracle of keeping me alive all of these days *(Rashi; Radak).*

[I.e., originally I thought that I was destined to die, *but now* my confidence springs from my miraculous escape from drowning since I am certain You would not have sustained me in this condition unless You intended me to live, for it is known that You do not cause miracles to happen for naught.]

[Accordingly...]

אוֹסִיף לְהַבִּיט אֶל הֵיכַל קׇדְשֶׁךָ — *I will gaze again* [lit. *I will continue to gaze*], *at Your Holy Temple!*

I know that it is Your intention to free me from here and again let me gaze upon Your Holy Sanctuary in the Temple, and that You will yet return me to the place of Your prophecy and Providence though I fled from it. The meaning of *gaze* in this context is *pray (Radak).*

...And I will return there with prayers of thanksgiving *(Metzudos).*

Sforno interprets this phrase as a petition: אַךְ, I ask *only* that אוֹסִיף לְהַבִּיט אֶל הֵיכַל קׇדְשֶׁךָ, *I be permitted again to gaze* ... .

According to *Alshich,* Jonah's prayer that he be permitted to return to *Eretz Yisrael* rather than be punished by permanent exile [see *Alshich* above], was motivated by the hope that his sufferings atoned for his guilt.

6. אֲפָפוּנִי מַיִם עַד־נֶפֶשׁ — *Waters encompassed me to the soul.*

I.e., they encompassed me until I was nearly at the point of death, but then the fish swallowed me. Compare the expression in *Psalms* 69:2: כִּי בָאוּ מַיִם עַד נָפֶשׁ, *for the waters have come to my soul (Radak).*

Mahari Kara paraphrases our verse: the waters rose up to my nose [homiletically suggested by the assonance of אַף, *nose,* to אֲפָפוּנִי, *encompassed me*] preventing me from breathing, until my נֶפֶשׁ, *soul,* was about to depart.

but — I will gaze again at Your Holy Temple!
6 *Waters encompassed me to the soul,*
the Deep whirled around me,
weeds were tangled about my head.
7 *To the bases of the mountains did I sink;*
the earth: its bars against me forever.

תְּהוֹם יְסֹבְבֵנִי — *The Deep whirled around me* [lit. *engulfed me; surrounded me*].

According to *Malbim,* this recounts the episode when Jonah was spit out of the דָּג, *male* fish's mouth and swallowed by the דָּגָה, *female* fish. This incident took place in the deepest part of the sea [see *commentary* to *v.* 2 and footnote to *v.* 1].[1]

סוּף חָבוּשׁ לְרֹאשִׁי —*Weeds were tangled about* [lit. *to*] *my head.*

I.e. the seaweed , known in French as *algae,* which grows in riverbanks and beneath the sea, and which tangles around the heads of fish swimming through it. By *my head* Jonah refers to the head of the fish in which he was imprisoned; while Jonah was inside it, he identified with the fish and spoke of the weeds as being entangled around his own head *(Radak).*

[The word סוּף is usually rendered as synonymous with קָנֶה, *reed.* Apparently, however, there is a distinction between the two. See *Isaiah* 19:6 קָנֶה וָסוּף קָמֵלוּ, *reed (?) and weed (?) shall wither.*]

Rashi following *Pirkei d'Rabbi Eliezer* [cited in footnote to *v.* 1] explains this phrase — as does *Targum: The Sea of Reeds* [יַמָּא דְסוּף] *was suspended above my head.* For [as *PdRE* notes], the fish's two eyes were like two windows through which Jonah gazed and saw everything in the sea. Now, God showed Jonah the place where the Israelites passed through the Sea of Reeds.

7. לְקִצְבֵי הָרִים יָרַדְתִּי — *To the bases of the mountains did I sink* [lit. *descend.*]

The very ends of the mountains, i.e., to their foundation on the ocean floor. קֶצֶב is synonymous with קֵץ, *end*; hence the implication of [bottom] *end, foundation, base.* As *Targum* renders: לְעִקָּרֵי טוּרַיָּא, to the foundations of the mountains *(Radak).*

הָאָרֶץ בְּרִחֶיהָ בַעֲדִי לְעוֹלָם — *The earth: its bars against me forever.*

[I.e., its bars *were closed* against me forever. The phrase *were closed* is not in the Hebrew, but is implied and is so understood by all expositors.]

While I sunk to the bases of the mountains *I thought* that the bars

1. See *commentary* to the parallel phrase אֲפָפוּנִי חֶבְלֵי מָוֶת in ArtScroll *Tehillim* 18:5 where *Midrash Shocher Tov* is cited noting a number of possible homiletic derivations of this rare word. Some have application here: It is related to אַף, *nose:* my misfortunes are so many that they reach my *nose* — i.e., they threaten to snuff out my very breath of life. They constantly roll over me like a never-ending אוֹפַן, *wheel.* My misfortunes come in pairs like אַפְפוּן, the *doubled thread of a loom.* Finally, the word is interpreted as if it were spelled עֲפָפוּנִי, i.e. misfortunes *fly and soar over my head like many* עוֹפוֹת, *birds.*

ח מִשַּׁחַת חַיַּי יְהוָה אֱלֹהָי: בְּהִתְעַטֵּף עָלַי
נַפְשִׁי אֶת־יְהוָה זָכָרְתִּי וַתָּבוֹא אֵלֶיךָ
ט תְּפִלָּתִי אֶל־הֵיכַל קָדְשֶׁךָ: מְשַׁמְּרִים
י הַבְלֵי־שָׁוְא חַסְדָּם יַעֲזֹבוּ: וַאֲנִי בְּקוֹל

of the earth above me were closed against me, and that I would never escape *(Rashi).*

I thought that I would never be able to return to the earth *(Ibn Ezra).*

— And that the depths of the sea would be my grave *(Radak).*

לְעוֹלָם — *Forever.*

This refers both to Jonah's statement in *v.* 5 and his statement here that the earth's bars were closed against him [i.e., in both cases Jonah feared that his doom was eternally sealed] *(Rashi).*

Mahari Kara understands לְעוֹלָם in its other sense: *to the world.* He interprets the phrase figuratively as: *the bars of the earth stood opposite me to* [*support*] *the world* [i.e., earth.]

[This follows *PdRE* where it is noted that God showed Jonah the 'pillars of the earth' in its foundations, our verse being cited in this connection.]

וַתַּעַל מִשַּׁחַת חַיַּי ה׳ אֱלֹהָי — *Yet* [(in the sense of the conversive: *But);* lit. *and*], *You lifted my life from the pit, HASHEM, my God.*

I.e., but now that You have let me survive in the fish's belly, I am confident that You [did not intend the earth's bars to be closed against me *forever,* but that You] have indeed *lifted my life from the pit* — this being the connatation of שַׁחַת, *pit* — and that I will yet return to dry land *(Radak).*

The *pit* or *grave* of our verse is a figurative reference to the *belly of the fish (Metzudos).*

8. בְּהִתְעַטֵּף עָלַי נַפְשִׁי — *While my soul was faint within me.*

I.e., Even when I was swooning from the misery of my predicament within the fish's belly, and I thought myself near extinction ... *(Radak).*

The word בְּהִתְעַטֵּף literally means wrapping oneself up. It refers to one swooning from misery, since such a person compresses his body as if he were shriveled. Thus, he appears to be bent and folded over as if being wrapped up. Cf. *Lamentations* 2:19: הָעֲטוּפִים בְּרָעָב, *who swoon from hunger (Metzudos).*

Rashi, following *Targum,* renders בְּאִשְׁתַּלְהָיוּת, *while in a swoon.*

אֶת ה׳ זָכָרְתִּי — *I remembered* [service to *(Targum)*] *HASHEM.*

With all of this, I remembered HASHEM and prayed to Him *(Radak).*

וַתָּבוֹא אֵלֶיךָ תְּפִלָּתִי אֶל־הֵיכַל קָדְשֶׁךָ — [*And*] *my prayer came to You, to Your holy Temple.*

Since You sustained me in the fish's belly, I am confident that my prayers reached You in Your *Holy Sanctuary* which refers to the heavens, as the Psalmist declared [*Psalms* 103:19]: *HASHEM has established His throne in the heavens.* It is with this similar con-

Yet, You lifted my life from the pit,
HASHEM, my God.
8 *While my soul was faint within me,*
I remembered HASHEM;
My prayer came to You,
to Your Holy Temple.
9 *Zealously guarding utter futilities*
they forsake their Kindness.

notation that it is written [*II Chronicles* 30:27]: *their prayer ascended to His holy dwelling place, to heaven (Radak).*[1]

9. מְשַׁמְּרִים הַבְלֵי־שָׁוְא — *Zealously guarding* [or: *those who zealously guard*] *utter* [lit. *worthless*] *futilities.*

A reference to the heathen nations of the world who worship idolatry *(Rashi).*

According to *Mahari Kara* and *Radak* [following *PdRE*], Jonah is referring to the sailors on board his ship, each of whom had vainly sought salvation from his own god.

Ibn Ezra notes the transitive-intensive nature of the verb מְשַׁמְּרִים, *guards.* He explains that it refers to the sailors who actively *encouraged each other* to support their idolatry.

[The translation *zealously guarding* reflects the intensive nature of the verb מְשַׁמְּרִים as compared with the more simple form שׁוֹמְרִים.]

[Compare again, a parallel in *Psalms* 31:7 which Jonah was undoubtedly familiar with: שָׂנֵאתִי הַשֹּׁמְרִים הַבְלֵי שָׁוְא, *I hate them that regard futile idols.*]

חַסְדָּם יַעֲזֹבוּ — *They forsake* [lit. *will forsake*] *their Kindness.*

By clinging to their idolatry they thereby relinquish the fear of God, Who is the Source of all their kindness and beneficence *(Rashi; Targum).*

Rashi continues that according to *PdRE* this verse refers to the ship's idolatrous sailors who [in a display of belief in God] חַסְדָּם יַעֲזֹבוּ, *abandoned their kindness,* which they had always performed on behalf of their idols [i.e., sacrifice, prayer, etc.] and they converted. [See also *comm.* to 1:5 citing *PdRE.*]

Radak interprets that although the sailors professed to give up their idols and turn to Hashem who is called חַסְדָּם, *their Kindness,* they will forsake Him when the danger is over. However, he suggests in an alternative rendering that חֶסֶד here does not mean *kindness* but has the

1. According to *Rashi* [following *PdRE* cited in footnote to *v.* 2], Jonah had been shown the depths of Gehinnom [implied by the word שַׁחַת, *pit.*] From there, he was brought up to the *bases of the mountain,* i.e., beneath the mountain upon which the Temple stood. There he stood beneath the הֵיכָל, *sanctuary,* in Jerusalem [where, according to *PdRE* he was shown the אֶבֶן שְׁתִיָּה, *Foundation Stone,* upon which the whole world 'rested' (see *Yoma* 54b), fixed in the depth.] Thus, when Jonah prayed that he be permitted to gaze again upon the Sanctuary [*v.* 5], and that his prayer might come there [this verse], he referred not necessarily to the Sanctuary as he remembered it from a prior pilgrimage, but to the Temple as he was seeing it then.]

ב תּוֹדָה אֶזְבְּחָה־לָּךְ אֲשֶׁר נָדַרְתִּי אֲשַׁלֵּמָה
יא יא יְשׁוּעָתָה לַיהוָה׃ וַיֹּאמֶר
יְהוָה לַדָּג וַיָּקֵא אֶת־יוֹנָה אֶל־

meaning of *shame* as in *Leviticus* 20:17: חֶסֶד הוּא, *it is a disgrace.* Our phrase accordingly means: *They* who zealously served their futile gods, now *abandoned their shame* — i.e., *their idolatry* which was their shame and disgrace. [*Mahari Kara* also interprets this verse as referring to the sailors' sincere conversion, after having cast off their idolatry.]

10. וַאֲנִי בְּקוֹל תּוֹדָה אֶזְבְּחָה־לָּךְ — *But as for me, with a cheer* [lit. *voice*] *of gratitude will I bring offerings to You.*

[Continuing *Rashi*, who, in his primary comment interprets this verse in conjunction with the previous one]: '... *But as for me,* in contrast to the idolatrous heathens, *I will bring offerings to You,* HASHEM, *with a cheer of gratitude.*'

Radak implies that קוֹל תּוֹדָה refers to the prayers of thanksgiving which will accompany the קָרְבַּן תּוֹדָה, *thanksgiving sacrifice,* he would offer in fulfillment of his vow.

Mahari Kara notes that Jonah is among the four categories of people who are required to render thanksgiving: Those who crossed the sea, those who traversed the wilderness, those who have recovered from an illness, and a prisoner who has been set free [*Berachos* 54b.]

... Therefore Jonah made this vow to bring a thanksgiving offering *(Malbim).*

אֲשֶׁר נָדַרְתִּי אֲשַׁלֵּמָה — *What I have vowed I will fulfill* [lit. *pay.*]

I.e., I shall fulfill whatever I vowed while inside the fish's belly *(Ibn Ezra).*

[We are not told specifically what this vow was. According to *PdRe* (cited in the footnote to *v.* 1) Jonah had made a vow to slaughter the Leviathan for the benefit of the righteous upon the redemption of Israel. It was only after Jonah said these words, promising to fulfill his vow, that his prayer was answered and the fish vomited him out.]

[In the literal sense, however, he refers to the vows he was *now* making: to offer a thanksgiving offering upon his return and thank God for his salvation.]

יְשׁוּעָתָה לַה׳ — *For the Salvation which is* HASHEM*'s* [lit. *to* HASHEM.]

I.e., I will fulfill my sacrificial vows *because of the salvation which* HASHEM *wrought for me (Rashi; Mahari Kara).*

Thus, *Rashi* interprets the ה of יְשׁוּעָתָה as substituting the pronominal prefix ל, *to,* synonymous with לִישׁוּעָה לַה׳, *for the salvation which is* HASHEM*'s.* Cf. *Psalms* 44:27 קוּמָה עֶזְרָתָה לָּנוּ, which means: קוּמָה לְעֶזְרָה שֶׁלָּנוּ, *arise for our help.*

According to *Michlol Yofi* the extra ה in the word intensifies the noun: HASHEM*'s great salvation.*

Radak interprets this as an independent phrase: *Salvation is* HASHEM*'s!* I.e., Hashem *alone* wrought this wonderous salvation for me.

10 *But as for me, with a cheer of gratitude*
will I bring offerings to You.
What I have vowed I will fulfill
for the salvation which is HASHEM's."
11 *Then HASHEM addressed the fish and it spewed*
Jonah out to dry land.

11. The Prayer is Heard.

When God saw the sincerity of Jonah's repentance, He responded to the prayer by inspiring the fish to swim to shore and spit up Jonah on the dry land (*PdRE*).

וַיֹּאמֶר ה׳ לַדָּג — *Then* [lit *and*] *HASHEM addressed* [lit. *said to*] *the fish.*

[I.e., He communicated His wish to the fish.] As *Radak* comments, He *aroused a desire in the fish* to spit out Jonah.

This follows *Rambam* [*Moreh Nevuchim* 2:48] who also notes that actual *speech* to the fish is not meant here; for God certainly did not transform the fish into a prophet and send it prophetic revelation.

[The fish is here referred to again in the male gender: דָּג. See *comm.* to *v.* 2 מִמְּעֵי הַדָּגָה.] [1]

וַיָּקֵא אֶת־יוֹנָה אֶל הַיַּבָּשָׁה — *And it spewed* [lit. *vomited out*] *Jonah out to* [*the*] *dry land.*

I.e., as a result of God having aroused the desire in the fish, *it spewed Jonah out upon dry land* (*Metzudos*).

[The verse does not specify *which* land. It probably means the coast of *Eretz Yisrael*, where he again was able to receive prophecy. However, it is quite possible that the fish spewed him for a distance and that the area near Nineveh is meant, thereby readying him for his renewed mission.]

Pirkei d'Rabbi Eliezer describes the tattered state Jonah was in when he landed on shore from his ordeal in the fish: his clothes torn, his hair fallen out and his skin shrivelled and swollen.

Harav David Feinstein notes the choice of the word וַיָּקֵא, *vomited out*, which is derived from קִיא, *vomit*. This, too, was part of Jonah's suffering: first, that he was referred to in such unflattering terms as though he were a filthy object to be expectorated; and second, because he was not placed gently on the shore but spewed out — tossed through the air — and presumably he fell heavily to the earth.

1. The *Talmud* (*Bechoros* 8a) relates that God communicated directly to three creatures: man, the serpent (in the Garden of Eden), and the fish of Jonah.

That God spoke to the fish, may have been meant as an implied reproof to Jonah. By his flight from *Eretz Yisrael*, Jonah intended to remove himself from the source of prophecy. Now, God showed him that not only could he not remove himself from God's power, but that even a fish could receive the word of God if such was the Divine Will (*Ohel David* II).

א הַיַּבָּשָׁה: וַיְהִי דְבַר־יְהוָה
ב אֶל־יוֹנָה שֵׁנִית לֵאמֹר: קוּם לֵךְ אֶל־נִינְוֵה
הָעִיר הַגְּדוֹלָה וּקְרָא אֵלֶיהָ אֶת־הַקְּרִיאָה
ג אֲשֶׁר אָנֹכִי דֹּבֵר אֵלֶיךָ: וַיָּקָם יוֹנָה וַיֵּלֶךְ אֶל־

III.

1. The second call.

וַיְהִי דְבַר ה׳ אֶל יוֹנָה – *And the word of HASHEM came* [lit. *was*] *to Jonah.*

[God now communicates with Jonah again, once more giving him the mission to Nineveh. Having repented from his initial refusal to carry out God's command, Jonah now receives an opportunity to demonstrate the perfection of his penitence for, as *Rambam* declares *(Hilchos Teshuvah* 2:1), complete repentance requires that the erstwhile sinner be presented with an opportunity to commit the same sin under identical circumstances — but refrain from doing so.]

שֵׁנִית – *A second time.*

— Only a *second* time did the Shechinah speak to him, but not a third time (R'Akiva in *Yevamos* 98a).[1]

2. קוּם לֵךְ אֶל־נִינְוֵה הָעִיר הַגְּדוֹלָה – *Arise! Go to Nineveh that great city.* [see *comm.* to parallel phrase in *v.* 1.]

[The prophet is not reproached for his former disobedience. God's point had been amply made. It suffices simply to reiterate the command.]

Ibn Ezra [as explained by *Hadar Ezer*] notes that in the literal sense, the word קוּם, *arise,* implies that Jonah strategically stationed himself in the closest approach to Nineveh, so that when God commanded him to go, he would merely

1. The Talmud, ibid. questions this view by citing the prophecy recorded in II *Kings* 14:25 [see *comm.* above to 1:1] which shows that Jonah received a *third* prophecy.

One answer given is that our verse means that Jonah received only two prophecies *concerning Nineveh* but never a third [accordingly, the verse in II *Kings* 14:25 presents no difficulty, for it speaks of Jeroboam's conquest of territory which had been taken from Israel by foreign conquerors].

A second answer suggests that the verse in II *Kings* which reads: [Jeroboam] *restored the border of Israel ... according to the word of HASHEM which He spoke by the hand of His servant Jonah the son of Amittai the prophet,* means [not that a *prophecy* regarding the restoration of these borders had been transmitted but] that an analogy was being made between the successful repentance of Nineveh and the restoration of Israel's borders. Although Jeroboam was wicked, God relented from His intention of evil toward Israel, just as He had relented in His decree against Nineveh through Jonah. [The verse in II *Kings* would accordingly be interpreted as: *Jeroboam restored the border of Israel* [in a manner which displayed God's forbearance], *analogous to the* manner in which *He had earlier effected* [the salvation of the Ninevites] *through His prophet Jonah.*

[Note that according to *Pirkei d'Rabbi Eliezer* ch. 10 Jonah's mission to Nineveh came after the matter of Jeroboam, while according to the Talmudic view cited above it preceded it. As *Radal* notes that these reflect indeed divergent opinions which he cannot reconcile. In any event, *later* prophecies to Nineveh were delivered by Nachum.]

III
1-3

And the word of HASHEM came to Jonah a second time, saying: [2] 'Arise! Go to Nineveh that great city, and cry out to her the proclamation which I tell you.'
[3] So Jonah rose up and went to Nineveh, in accor-

have to *rise up* and proceed.

God repeated the description of Nineveh as הָעִיר הַגְּדוֹלָה, *that great city*, to appease Jonah and to suggest that only because of its size did God have compassion upon it (*Abarbanel*).

וּקְרָא אֵלֶיהָ – *And cry out* [lit. *call*] *to her.*

I.e., *prophesy* concerning her (*Targum*).

[The implication is somewhat gentler than the first command. Now the command is: וּקְרָא אֵלֶיהָ, cry out *to* her, instead of וּקְרָא עָלֶיהָ, cry out *against* her (1:2).] As *R'Bachya* explains: קְרָא עָלֶיהָ has a connotation of proclaiming trouble as in *Lam.* 1:16 קָרָא עָלַי מוֹעֵד, while קְרָא אֵלֶיהָ has a favorable connotation, as in *Ezek.* 36:29: וְקָרָאתִי... אֶל, *I will call out to* [i.e. summon] *the grain and make it abundant.*

אֶת הַקְּרִיאָה אֲשֶׁר אָנֹכִי דֹּבֵר אֵלֶיךָ – *The proclamation which I tell* [to] *you.*

I.e. which I have already told you previously [following *Radak's* own interpretation to 1:2] and which I now reiterate to you, that you should proclaim to her: *'Forty days more and Nineveh shall be overturned!' (Radak).*

That this was the message now implied is self-evident since it was the message which Jonah actually delivered [*v.* 4]. It was therefore unnecessary to record it here (*Metzudos*).

[Not all agree with *Radak's* interpretation that in 1:2 Jonah was given this same prophecy to deliver to Nineveh. For example *Alshich* maintains that originally Jonah was not given a specific message to deliver and therefore he was not guilty of suppressing prophecy (see *comm.* to 1:2). According to them, our phrase would be interpreted, *which I tell you now,* or at a later, unspecified time.]

Compare the similar expression to Moses [*Exod.* 6:29]: דַּבֵּר אֶל פַּרְעֹה... אֵת כָּל־אֲשֶׁר אֲנִי דֹּבֵר אֵלֶיךָ, *speak to Pharaoh all the things that I tell you* [where the implication is apparently future tense: 'That I *will* tell you'.][1]

3. וַיָּקָם יוֹנָה וַיֵּלֶךְ אֶל־נִינְוֵה – *So* [lit. *and*] *Jonah rose up and* [he] *went to Nineveh.*

[See *Ibn Exra* above.]

The same expression וַיָּקָם וַיֵּלֶךְ, *he rose up and went* is used regarding Abraham when he set out to comply with God's command to slaughter

1. Cf. *Yalkut Shimoni* 343: Why did God not tell Jonah [the specific prophecy] at once [— instead of keeping him in suspense?] — In order to endear the commandment to him and reward him for each and every step ... As Rav Hana said, God first places the righteous in doubt and then informs him of the matter [see *Rashi* to *Gen.* 12:1 s.v. *To the land that I will show you.*]

ג נִינְוֵה כִּדְבַר יהוה וְנִינְוֵה הָיְתָה עִיר־גְּדוֹלָה
ד־ה ד לֵאלֹהִים מַהֲלַךְ שְׁלֹשֶׁת יָמִים: וַיָּחֶל יוֹנָה
לָבוֹא בָעִיר מַהֲלַךְ יוֹם אֶחָד וַיִּקְרָא וַיֹּאמַר
ה עוֹד אַרְבָּעִים יוֹם וְנִינְוֵה נֶהְפָּכֶת: וַיַּאֲמִינוּ

his son *(Gen.* 22:3). The *Midrash* there (*Bereishis Rabbah* 55:8) accounts for the apparent redundancy of verbs (for it is unnecessary to specify that *he rose up* — how else could he go? [*Matnas Kehunah,* ibid.]) by noting that Abraham was rewarded separately for each act: for *rising up* and for *going.* [Perhaps a similar exegesis can be derived here as well.]

כִּדְבַר ה׳ — *In accordance with God's command* [lit. *word*].

—[His sole purpose in going was because this was God's command.]

וְנִינְוֵה הָיְתָה — *Now* [lit. *And*] *Nineveh was.*

The city existed until the Medean conquest, long after Jonah's prophecy was transcribed. Nevertheless, the past tense is used because the narrative was intended for generations far off into the future, after Nineveh's destruction, as a lesson on the efficacy of repentance *(Daas Sofrim).*

עִיר גְּדוֹלָה לֵאלֹהִים — *An enormously large city* [lit. *a city great to God*].

The translation *enormously large* for the Hebrew which literally means *great* (or *large*) *to God* follows *Radak* who explains that when Scripture wishes to emphasize something's size or importance it idiomatically attaches God's name to the noun, e.g. [*Ps.* 36:7]: הַרְרֵי אֵל, *enormously high mountains;* [ibid. 80:11]: אַרְזֵי אֵל, *enormously tall trees;* [*Song of Songs* 8:6]: שַׁלְהֶבֶתְיָה, *an exceedingly intense flame;* [*Jeremiah* 2:31]: מַאְפֵּלְיָה, *total darkness (Radak).*

R'Bachya suggests that the connotation of the phrase is that something of such great power is not to be attributed to human resources, but to the power of God.

According to *Rashbam* [in his *comm.* to *Gen.* 27:7], this phrase means: *In all of God's world there was never a city as large as Nineveh.* He cites a similar meaning for *Gen.* 10:9 where Nimrod is described as a mighty hunter לִפְנֵי ה׳ [lit. before HASHEM] i.e. *an exceedingly mighty hunter.*

Ibn Ezra [to 1:2] conjectures that this phrase implies that Nineveh had previously been a city of God-fearing people but had in Jonah's time deteriorated, and become sinful. [*Abarbanel* disagrees since nowhere else in Scripture is it suggested that this wicked Assyrian city was righteous or God-fearing.]

מַהֲלַךְ שְׁלֹשֶׁת יָמִים — *A three-day journey* [lit. *walk*].

Either across the city's diameter *(Radak);* or according to *Ibn Ezra,* around its circumference, which would equal one day from end to end.

The *Talmud* [*Pesachim* 93b] estimates that a man walks ten *parsas* a day [approximately 26 miles/41 kilometers.] Our verse therefore speaks of a distance of about 78 miles.

[According to either *Radak* or *Ibn Ezra,* Nineveh would have been

III dance with God's command. Now Nineveh was an
4 enormously large city, a three-day journey. [4]Jonah
commenced to enter the city the distance of one day's
journey, then he proclaimed and said, 'Forty days
more and Nineveh shall be overturned!'

enormously large. Perhaps the 'city' referred to a metropolitan area which included Nineveh and all the towns around it.]

4. The prophecy is proclaimed.

וַיָּחֶל יוֹנָה לָבוֹא בָעִיר מַהֲלַךְ יוֹם אֶחָד – [*And*] *Jonah commenced to enter* [*into*] *the city* [the distance of] *one day's journey* [lit. *walk*].

I.e., about a third of the distance into the city *(Radak).*

Perhaps this is where the greatest concentration of citizens and commercial establishments were located *(Harav David Feinstein).*

וַיִּקְרָא וַיֹּאמַר – *Then* [lit. *and*] *he proclaimed, and* [*he*] *said.*

[The implication is that Jonah proclaimed his message of judgment as he walked.]

Malbim translates וַיָּחֶל יוֹנָה, *Now Jonah waited ... one day,* before he began to proclaim his message. He was not sure when the forty-day grace period was to begin. If he began to proclaim his prophecy as soon as he entered Nineveh, the people on the outskirts of the city would begin counting forty days then, but those furthest in would not know of the prophecy until the third day. Therefore, he assumed that the forty days should begin on the second day, the average location in the city.

[Compare *Rashi*'s interpretation of וַיָּחֶל as *waited* in *Genesis* 8:10.]

According to *R' Bachya,* when Jonah arrived at the city, he had not yet been told what message he was to deliver. He interptets וַיָּחֶל as being from the root יחל, *wait, hope,* as: *he waited in anticipation* for God to reveal to him exactly what his prophecy should be. The message was not given to Jonah until after one day had passed, after which he walked about proclaiming it. God purposely waited so the suddenly revealed prophecy would be more dramatically impressed upon the citizenry seeing that it was proclaimed in the *center of the city.* This accounted for Nineveh's utter frenzy and the swiftness of its response.

עוֹד אַרְבָּעִים יוֹם וְנִינְוֵה נֶהְפָּכֶת – *Forty days more and Nineveh shall be* [lit. *is*] *overturned!*

Utterly destroyed [i.e., by Divine intervention] *(Rashi).*

⇐§ The meaning of the prophecy.

That Nineveh survived thanks to its repentance was not a contradiction of Jonah's prophecy. It reveals one of the principles of prophetic communication, and is expounded by *Derech Hashem* (III 4:7) as follows: It is further possible for a prophet to comprehend the truth of his prophecy [as it is indeed transmitted and meant to be understood] yet not to perceive all of the [hidden, later to be understood] truths which may be included in it. For example, Jonah's prophecy. He was told *Nineveh shall be 'overturned'.* This statement [although *initially* carrying but one intent, as explained by *Ibn Ezra* below, and which Jonah correctly understood], actually contained two true meanings: one, the punishment due them as a result of their sins [i.e., *physical destruction*]; and second, what was revealed before God that would actually occur, that they would be transformed from evil to good [i.e., *spiritually overturned.*] However, if *only* the *punishment* had been implied by the prophecy, then God would have revealed to His prophets, and especially to Jonah, that He was later relenting, and that a new decree [of survival in response to repentance] had supplanted the first.

This follows *Sanhedrin* 89b where the dual meaning of נֶהְפָּכֶת, *overturned*, is cited to explain why God did not notify Jonah that the Ninevites were forgiven, in apparent contradiction to the doctrine of *Amos* 3:7 that God makes no decision affecting humanity without first informing His prophets. In the case of Jonah's prophecy, however, the possibility of a 'spiritual upheaval' as opposed to physical destruction was already implicit in the original prophecy, thus no further notification was necessary (see *Rashi* and *Maharsha* ibid., and *comm.* to 4:1).

[The initially intended meaning of the prophecy, as noted however, was the one Jonah understood: that the city would be destroyed. Therefore, he felt that in the aftermath of the repentance, he would be considered a false prophet since his prophecy, as he understood it, had not been fulfilled *(Harav David Feinstein).*]

As *Ibn Ezra* maintains, literal *destruction* was clearly the original intent, but God later relented in response to the repentance. As *Jeremiah* 18:7 notes: *For one moment will I* [*God*] *decree on a nation or kingdom desolation and destruction. But if that nation repents of its evil ... I will withhold that evil decree which I considered for it.* [Thus, in retrospect, it became clear why God used the term נֶהְפָּכֶת, *overturned*, which allowed for a reversal of the decree while still being true to the prophetic prediction as verbalized by the prophet. The absolute term נֶחְרֶבֶת, *destroyed*, however, would not have been open to this second interpretation. Consequently, God would not have reversed the decree without explicitly informing the prophets.]

[See ArtScroll *Bereishis* p. 706 where *Radak* and *Abarbanel* suggest a figurative interpretation of *Genesis* 19:25 regarding the *overturning* of Sodom, taking it as 'reversed': what had previously been a fertile region, He now turned into barren desolation — utterly devastating it.]

Radak suggests that the term נֶהְפָּכֶת, *overturned*, is used here because it is suggestive of the utter destruction of Sodom which the Torah describes with the same terms [*Genesis* 19:25: וַיַּהֲפֹךְ אֶת הֶעָרִים הָאֵל, *He overturned these cities*, and *Deuteronomy* 29:22: כְּמַהְפֵּכַת סְדֹם וַעֲמֹרָה, *like the overturning of Sodom and Amorrah.* The analogy is appropriate since the sins of both cities were similar. [And since everyone was presumably aware of the historical fate of Sodom, perhaps hearing the word *overturn* in the prophet's augury lent his message even more credence and spurred on their motivation to repent.]

5. The Ninevites' Repentance

The voice of the prophet was so stentorian that it reached every corner of the city and all who heard his words resolved to turn aside from their ungodly ways *(Midrash Yonah).*

וַיַּאֲמִינוּ אַנְשֵׁי נִינְוֵה בֵּאלֹהִים — [*And*] *the people of Nineveh had faith in God.*

I.e., in the prophecy they heard in God's Name *(Ibn Ezra).*

5 The people of Nineveh had faith in God, so they proclaimed a fast and donned sackcloth, from their

The verb הֶאֱמִין signifies an acknowledgment that we begin with the faith that what we are told is אָמֵן, a *firm, fixed dependable point;* and we make it אוֹמֵן, our *guide and educator (Rav S. R. Hirsch* to *Exodus* 4:31).

◆§ Why did the Ninevites so readily accept Jonah's prophecy?

— The sailors had gone to Nineveh and related to the Ninevites how they had cast Jonah into the sea and about his miraculous rescue, etc., thereby testifying to his status as a prophet, with the result that his Word carried supreme credibility *(Ibn Ezra; Radak).*

Abarbanel observes, however, that there is no mention of the Ninevites having faith in *Jonah.* Presumably he was not required to prove himself through the performance of a sign or miracle; it was taken for granted that the Ninevites would accept his warning if they had faith in God. *Abarbanel* explains that only a prophet who delivers oracles *contrary* to the dictates of the Torah is expected to prove himself. Jonah, however, explained that the impending disaster was caused by the sinfulness of the city and not by some unnatural phenomenon. Seeing that his words were true and correct they fully believed his prophecy. The phrase *they believed in God* is to be understood as: they believed that God had the power to destroy the city if He so wished, and that He loves the righteous and abhors injustice. From Jonah's words they were stirred to repentance.

[However, see *Rambam, Hilchos Yesodei HaTorah ch.* 10, where he maintains that even a righteous person who claims to be a prophet must prove himself by foretelling future events, although he is not required to perform miracles.]

The faith of the Ninevites, however, was not entirely wholehearted. Their repentance stemmed from *fear* of the powers of a *Divinity* (אֱלֹהִים) to execute retribution from His subjects, rather than from recognition of *HASHEM* as the Supreme Being. In this way the Ninevites were inferior to the sailors on Jonah's ship who at first referred to Hashem by the general appellation, known even to the gentiles: אֱלֹהִים, *God,* but who later are described as fearing *HASHEM* greatly [1:16] *(Hegyon Hanefesh).*

[It should also be noted in this context that Jonah did not employ the Four-Letter Name, HASHEM, in addressing the Ninevites as He did when He addressed the sailors in 1:9.]

The Ninevites were also spurred on to repent by assuming that God would not have sent a prophet to foretell their impending doom had He not intended them to use the forty day grace period to mend their ways and possibly avert the Decree *(Malbim* to *v.* 9).

וַיִּקְרְאוּ־צוֹם — *So* [lit. *and*] *they proclaimed a fast.*

— The proclamation of a fast is one form of prayer to abolish an evil decree. Cf. *Joel* 1:14: *Sanctify a fast, call a solemn assembly ... and call out to HASHEM.* See also

ו שַׂקִּים מִגְּדוֹלָם וְעַד־קְטַנָּם: וַיִּגַּע הַדָּבָר אֶל־
מֶלֶךְ נִינְוֵה וַיָּקָם מִכִּסְאוֹ וַיַּעֲבֵר אַדַּרְתּוֹ
ז מֵעָלָיו וַיְכַס שַׂק וַיֵּשֶׁב עַל־הָאֵפֶר: וַיַּזְעֵק
וַיֹּאמֶר בְּנִינְוֵה מִטַּעַם הַמֶּלֶךְ וּגְדֹלָיו לֵאמֹר

Esther's call for a three-day fast in *Esther* 4:16.[1]

They repented in a spontaneous expression of remorse even *before* the king's decree in *vs.* 7-8 *(Radak).*

[Thus, Jonah's anticipation, as noted in *Mechilta* and *PdRE,* was fully justified: 'The gentiles are near to repentance.' (See *Rashi* to 1:3, and *Overview).*]

וַיִּלְבְּשׁוּ שַׂקִּים — *And* [*they*] *donned sackcloth.*

— Another manifestation of grief which usually accompanied fasting. See *I Kings* 21:27: ... *When Ahab heard these words he rent his clothes, put sackcloth on his flesh and fasted; he lay in sackcloth and walked slowly* — See also *Psalms* 35:13, and *Esther* 4:1.

מִגְּדוֹלָם וְעַד קְטַנָּם — *From their great* [*and*] *to their small.*

[I.e., both the upper and lower classes or: both the old and young. In any event: *All* the Ninevites.]

6. וַיִּגַּע הַדָּבָר אֶל מֶלֶךְ נִינְוֵה — *When* [lit. *and*] [*the*] *word reached* [*to*] *the king of Nineveh.*

I.e., the *word* which the prophet was proclaiming throughout the city *(Radak).*

The king is not identified. According to the *Midrash* [*Yalkut Shimoni* 550:3] he was Osnapper [mentioned in *Ezra* 4:10. *Rashi* there further identifies him with Sennacheriv the mighty king of Assyria. (See also II *Kings* 19:36-37 where Nineveh is mentioned as the city to which Sennacheriv later returned after his failure to capture Jerusalem, and in which he was murdered by his sons. However, that campaign was at least sixty years after Jonah's visit).]

According to *Pirkei d'Rabbi Eliezer* ch. 43, this king was the Pharaoh of the Exodus who had first-hand acquaintance with God's might at the Sea of Reeds. As the *Yalkut* notes, God spared him so he would recount His fame, and he became king of Nineveh. Under his rule, the Ninevites drew up felonious contracts, stole from each other, lived lewdly, and perpetrated other evils. When word of the decree reached him, he was seized with fear and terror, and he covered himself with sackcloth and ashes. With his own mouth he proclaimed and published this decree through Nineveh: 'Let neither man nor beast, herd nor flock taste anything

1. Fasting and wearing of sackcloth are not repentance in themselves, but they help prepare one for a sincere submission to God's will. Nevertheless, the two are quite different. The wearing of sackcloth has a symbolic effect. It represents a denial of the quest for physical comfort and material gain, and a recognition that only basic necessities are worthy of attention. Fasting, by weakening the body and pointing up the frailty of the faster, helps foster humility and submissiveness. *Rabbeinu Yonah* lists it as the seventh factor in repentance *(Shaarei Teshuvah* 1:22).

great to their small.
[6] *When word reached the king of Nineveh, he rose*
from his throne and removed his robe from upon
himself. He covered himself with sackcloth and sat
on ashes, [7] *and had it promulgated and declared*
throughout Nineveh:

'By the counsel of the king and his nobles,
the following:

for three days at the risk of being burned alive for disobedience; let them neither feed nor drink water, for know that there is no God beside Him in all the world; all His words are truth, and all His judgments are true and faithful!' *(Yalkut, Exodus* 176).

וַיָּקָם מִכִּסְאוֹ – *[And] he rose from his throne.*

In order to sit on the ground *(Metzudos).*

[The king – by coming down from his own throne – acknowledges his subjection to the King of Kings. Compare Eglon's rising up from his throne in deference to God's Word [*Judges* 3:20, for which act the Sages *(Ruth Rabbah* 2:9) say, Eglon was rewarded that Ruth and David – who both sat upon the throne of God – descended from him. (See *Bava Basra* 91b).]

וַיַּעֲבֵר אַדַּרְתּוֹ מֵעָלָיו – *And removed* [lit. *passed*] *his robe from upon himself.*

– A further step in his progressive humbling of himself before God in deference to the prophecy *(Alshich).*

Rashi following *Targum* explains אַדַּרְתּוֹ as לְבוּשׁ יְקָרֵיהּ *his precious robe;* while *Mahari Kara* and *Radak* interpret: *his majestic vestment,* the word אדר, as explained by *Ibn Janach* signifying greatness and importance. Cf. also *Gittin* 56b which specifically defines אַדִּיר as pertaining to royalty.

וַיְכַס שַׂק – [And] *he covered himself with sackcloth.*

[See in *v.* 5.]

וַיֵּשֶׁב עַל הָאֵפֶר – *And* [*he*] *sat on ashes.*

– As a further act of repentance and a display of his sincere humility and grief in the face of the prophecy *(Alshich).*

7. וַיַּזְעֵק וַיֹּאמֶר בְּנִינְוֵה – *And* [he] *had it promulgated and declared throughout Nineveh* [lit. *and he caused it to be cried out and said in Nineveh.*]

[As explained earlier, the people's spontaneous remorse began as soon as they heard Jonah. The king's decree lent royal authority to the prevailing mode. The repentance now became obligatory upon every citizen.]

According to *Ibn Ezra,* however, the chronological sequence of events was that this royal edict *preceded* the people's fasting and other manifestations of repentance in *v.* 5.

מִטַּעַם הַמֶּלֶךְ וּגְדֹלָיו לֵאמֹר – *By* [the] *counsel of the king and his nobles, the following* [lit. *to say*]:

The above, following *Metzudos*

הָאָדָם וְהַבְּהֵמָה הַבָּקָר וְהַצֹּאן אַל־יִטְעֲמוּ
ח מְאוּמָה אַל־יִרְעוּ וּמַיִם אַל־יִשְׁתּוּ׃ וְיִתְכַּסּוּ
שַׂקִּים הָאָדָם וְהַבְּהֵמָה וְיִקְרְאוּ אֶל־אֱלֹהִים
בְּחָזְקָה וְיָשֻׁבוּ אִישׁ מִדַּרְכּוֹ הָרָעָה וּמִן־
ט הֶחָמָס אֲשֶׁר בְּכַפֵּיהֶם׃ מִי־יוֹדֵעַ יָשׁוּב וְנִחַם

[and implication of *Rashi*] was part of the decree. They were to proclaim: 'By counsel of the king and officials of the kingdom it has been decreed as follows!'

The translation of מִטַּעַם as *counsel* follows *Rashi*, (מֵעֵצַת); *Mahari Kara* following *Targum* renders *by decree*.

Ibn Ezra and Radak render similar to *Rashi* but add the nuances: by the king's counsel, knowledge and sound judgment [based upon טַעַם, *taste, discernment (Metzudos)*.] Cf. *Job* 12:20; וְטַעַם זְקֵנִים יִקָּח; *He takes away the discretion of the aged; Psalms* 34:1: בְּשַׁנּוֹתוֹ אֶת טַעְמוֹ, *when he disguised his discernment* [or *sanity*].

הָאָדָם וְהַבְּהֵמָה הַבָּקָר וְהַצֹּאן — [The] *man and* [the] *cattle,* [the] *herd or* lit. *and*] [*the*] *flock.*

The king decreed that animals, as well, be included in the fast *(Radak).*

Cattle refers to the domestic animals: they are to *taste* nothing; the *herd* and *flock* are those animals that graze in the fields: *they shall not graze;* and *no one* shall drink water *(Malbim).*

The withholding of food from beasts was instituted because it would instill added grief and penance for their owners *(Metzudos).*

The Ninevites said to God: 'Lord of the Universe! The beast has no knowledge yet You treat it favorably [by providing for it and protecting it *(Eitz Yosef)*]. Then treat us also as the beast of the field!' *(Shmos Rabbah* 45:1).

8. וַיִּתְכַּסּוּ שַׂקִּים הָאָדָם וְהַבְּהֵמָה — [*And*] *they are to cover themselves with sackcloth,* — [both] [*the*] *man and* [*the*] *beast.*

— The beasts referred to here were the royal horses which usually were richly bedecked. Even they were to be covered in sackcloth as a sign of royal repentance and humility. The *man* here refers to the nobility *(Rid).*

וְיִקְרְאוּ אֶל־אֱלֹהִים בְּחָזְקָה — *And let them call out* [i.e. *pray; implore (Targum)*] *mightily* [i.e. wholeheartedly *(Radak)*] *to God.*

How did they pray?

— They separated the animals from their young, and they said, 'Master of the Universe! If You will not have mercy on us, we will not show mercy to these' (*Rashi;* comp. *Taanis* 16a).[1] [Thus the Talmud understands בְּחָזְקָה as denoting that they were to implore God *hardheartedly;* using the animals to force compassion from God.]

Furthermore, they held their in-

1. The men stood on one side and the women on the other, and their children stood apart by themselves. All the male and female animals were separated and their offspring were placed separately. The children, wishing to nurse, cried for their mothers, and the mothers yearned for their offspring, and all began to cry and bellow *(PdRE* ch. 43).

III
8

Man and cattle, herd or flock
shall not taste anything;
they shall neither graze, nor drink water;
8 *they are to cover themselves with sackcloth*
— both man and beast—
and let them call out mightily to God.
Everyone is to turn back from his evil way,
and from the robbery which is in his hands.

fants heavenward and cried out to the Holy One, Blessed be He: 'For the sake of these innocent babes who have never tasted sin, hear our prayers and cause us not to perish!' *(Midrash Yonah).*

וְיָשֻׁבוּ אִישׁ מִדַּרְכּוֹ הָרָעָה — [And] *everyone is to turn back from his evil way.*

— I.e. from his sins, in general *(Radak).*

[For their repentance was not to content itself with the external symbols of fasting and donning sackcloth, but it was to be a sincere turning away from past iniquities and a return of all ill-gotten gains.]

וּמִן הֶחָמָס אֲשֶׁר בְּכַפֵּיהֶם — *And from the robbery which is in his* [lit. *their*] *hands.*[1]

[The *Talmud (Taanis* 16a) understands this literally as: contraband in one's possession [or as the sins that were actually done with their *hands*, in this case building with stolen materials — *(Maharsha)*] — *'Even if one had stolen a beam and built it into his castle he was to raze the entire castle, to the ground and return the beam to the owner.'*

[Such acts as razing buildings to retrieve stolen materials, while highly commendable, are not required by halachah. A Rabbinic ordinance known as תַּקָּנַת הַשָּׁבִים, *ordinance for penitents*, provides that in such cases monetary compensation is sufficient 'to make matters easier for repentant robbers'. See *Bava Kamma* 66b.]

According to a view expounded by R' Yochanan in *Yerushalmi Taanis* 2:1, however, they returned only the contraband בְּכַפֵּיהֶם, in their *immediate possession.* That which was out of sight or stored away, they kept.

Mahari Kara explains the phrase as denoting open crimes of which the victim is aware; while *Radak* maintains that it was their חָמָס, *robbery,* that was equal to all their

1. The symbolism of *which is in their hands* is poignant.

Midrash Lekach Tov [cited in ArtScroll *Eichah* 3:41] comments: We should concentrate on the evil we cause with our hands; when we repent and 'cast it away from our hands' our prayers will be answered. [Good *intentions* are not enough; they must be consistent with a level of active expression.]

As the Sages [*Taanis* 16a] comment: One who has sinned and confesses his sin but does not repent may be compared to a man holding a dead reptile in his hand: although he may immerse himself in all the waters of the world his immersion is to no avail to him. But when he casts it away, as soon as he immerses himself in forty *seahs* of water [the minimum requirement for ritual purification], he becomes ritually pure.

ג י הָאֱלֹהִים וְשָׁב מֵחֲרוֹן אַפּוֹ וְלֹא נֹאבֵד: וַיַּרְא
י הָאֱלֹהִים אֶת־מַעֲשֵׂיהֶם כִּי־שָׁבוּ מִדַּרְכָּם

other crimes, and which had sealed their doom.

[In general, the phrase is taken figuratively to denote the *injustices of which they were guilty*].

9. מִי יוֹדֵעַ יָשׁוּב וְנִחַם הָאֱלֹהִים – *He who knows – let him repent* [lit. *turn*] *and God will be relentful.*

I.e., *whoever is cognizant of the sins he has committed – let him repent* [*and then* (or: *and perhaps*) *God will relent*] *(Rashi).*

This refers to those *secret sins* of which only the perpetrator is aware. The meaning then is: He who knows – within himself – that he has sinned, shall repent of his wickedness, and God will relent *(Mahari Kara).*

– Whoever is rational, or whoever is aware that he committed evil ... *(Ibn Ezra).*

– Whoever knows the way of repentance *(Radak*'s alternate interepretation).

[*Harav David Feinstein* notes that the word וְנִחַם, *and will relent,* stands independently, separated as it is by the disjunctive cantillation *(trop)* on the preceding word יָשׁוּב which is a *zakef katan,* a semi-pause, and the cantillation under וְנִחַם itself, a *tipcha,* which also is a semi-pause. Thus, the phrase may be interpreted as referring to God's forgiveness, וְנִחַם הָאֱלֹהִים, as in the simple meaning above, or homiletically as citing the essentials of repentance: יָשׁוּב, *let him* (the sinner) *repent* (i.e., remorse over his misdeeds of the past), וְנִחַם, *and let him* (the sinner) *relent* (i.e., let him resolve never to commit those sins in the future). Then וְנִחַם הָאֱלֹהִים, God will relent (the sinner will gain forgiveness).]

Or, the verse can be interpreted with *God* as the subject: *Who knows but that God may turn and relent?* – Perhaps upon seeing us repent from our evil ways God, too, will turn and relent *(Ibn Ezra*'s alternate interpretation; and *Radak*'s primary interpretation).

[The word for repentance, תְּשׁוּבָה, *teshuvah,*is related to the verb שׁוּב, *return.* Repentance implies a return to an earlier state of sinlessness and purity. In its loftiest sense, it means a return to the state of Adam before his sin – the total spiritual redemption of creation. (See *Overview).*]

וְנִחַם הָאֱלֹהִים – *And* [*the*] *God will be relentful* [lit. *be comforted* from a previous feeling; or *reconsider.*]

I.e., He will be compassionate towards us *(Targum).*

– He will be moved to change His intention (יִתְעַשֵּׁת) and relent from the calamity *(Rashi).*

[Compare the captain's statement to Jonah in 1:6: *Perhaps (the) God will pay us mind and we will not perish.*]

[הָאֱלֹהִים, *THE God,* i.e., stressing His Attribute of Justice. Even as *The Elohim* dispenser of Strict Justice, He will be relentful of punishment in the face of sincere repentance.]

[The concept of God anthropopathically allowing His 'mind' to be changed, and alter His decisions has been discussed in ArtScroll *Bereishis* 6:6.]

[The Torah, in so describing God's emotions, 'speaks in the language of man.' Although this cannot be understood in human terms because God knows beforehand what man will do and, therefore, He cannot 'change His mind' in the ordinary sense. This doctrine that God alters His decision in

[9] *He who knows — let him repent*
and God will be relentful;
He will turn away from His burning wrath
so that we perish not.'

[10] *And God saw their deeds, that they repented*

response to man's actions is basic to repentance, and is mentioned many times in Scripture. (See e.g. *Exodus* 32:12, 14; *Judges* 2:18; II Samuel 24:16; *Jeremiah* 18:8, 10; 26:19; *Joel* 2:13, 14; *I Chronciles* 21:15, and frequently).]

[See further *v.* 10, and full discussion of Repentance in *Overview.*]

וְשָׁב מֵחֲרוֹן אַפּוֹ וְלֹא נֹאבֵד — [*And*] *He will turn away from His burning wrath* [Or: *His fierce anger* (lit. *the vexation of His anger,* Or: *the annoyance of His anger)*] *so that* [lit. *and*] *we perish not.*

They surmised that God would not have sent His prophet to portend the calamity unless He intended thereby to grant them the opportunity to repent *(Malbim).*

[The concept of God being 'wrathful' is again an example of attributing emotion to God and expressing it in human terms (anthropopathism). According to *Ramban* in *Exodus* 32:11, God's 'anger' is esoterically manifested when He allows His מִדַּת הַדִּין, *Attribute of Strict Justice,* to prevail.]

[*Rashi* in *Exodus* 15:8 explains that the expression חֲרוֹן אַף metaphorically means *the heat of the nostrils,* since when one is angry the nostrils flare up and become 'hot.' Conversely, when one's wrath subsides, he is figuratively described as נִתְקָרְרָה דַעְתּוֹ, *his mind has become 'cooled.' Rashi* observes that it is permissible to describe God in such anthropopathic terms and attribute to Him human frailties and limitations כִּבְיָכוֹל (as if it were possible to so speak of God) — in order to help people better comprehend the matter.]

10. Their repentance is accepted.

וַיַּרְא הָאֱלֹהִים אֶת מַעֲשֵׂיהֶם — *And* [*the*] *God saw their deeds.*

The verse does not read: *and God saw their sackcloth and their fasting,* but 'God saw their *deeds,* that they repented of their evil ways' (*Taanis* 16a).[1]

According to *Abarbanel,* they repented of the חָמָס, *robbery and injustice,* but they did not change their pagan *beliefs* which remained

1. The *Mishnah* and *Gemara* (ibid.) record that when fast days were decreed in *Eretz Yisrael* for rain, the ark was taken out to the open spaces of the city, ashes were placed in the ark, on the head of the *Nassi,* and the head of the *Av Beis Din.* Everyone present put ashes on his own head, and donned sackcloth in order to express thereby the idea that 'we consider ourselves animals (before God)' [because sackcloth is woven of the hair of animals *(Rashi)*; or because animals are covered with inferior sackcloth *(Maharsha).*]

The elder among them would address them with words of admonition to repentance as follows: 'Brethren, neither sackcloth nor fastings are effective [these merely act to help foster humility and submissiveness *(Maharsha)*], but only penitence and good deeds. For concerning Nineveh, the verse does not read: *and God saw their sackcloth and their fasting,* but *God saw their* deeds *that they repented of their evil ways.'*

ד הָרָעָה וַיִּנָּחֶם הָאֱלֹהִים עַל־הָרָעָה אֲשֶׁר־
א־ב א דִּבֶּר לַעֲשׂוֹת־לָהֶם וְלֹא עָשָׂה: וַיֵּרַע אֶל־
ב יוֹנָה רָעָה גְדוֹלָה וַיִּחַר לוֹ: וַיִּתְפַּלֵּל אֶל־

with them. Hence the verse specifies that God saw their *deeds*, i.e., their improved level of personal consideration and social interaction. Nevertheless, the verse continues, God relented and forgave them because חָמָס was the reason for their doom to begin with.

[On the definite article ה, *the*, in הָאֱלֹהִים, *the God*, see below.]

כִּי שָׁבוּ מִדַּרְכָּם הָרָעָה — *That they repented from their evil way.*

They repented, and returned to their rightful owners even lost objects found in a field, vineyard, market place, or street. They even tore down the royal palace and returned to their rightful owners the stolen bricks in the structure. Any vineyard which had two stolen seedlings or two stolen trees was uprooted and returned to the rightful owner. If a garment contained two strands of stolen thread, it was unravelled and the threads were returned to their owner. They acted righteously and judiciously, everyone repented of his sins, and willfully submitted to punishment of death due him by Torah law. If one were to discover a hidden treasure in a house he purchased, the judge would go so far as to search up to thirty-five generations to establish original ownership of the treasure and make restitution to the rightful heirs (*Yalkut Shimoni* 550).[1]

Reb Avrohom Gold calculates exactly thirty-five generations from the Deluge until the period of Jonah's prophecy to Nineveh. This accounts for the thirty-five generation search for stolen property.

Rav Yitzchak said: Four things cancel an evil decree: צְדָקָה *charity*, צְעָקָה, *supplication*, שִׁנּוּי הַשֵּׁם, *change of name, and* שִׁנּוּי הַמַּעֲשֶׂה, *change of conduct* ... Some add שִׁנּוּי מָקוֹם, *change of place.*

... Change of conduct is derived from our verse: *God saw their deeds ... and God relented concerning the calamity He said He would bring upon them and He did not carry it out (Rosh Hashanah* 16b).

וַיִּנָּחֶם הָאֱלֹהִים עַל הָרָעָה אֲשֶׁר־דִּבֶּר לַעֲשׂוֹת לָהֶם — *And* [*the*] *God relented concerning* [lit. *upon*] *the calamity* [lit. *evil*] *He had said He would bring upon* [lit. *do to*] *them.*

[The definite article הָ, *the*, in הָאֱלֹהִים emphasizes that it was God in His manifestation as *Elohim*, the Dispenser of Strict Justice, Who relented. Such was the sincerity of the Ninevite repentance that even Divine *Justice* was moved to mercy.

See *Bereishis Rabbah* 33:3: Praiseworthy are the righteous who turn the Attribute of Justice into the

1. One of the Seven Noachide Laws is the responsibility for a community to have a system of laws and justice. Without such a system, society cannot function. The penalty for violating the Noachide Laws is death (see *Rambam, Genesis* 34:13). From the fact that the Ninevites submitted to the punishments due them under Torah law (see *comm.*), it would appear that the Ninevites did have a judicial system to adjudicate such matters *(Harav David Cohen).*

from their evil way; and God relented concerning the calamity He had said He would bring upon them and did not act.

IV 1-2

This displeased Jonah greatly and it grieved him.
2 He prayed to HASHEM, and said: 'Please

Attribute of Mercy ... as we find *And Elohim* (i.e., in His Attribute of Justice) *remembered Noah.*]

[*On* וַיִּנָּחֶם, see *commentary* to previous verse, s.v. וְנִחַם.]

Rav S.R. Hirsch renders a similar phrase in *Exodus* 32:12: *He allowed Himself to be moved to change His mind* [concerning the calamity He said He would bring upon them.]

Any prophecy foretelling suffering upon people is always subject to the condition that they do not repent; if they *do* repent, however, they will be forgiven. This refusal to make unalterable an adverse prophecy is one of God's Attributes. The concept is found in the Torah [see *Exodus* 32:14]. See *Jeremiah* 18:7: *'For one moment will I* [*God*] *decree on a nation or kingdom desolation and destruction. But if that nation repents of its evil, I will withhold that evil decree which I considered for it.'* See *Ezekiel* 33:19 *(Radak).* [Cf. *comm.* to *v.* 4, and *Overview.*]

וְלֹא עָשָׂה — *And* [*He*] *did not act* [lit. *do.*]

— He did not carry it out *then,* but as *Pirkei d'Rabbi Eliezer* notes, God indulged them for a period of forty years equal to the forty days He had sent Jonah. Then, they returned to their many evil deeds — even more so than previously — and they were swallowed up like the dead. [However Nineveh was later rebuilt *(Radal)* and under the rule of Sennacheriv, Assyria, was indeed the instrument of God in punishing Israel.]

IV.

1. Jonah's anguish.

וַיֵּרַע אֶל־יוֹנָה רָעָה גְדוֹלָה — *This displeased Jonah greatly* [lit. *and it was evil to Jonah a great evil.*]

The fact that God had relented from His intended punishment of the Ninevites, contrary to what Jonah had been told to prophesy, displeased Jonah greatly *(Ibn Ezra; Metzudos).*

— He knew that the Israelites would not heed the prophets' call as had the Ninevites, and that eventually they would be conquered by the Assyrians [of which Nineveh was the capital city] *(Sforno).*

— He saw himself as the instrument for an indictment against Israel who had not repented despite many years of prophetic ad-

ד יהוֹה וַיֹּאמַר אָנָּה יהוה הֲלוֹא־זֶה דְבָרִי עַד־
ב הֱיוֹתִי עַל־אַדְמָתִי עַל־כֵּן קִדַּמְתִּי לִבְרֹחַ
תַּרְשִׁישָׁה כִּי יָדַעְתִּי כִּי אַתָּה אֵל־חַנּוּן

monition. The *Talmud* says מְגַלְגְּלִין חוֹבָה עַל יְדֵי חַיָּב, *guilt is brought about through an evil* [lit. *guilty*] *person (Shabbos* 32a). Therefore Jonah was displeased because he feared that the fact that Israel's חוֹבָה, *guilt,* was reflected, not as a result of an admonition of repentance he would deliver to Israel, but as a result of his indirect mission to Nineveh. That Jonah would thereby be a *cause* of Israel's condemnation would tend to prove that *he,* too, was a guilty person, otherwise he would not have been selected for the task *(Harav David Feinstein).*

According to *Rashi,* because Jonah said: Now [that my prophetic message failed to materialize] the nations will claim that I am a false prophet *(Rashi).*

[The above is based on *Pirkei d'Rabbi Eliezer.* As *Radal* ad. loc. explains, Jonah's concern was not motivated by *pride,* as this would be out of character for one whom God had chosen as a prophet. Rather his concern was that wicked scoffers would not attribute the annulment of the decree to their repentance. Instead, they would complacently say that Jonah's prophecy was unfounded to begin with, or that God lacked the power to punish them. The result would be that the institution of prophecy would be discredited. This, Jonah feared, would result in חִלּוּל ה׳, the profanation of the Name of HASHEM (see *Overview).*]

וַיִּחַר לוֹ – *And it grieved him.*

– Because of Israel who did not repent *(Radak).*

As explained above, he feared that the Ninevites' repentance would reflect adversely on the Israelites who, in spite of repeated prophetic warnings, had not repented. Thus Jonah felt that he had, in effect, condemned Israel by contrast *(Mechilta Bo)* [see *comm.* to 1:3].

[The rendering of וַיִּחַר as *grieved* follows *Rashi* to *Numbers* 16:15, where he explains it as *grief, annoyance* (נִצְטַעֵר מְאֹד). *Targum* here and *Onkelos* to *Exodus* 15:7 render וּתְקֵיף לֵיהּ, *and he became angered.*

Rashi to *Exodus* 15:8 explains the root חרה as denote *burning,* hence heated *anger* (see *comm.* to 3:9).

Rav S.R. Hirsch to *Gen.* 4:5 similarly renders *burnt,* denoting 'irritation provoked by something we consider unfair.']

⋖§ When did the events of this chapter occur?

[According to the *Talmud (Sanhedrin* 89a), Jonah was not told that Nineveh would be spared (see *comm.* 3:4). From the fact that Nineveh still stood, he realized that his prophecy would not be fulfilled in its literal sense. Therefore, the events of this chapter which tell of Jonah's grief at the survival of Nineveh, could only have taken place *after the forty days had passed.* The first four verses recapitulate Jonah's grief and God's rhetorical question indicating the intention to show him the error of his thinking. The rest of the chapter reviews the events in greater detail.]

Ibn Ezra, seeking the literal meaning, comments that the chapter begins with an event that occurred after the forty days elapsed. Then, *v.* 5 reverts to a sequence of events that happened during the forty days.

Radak, however, interprets the entire chapter as being in chronological order.

IV *HASHEM, was this not my contention when I was still*
2 *on my own soil? I therefore had hastened to flee to*
Tarshish for I knew that You are a gracious and com-

He comments that Jonah learned prophetically *during* the forty days that Nineveh would be spared. Thus, his grief at the beginning of the chapter occurred while he was still in the city. Then he left *(v.* 5) and awaited further events, anticipating that the repentance would spend itself and the Ninevites would return to their wicked ways before the forty days had elapsed.

According to *Abarbanel* and *Malbim* [see 1:3], Jonah's grief flowed from his prophetic foreknowledge that the Ninevites' repentance would make them [i.e. Assyria] worthy of their later role as the *rod of God's anger* in becoming God's instrument to punish Israel in later years.

2. וַיִּתְפַּלֵּל אֶל־ה׳ וַיֹּאמַר — *[And] he prayed to HASHEM, and [he] said.*

The *prayer* is given in the following verse: *'Please take my life from me.'* He prefaced it by the statement beginning with, *'Please, HASHEM' (Radak).*

According to *Sforno* the phrase וַיִּתְפַּלֵּל אֶל־ה׳, *and he prayed to God* stands alone and refers to a prayer not recorded in Scripture. [After he completed his prayer, וַיֹּאמַר, *he said,* referring to the following which he said independently.] He explains that the prayer was that God should not send him on a similar mission [threatening doom] to Israel.

אָנָּה ה׳ — *Please, HASHEM!*

An introductory phrase meaning, as *Targum* reads קַבֵּיל בָּעוּתִי ה׳, *accept my petition, HASHEM.*

הֲלוֹא־זֶה דְבָרִי עַד הֱיוֹתִי עַל אַדְמָתִי — *Was this not my contention* [lit. *word*] *when I was still on my own soil* [lit. *upon my ground*]*?*

This was what I feared from the start: that the Ninevites would repent and be spared and that their repentance would cause evil to befall Israel *(Radak).*

The phrase עַד הֱיוֹתִי [lit. *until my being*], means *while I yet was,* as in *Job* 1:18: עַד זֶה מְדַבֵּר, *while he was yet speaking (Radak).*

עַל־כֵּן קִדַּמְתִּי לִבְרֹחַ תַּרְשִׁישָׁה — *I therefore had hastened* [lit. *preceded*] *to flee to Tarshish.*

— Attempting thereby to avoid receiving a second prophetic communication regarding this matter *(Radak)* [see *commentary* to 1:3.]

כִּי יָדַעְתִּי כִּי אַתָּה אֵל חַנּוּן וְרַחוּם — *For I knew that You are a gracious and compassionate God.*

— I was aware that if they would repent You would accordingly not destroy them, and they would consider me a false prophet *(Rashi;* see on *v.* 1).

I therefore found the prophecy difficult, and I was recalcitrant because I deemed it better that they not repent and ultimately perish because of their sins, because if they were to survive they would become the whip with which Israel would be punished. According to the Sages' interpretation, however, [*PdRE* and *Mechilta*] the implication is: I knew that their repentance would be accepted by You and that their example would ultimately

וְרַחוּם אֶרֶךְ אַפַּיִם וְרַב־חֶסֶד וְנִחָם עַל־
ג הָרָעָה: וְעַתָּה יהוה קַח־נָא אֶת־נַפְשִׁי מִמֶּנִּי
ד כִּי טוֹב מוֹתִי מֵחַיָּי: וַיֹּאמֶר יהוה הַהֵיטֵב
ה חָרָה לָךְ: וַיֵּצֵא יוֹנָה מִן־הָעִיר וַיֵּשֶׁב מִקֶּדֶם

cause evil to befall recalcitrant Israel which ignored prophetic calls to repent *(Metzudos).*

[Jonah maintains that he *knew all along* that it is the 'nature' of God to be forgiving if the Ninevites repented. Unlike the captain who *conjectured* that *perhaps* God will relent in response to repentance (1:17), Jonah *knew* that forgiveness was one of God's characteristics.

Jonah's description here of God's Attributes calls to mind the 'Thirteen Attributes' which God revealed to Moses in *Exodus* 34:6-7: *'*HASHEM*,* HASHEM*, God, compassionate and gracious, slow to anger, abounding in kindness and truth, storing up mercy for thousands (of generations), forgiving iniquity, rebellion and carelessness, and cleanses ...'*]

אֵל – *God.*

Rashi, in commenting on the use of this Name among God's Thirteen Attributes of Mercy (*Exodus* 34:6) notes that, *in this context,* אֵל [unlike אֱלֹהִים which describes God as *just*] refers to His Attribute of *Mercy. Ibn Ezra* there interprets that it means *powerful* to act as His wisdom dictates [i.e., to be merciful even though strict justice might dictate otherwise].

חַנּוּן – *Gracious.*

– To assist those who have fallen but cannot rise (*Ibn Ezra* to *Exodus* 34:6); to reward those who are not fully deserving (*Sforno,* ibid.).

וְרַחוּם – *And compassionate* [or: *merciful.*]

– Like a father to his childen to prevent them from falling *(Ibn Ezra, ibid.);* to lighten the punishment when the sinner calls You (*Sforno,* ibid.).

אֶרֶךְ אַפַּיִם – *Slow to anger* [lit. *long of anger.*]

You defer Your anger, and, in the hope that the sinner will repent, You do not hasten to punish him (*Rashi,* ibid.).[1]

וְרַב חֶסֶד – [*And*] *abounding in kindness.*

– To those who are in need of His kindness because they lack merit (*Rashi* to *Exodus* 34:6); according to *Ibn Ezra* (ibid.) this kindness extends both to the righteous and to the wicked.

וְנִחָם עַל הָרָעָה – *And relentful of* [lit. *upon*] *punishment* [lit. *evil (intention).*]

[See *commentary* to 3:9 and 3:10.]

3. וְעַתָּה ה׳ קַח־נָא אֶת נַפְשִׁי מִמֶּנִּי – *So* [lit. *and*], *now* HASHEM*, please take my life* [lit. *soul*] *from me.*

1. [*Rashi* to *Exodus* 15:8 explains that אַפַּיִם, literally means *nostrils,* but is figuratively applied to anger since, when one is angry, breath issues from his nostrils and they flare up (and Scripture anthropomorphically attributes this to also God, when He is in anger). When one is angry, his breathing becomes short, but when his anger subsides his breathing becomes long. Consequently the concept of אֶרֶךְ אַפַּיִם (long of breath) signifies *subsided, deferred anger.*]

passionate God, slow to anger, abounding in kindness, and relentful of punishment. [3] *So now HASHEM, please take my life from me, for better is my death than my life.'*

[4] *And HASHEM said, 'Are you that deeply grieved?'*

[5] *Jonah had left the city and stationed himself at*

— And spare me the sight of the destruction of my people [which Jonah foresaw would eventually befall Israel in punishment for their obduracy *(Ibn Ezra)*] since I was instrumental in bringing it about. Similar to this was Moses' declaration to God [*Exodus* 32:32]: [*If You will not forgive their sin*] *then blot me out from Your Book which You have written (Radak).*

As the *Mechilta* notes: This was a sign of supreme love for Israel: All our ancestral leaders offered their lives on behalf of Israel [see footnote to 1:12 and *Overview.*]

[Compare also Elijah's request that he die in *I Kings* 19:4.]

כִּי טוֹב מוֹתִי מֵחַיָּי — *For better is my death than my life.*

Since they will accuse me of being a false prophet *(Mahari Kara)* [which will result in a חִלּוּל ה׳, *Profanation of God's Name* (see *commentary* to *v.* 1 and *Overview).*]

4. הַהֵיטֵב חָרָה לָךְ — *Are you that deeply grieved?*

God asked the question, but said no more. The question was rhetorical as if to imply that Jonah would yet be shown that his displeasure was improper *(Radak).*

Radak continues: the word הֵיטֵב connotes an intensification of whatever is under discussion. Thus טָחוֹן, *ground,* becomes טָחוֹן הֵיטֵב, *well ground;* חָרָה, *grieved,* becomes הֵטִיב חָרָה, *deeply grieved.*

Sforno renders: Are you that deeply grieved that you were the instrument of the *goodness* [הַהֵיטֵב] I granted to Nineveh? [See *commentary* to חָרָה in *v.* 1 and 3:9.]

Others render: *Is it correct (הַהֵיטֵב) for you to be grieved?:* Does My compassion to them deserve your anger? *(R' Eliezer of Beaugency).*

R' M. Hirsch notes that in contrast to the cantillation [*trop*] in *v.* 9 where הַהֵיטֵב חָרָה is treated as one unit, in our verse הַהֵיטֵב is separated by accent from חָרָה and should accordingly be rendered in the infinitive: *So to do good grieves you?* It was a rhetorical question, one which does not require an answer, and therefore received none. In silence the prophet left the city.

Here, God reminded Jonah of the principle enunciated in *Jeremiah* 28:9 that prophecies of evil tidings are always subject to annulment based on repentance. Prophecies of good tidings, however, are inviolable. Therefore, Jonah could not be accused of a false prophecy since a prophecy of destruction is *ipso facto,* subject to change *(Malbim).*

5. Jonah observes Nineveh.

וַיֵּצֵא יוֹנָה מִן הָעִיר — [*And*] *Jonah* [*had*] *left the city.*

לָעִיר וַיַּעַשׂ לוֹ שָׁם סֻכָּה וַיֵּשֶׁב תַּחְתֶּיהָ בַּצֵּל
ו עַד אֲשֶׁר יִרְאֶה מַה־יִּהְיֶה בָּעִיר: וַיְמַן יהוה־
אֱלֹהִים קִיקָיוֹן וַיַּעַל | מֵעַל לְיוֹנָה לִהְיוֹת
צֵל עַל־רֹאשׁוֹ לְהַצִּיל לוֹ מֵרָעָתוֹ וַיִּשְׂמַח
ז יוֹנָה עַל־הַקִּיקָיוֹן שִׂמְחָה גְדוֹלָה: וַיְמַן

[For the chronology of these events, see *comm.* to *v.* 1.]

וַיַּעַשׂ לוֹ שָׁם סֻכָּה וַיֵּשֶׁב תַּחְתֶּיהָ בַּצֵּל — *He made himself a booth* [or: *shelter*] *there, and sat under it in the shade.*

— He knew that he would remain there for the duration of the forty-day period so he built the booth to protect him from the sun. What he did not know, however, was the important role this booth he had built was to play in God's object lesson to him *(Bacharach).*

The *booth* was probably a temporary shelter of branches and foliage which would soon wither under the heat of the sun [see *Radak* next verse s.v. לְהַצִּיל.]

עַד אֲשֶׁר יִרְאֶה מַה יִּהְיֶה בָּעִיר — *Until he would see what would occur in the city.*

— To see if his prophecy would be fulfilled *(Mahari Kara).*

— He thought that [since, in the final analysis man has free will], they would possibly not maintain their penitence and the decree against them would be reinstated *(Radak).*

— [According to the *Talmud* from which it would appear that this occurred *after* the forty days (see *comm.* to *v.* 1), Jonah may have wished to observe whether or not repentance would endure beyond the passing of the deadline for the prophesied calamity.]

6. The kikayon. God's object lesson.

וַיְמַן ה׳ אֱלֹהִים — *Then* HASHEM, *God, designated.*

[I.e., God provided for this occasion through His Divine Providence. Thus, the growth of this plant is attributed specifically to God Who engineers Providence through His established laws of nature. (See also on 2:1)]

The use of the two Names, ה׳ אֱלֹהִים, in this connection indicates that He manifested two Attributes: Strict Justice *in combination with* Mercy. See also *commentary* to 2:2 and 2:7.

קִקָיוֹן — *A kikayon.*

Rashi identifies it only as a plant containing many leaves, which provides shade.

Ibn Ezra cites 'the wise men of Spain' who identify the plant as דַּלַּעַת [gourd] or קרה [?], but he concludes that it is unnecessary to identify it [i.e., presumably because such speculation diverts from the lesson of the narrative. All that matters is that the plant grew suddenly at God's command, just as the great

IV the east of the city. He made himself a booth there,
6 and sat under it in the shade until he would see what
would occur in the city.

[6] *Then HASHEM, God, designated a kikayon, which rose up above Jonah to form a shade over his head to relieve him from his discomfort. And Jonah rejoiced greatly over the kikayon.*

fish swallowed Jonah at God's command.]

— It is a tall plant producing long, shady leaves. The *Mishnah* [*Shabbos* 21a] mentions שֶׁמֶן קִיק, 'kik oil', which Resh Lakish in the *Talmud* identifies as 'the *kikayon* of Jonah.' Rabbah bar Bar Chanah said that he saw the species of Jonah's *kikayon* and that it resembled a צְלוּלִיבָא. It grows in ditches, is set up in the entrance of shops [to provide shade and fragrance], and oil is manufactured from its kernels. The *Geonim* define צְלוּלִיבָא as a non-fruit-bearing plant which grows in abundance. From its kernels a medicinal oil is produced which is drunk by people suffering from cold *(Radak)*.

[Many conjecture this to be the *Ricinus communis* (castor-oil plant) which grows wild in *Eretz Yisrael* and produces large, shady leaves.]

וַיַּעַל מֵעַל לְיוֹנָה לִהְיוֹת צֵל עַל רֹאשׁוֹ — *Which rose up above Jonah to form* [lit. *be*] *a shade over his head.*

לְהַצִּיל לוֹ מֵרָעָתוֹ — *To relieve* [lit. *save*] *him from his discomfort* [lit. *from his evil.*]

— I.e., from the heat of the sun *(Rashi)*.

He was unusually sensitive to the sun's heat due to his exposure to the salt-water *(Mahari Kara)*, or from the effect on his skin of his stay in the fish's belly *(Ibn Ezra)*.

According to *Radak*, מֵרָעָתוֹ [*his evil*] refers to the discomfort of the sun's heat which beat upon him, *and which withered the 'booth'* that he had erected for shade.

— The *kikayon* in this sense is more sturdy that the hut which had protected him, since the latter withers from the sun, but the *kikayon* draws nourishment and moisture, from the earth *(Metzudos)*.

Furthermore, the shade of the *kikayon* compensated for the inadequacy of his 'booth' which provided him with only a meager amount of shade *(Malbim)*.

וַיִּשְׂמַח יוֹנָה עַל הַקִּיקָיוֹן שִׂמְחָה גְדוֹלָה — *Jonah rejoiced greatly over the kikayon* [lit. *and Jonah rejoiced over the kikayon a great happiness.*]

— Since it provided him with permanent shade *(Metzudos)*.

— And since Jonah perceived this miraculous phenomenon as a sign of Divine approval for his stationing himself there to witness the just desserts of the wicked *(Malbim)*.

הָאֱלֹהִים֙ תּוֹלַ֔עַת בַּעֲל֥וֹת הַשַּׁ֖חַר לַֽמָּחֳרָ֑ת
ח וַתַּ֥ךְ אֶת־הַקִּֽיקָי֖וֹן וַיִּיבָֽשׁ׃ וַיְהִ֣י ׀ כִּזְרֹ֣חַ
הַשֶּׁ֗מֶשׁ וַיְמַ֨ן אֱלֹהִ֜ים ר֤וּחַ קָדִים֙ חֲרִישִׁ֔ית
וַתַּ֥ךְ הַשֶּׁ֛מֶשׁ עַל־רֹ֥אשׁ יוֹנָ֖ה וַיִּתְעַלָּ֑ף
וַיִּשְׁאַ֤ל אֶת־נַפְשׁוֹ֙ לָמ֔וּת וַיֹּ֕אמֶר ט֥וֹב
ט מוֹתִ֖י מֵחַיָּֽי׃ וַיֹּ֤אמֶר אֱלֹהִים֙ אֶל־יוֹנָ֔ה
הַהֵיטֵ֥ב חָרָה־לְךָ֖ עַל־הַקִּֽיקָי֑וֹן וַיֹּ֕אמֶר

7. The destruction of the kikayon.

וַיְמַן הָאֱלֹהִים תּוֹלַעַת — *And God designated a worm.*

I.e., He providentially provided for a worm to be near the *kikayon* for this very purpose *(Radak).*

[God is once more described as הָאֱלֹהִים, *THE God,* to emphasize that He was now acting in manifestation of His attribute of being *the Elohim,* dispenser of Strict Justice.]

בַּעֲלוֹת הַשַּׁחַר לַמָּחֳרָת — *At dawn of the morrow.*]

— I.e., the day following his joy over the *kikayon (Ibn Ezra).*

It struck at *dawn,* presaging the time when Jonah's greatest need for shade would begin *(Abarbanel).*

וַתַּךְ אֶת־הַקִּיקָיוֹן וַיִּיבָשׁ — [*And*] *it attacked* [lit. *struck*] *the kikayon so that* [lit. *and*] *it withered.*

The worm attacked it at its roots cutting off its nourishment so that it withered. Accordingly, Jonah's joy over the plant lasted but one day; by the next morning the *kikayon* had withered *(Radak).*

8. וַיְהִי כִּזְרֹחַ הַשֶּׁמֶשׁ — *And it happened, that when the sun rose.* [*And Jonah was unprotected*]...

וַיְמַן אֱלֹהִים רוּחַ קָדִים חֲרִישִׁית — *That* [lit. *and*] *God designated a stifling east wind.*

חֲרִישִׁית, a Biblical term for a hot oppressive wind which the Sages [*Gittin* 31b] explained as a wind which, when it blows, *stifles (stills)* [חֲרִישִׁית from חרש, *silent*] all other winds *(Rashi).* [I.e., a wind so oppressively hot that it nullifies the coolness of all other breezes *(Rashi, Gittin* ad. loc.).] *Targum,* too, renders it as שְׁתִיקָא, *silent.*

Note that God similarly caused a *powerful east wind* to blow back the waters of the Sea of Reeds at the Exodus [*Exod.* 14:21]. *Rashi there, citing the Mechilta* notes that 'the east wind is the most powerful of all winds. This is the wind by which the Holy One, Blessed be He, exacts punishments from the wicked. See *Jer.* 18:17; *Hosh.* 13:15; *Ezek.* 27:26; *Isaiah* 27:8 *(Reb Avrohom Gold).*

Radak explains that God added to Jonah's misery by causing a temporary, hot eastern wind to blow. According to him, the implication of חֲרִישִׁית [related to חרש, *deaf*], is 'strong' since it *deafens* those who hear it howl.

Mahari Kara agrees with the latter interpretation and adds that the

7 Then God designated a worm at the dawn of the
morrow and it attacked the kikayon so that it
withered. 8 And it happened when the sun rose that
God designated a stifling east wind; the sun beat
upon Jonah's head and he felt faint. He asked for
death saying: 'Better is my death than my life!'
9 And God said to Jonah 'Are you so deeply
grieved over the kikayon?'

wind swept away what was left of Jonah's hut and *kikayon.*

— Jonah was entirely at the mercy of this wind since there was no barrier against it, stationed as he was to the east of the city *(Metzudos).*

[The term וַיְמַן ה׳, *HASHEM designated, appointed,* appears four times in our narrative to emphasize the manifestation of Providence inherent in these occurrences.]

וַתַּךְ הַשֶּׁמֶשׁ עַל רֹאשׁ יוֹנָה וַיִּתְעַלָּף — [*And*] *the sun beat upon Jonah's head and he felt faint.*

— Jonah could not endure the combination of sultry wind and oppressive sun beating upon his [unprotected] head *(Metzudos).*

He became depressed and terrified at his inability to control himself in the face of the heat [aggravated by his extra-sensitivity to the sun since his stay in the fish (see *Mahari Kara* and *Ibn Ezra* to *v.* 6). He nearly died as a result *(Radak).*

וַיִּשְׁאַל אֶת נַפְשׁוֹ לָמוּת — *He asked for death* [lit. *and he asked his soul to die.*]

He figuratively asked his soul to depart from him so he might die *(Metzudos).*

[Unlike *v.* 3 he does not ask God for death, but communes with himself.]

טוֹב מוֹתִי מֵחַיָּי — *Better is my death than my life.*

Since I am enduring so much agony *(Metzudos).*

A righteous man finds death difficult since he would thereby forfeit his opportunity to perform *mitzvos;* and therefore he prays for long life. But Jonah, feeling himself the irremediable sinner, seeks death as preferable to life *(Alshich).*

9. וַיֹּאמֶר אֱלֹהִים — *And God said.*

A similar question is asked in *v.* 4 where God is designated by His Attribute of Mercy: HASHEM. In repeating Himself, God's anger, as it were, bestirred in Him as reflected by the use here of אֱלֹהִים, signifying Strict Justice *(Daas Soferim).*

הַהֵיטֵב חָרָה לְךָ עַל הַקִּיקָיוֹן — *Are you so deeply grieved over the kikayon?*

I.e., not merely about the loss of shade, but about the fate of the *kikayon itself,* in contrast to the joy you experienced at its growth? *(Alshich).*

God is setting the stage for the object-lesson He wishes to impress upon His prophet *(Ibn Ezra).*

Unlike *v.* 4, where the question was merely rhetorical, here it is a genuine inquiry as to whether the loss of the *kikayon* had seriously

י הֵיטֵב חָרָה־לִי עַד־מָוֶת׃ וַיֹּאמֶר יהוה
אַתָּה חַסְתָּ עַל־הַקִּיקָיוֹן אֲשֶׁר לֹא־עָמַלְתָּ
בּוֹ וְלֹא גִדַּלְתּוֹ שֶׁבִּן־לַיְלָה הָיָה וּבִן־לַיְלָה
יא אָבָד׃ וַאֲנִי לֹא אָחוּס עַל־נִינְוֵה הָעִיר
הַגְּדוֹלָה אֲשֶׁר יֶשׁ־בָּהּ הַרְבֵּה מִשְׁתֵּים־
עֶשְׂרֵה רִבּוֹ אָדָם אֲשֶׁר לֹא־יָדַע בֵּין־יְמִינוֹ

upset him. The answer follows in the affirmative *(Rav M. Hirsch).*

הֵיטֵב חָרָה־לִי עַד־מָוֶת – *I am greatly grieved, to [the point of] death.*

I.e., to the point of *choosing death* because of the loss of the *kikayon* and the extreme discomfort that followed. Or, I will be grieved *until I die,* and will never be consoled *(Metzudos).*

—I am justified in being grieved because the absence of the *kikayon* will bring about my death *(Malbim).*

10. וַיֹּאמֶר ה׳ – *And HASHEM said.*

He is designated here as *HASHEM,* signifying His Attribute of Mercy, since the content of this verse reflects God's *compassion (R' Bachya).*

אַתָּה חַסְתָּ עַל הַקִּיקָיוֹן אֲשֶׁר לֹא־עָמַלְתָּ בּוֹ וְלֹא גִדַּלְתּוֹ – *You took pity on the kikayon for which you did not labor, nor did you make it grow.*

— I.e., you took pity on something you did not even make *(Ibn Ezra).*

Something *for which you did not labor*: you neither plowed, sowed, nor watered it *(Rashi).*

— You grieved over its loss not because it was your handiwork, but only because you recognized its usefulness to you in providing shade. [This follows *Malbim* who notes that the root חוס indicates compassion based on the *need* for something. (See next verse and Epilogue below).]

And although you pitied it only because of your discomfort ... nevertheless you had nothing to do with it ... and one usually grieves the loss of something he toiled over *(Radak).*

The hut over which Jonah labored with his own hands did not endure. It withered away naturally, and over that, interestingly, Jonah had neither rejoiced nor grieved. God therefore did not use it for His analogy. But over the *kikayon,* for which he neither toiled nor caused to grow, but which grew miraculously as a result of God's compassion, over *that* Jonah rejoiced, and it was over that that he now sat and wept grievously to the point of seeking death! ... *(Bacharach).*

שֶׁבִּן־לַיְלָה הָיָה וּבִן־לַיְלָה אָבָד – *Which materialized overnight and perished overnight* [lit. *which was a son of a night and perished a son of a night,* i.e., *rapidly.*]

The *kikayon*'s short existence is stressed. It sprang up overnight and at the end of the following night — by daybreak — the plant had withered *(Ibn Ezra; Radak).*

*And he said, 'I am greatly grieved to the point of
death.'*
10 *HASHEM said, 'You took pity on the kikayon for
which you did not labor, nor did you make it grow;
which materialized overnight and perished overnight.* 11 *And I — shall I not take pity upon Nineveh
that great city, in which there are more than a
hundred and twenty thousand persons who do not
know their right hand from their left, and many*

11. וַאֲנִי — *And I.*

[The pronoun וַאֲנִי, *And I,* is emphatic, in contrast with אַתָּה, *you* in *v.* 10.]

לֹא אָחוּס עַל נִינְוֵה הָעִיר הַגְּדוֹלָה — *Shall I not take pity upon Nineveh that great city.*

[After having told Jonah that his grief at the loss of the kikayon, which was not his handiwork, was based only on its usefulness to him (see *v.* 10), God concludes His argument: 'Should I — in response to their repentance — not show pity on the Ninevites who *are My handiwork, and also have usefulness to Me* inasmuch as they play a part in My scheme for Creation?!' (See Epilogue below).]

The analogy is not exact for God cannot be said to *toil* over His handiwork. Nevertheless it is couched in human terms, so that the message would be clearly understood: You took pity on something you did nothing to create, how shall I, by contrast, refrain from taking pity on *My* handiwork? *(Ibn Ezra).*

The Ninevites are *My* handiwork; how could I not take pity on such a large city? *(Metzudos).*

— [A city which is in existence such a long period of time, unlike the *kikayon* which was only a day old.]

Harav David Feinstein points out that God's compassion extends to all His creatures. As God said in silencing the angels who wished to sing His praises after the Egyptians drowned in the Sea of Reeds: מַעֲשֵׂה יָדַי טוֹבְעִים בַּיָּם וְאַתֶּם אוֹמְרִים שִׁירָה, *'My handiwork is drowning in the sea and you presume to sing praise?' (Megillah* 10b).]

אֲשֶׁר יֶשׁ־בָּהּ הַרְבֵּה מִשְׁתֵּים־עֶשְׂרֵה רִבּוֹ אָדָם — *In which there are more* [lit. *many*] *than a hundred and twenty thousand* [lit. *twelve myriads*] *persons.*

— I.e., male and female *(Radak).*

— Who have not sinned *(Ibn Ezra).* [Presumably, referring to the infant population, as below. According to *Ibn Ezra,* therefore, since the city had been condemned for its sinfulness the *total* population of the city, allowing for those who apparently *were* sinners, was significantly greater than the hundred and twenty thousand mentioned here!]

אֲשֶׁר לֹא־יָדַע בֵּין יְמִינוֹ לִשְׂמֹאלוֹ — *Who do not know their right hand from their left* [lit. in the collective singular: *who did not know*

ד
יא

לִשְׂמֹאלוֹ וּבְהֵמָה רַבָּה׃

[*The following verses from the end of* Micah *are a tender appeal to God for mercy and forgiveness. They are recited after* Maftir Yonah *on Yom Kippur.*]

מיכה
ז
יח־כ

יח מִי־אֵל כָּמוֹךָ נֹשֵׂא עָוֺן וְעֹבֵר עַל־פֶּשַׁע לִשְׁאֵרִית
יט נַחֲלָתוֹ לֹא־הֶחֱזִיק לָעַד אַפּוֹ כִּי־חָפֵץ חֶסֶד הוּא׃ יָשׁוּב
יְרַחֲמֵנוּ יִכְבֹּשׁ עֲוֺנֹתֵינוּ וְתַשְׁלִיךְ בִּמְצֻלוֹת יָם כָּל־
כ חַטֹּאתָם׃ תִּתֵּן אֱמֶת לְיַעֲקֹב חֶסֶד לְאַבְרָהָם אֲשֶׁר־
נִשְׁבַּעְתָּ לַאֲבֹתֵינוּ מִימֵי קֶדֶם׃

between his right to his left.]

— This refers to the innocent children who would have been swept away only by virtue of their fathers' iniquities. But having repented, no punishment was due them *(Rashi; Radak).*

Or, to the adults who were too simple-minded to deserve punishment *(Hegyon HaNefesh).*

— Those who cannot differentiate between the service of Hashem and their idolatrous ways, in contrast to Israel who, by having received the Torah, are more accountable for their actions than are the Ninevites, and who, by implication are deserving of more severe punishment for having practiced idolatry *(Malbim).*

וּבְהֵמָה רַבָּה — *And many beasts* [as well]!

This figuratively refers to the adults who had beast-like sensibilities inasmuch as they do not know their Creator *(Rashi).*

And many beasts, literally. Certainly *they* are innocent and deserving of compassion. Especially since they were *many! (Radak).*

Epilogue:

The kikayon and God's mercy — an explanation

In this final chapter, we find Jonah making two separate objections: 1 — He had originally wished to avoid going to Nineveh because he knew that God would have mercy on its people, and now that the city had been spared, Jonah did not wish to live (*vs.* 2-3). 2 — After the withering of the *kikayon* Jonah was grieved, and again he asked for his death (*vs.* 8-9).

To Jonah's first objection, God did not reply directly, but to the second, He responded with a קַל וָחוֹמֶר, *a fortiori* argument, comparing Jonah's concern for the *kikayon* with his lack of concern for the people of Nineveh. A proper understanding of this dialogue is essential for a comprehension of the lesson of the *Book of Jonah.*

Jonah's objection to God's acceptance of the *teshuvah* of Nineveh may be based on the following:

— Nineveh's repentance would serve as an indictment of Israel's failure to repent (see *commentary* to 1:2-3 and *Overview).*

IV 11 *beasts as well?'*

[The following verses from the end of *Micah* are a tender appeal to God for mercy and forgiveness. They are recited after *Maftir Yonah* on Yom Kippur.]

Micah VII 18-20

18 *Who is a God like You, Who pardons iniquity, and forgives the transgression of the remnant of His heritage? He does not maintain His anger forever, because He delights in mercy.* 19 *He will again have compassion on us; He will suppress our iniquities; and You will cast all their sins into the depth of the sea.*
20 *You will show truth to Jacob, loyal love to Abraham, as You have sworn to our fathers from days of old.*

— Jonah would be condemned as a false prophet (*Rashi, v.* 4:2). Jonah's concern would be because of חִלּוּל הַשֵּׁם (see *Overview*) or a general derogation of all prophecy which would result from the failure of his own to be fulfilled.

— By its survival, Nineveh would become the *rod of God's wrath* against Israel in future years (*commentary* to 1:3).

God's response was preceded and illustrated by the growth and subsequent withering of the *kikayon*. It would seem that two factors were involved in the sparing of Nineveh: the extent of the repentance, and the usefulness of Nineveh in the general scheme of Creation (as indicated by the comparison to the *kikayon* which, while insignificant in itself, had utility to Jonah).

Rosh Hashanah 16b cites the principle that God judges a person בַּאֲשֶׁר הוּא שָׁם, *in his present state* (*Genesis* 21:17). This was first enunciated in Scripture when a miracle occurred to save the life of Ishmael. The *Midrash* explains that the angels complained that Ishmael should not be saved because his descendants would murder and oppress Jews. God replied that people are judged on the basis of their current state of deservedness and, on that basis, Ishmael deserved to live. Thus, while Jonah's objections had validity, they could not override the fact that the Ninevites *had* repented sufficiently to earn God's mercy.

As *Rambam* notes in his *Introduction* to *Mishnah*, the existence of the entire universe is justified for the sake of a single righteous person. Since man does not live in isolation and the world is interdependent, the righteous person benefits to some extent — no matter how minute — from all aspects of Creation. In *Rambam*'s example, the erection of a huge palace may be justified only because, a century later, a scholar may sit in its shade. Thus, Jonah, as God's prophet, needed the *kikayon* and was dismayed when it died, exposing him to the unbearable sun and wind.

But he contended, the continued existence of Nineveh would result in harm to Israel — that being so, Nineveh was harmful to God's purpose.

God showed him by means of the *a fortiori* argument that the existence of a large city with a huge human and animal population was surely as necessary to the total scheme of creation as was a single *kikayon*. There could be numerous benefits that would accrue from the survival of Nineveh; that Jonah did not recognize these benefits did not alter this fact.

This idea may be supported by the use of the root חוס take 'pity' (see *vs.* 10, 11). *Malbim* explains that חוס [pity] refers to consideration of *the need* for something, as opposed to רחמים, *mercy*, which implies compassion even when its object is *un*deserving. One is חס at the loss of his own property, but he has רַחֲמִים at the suffering of a total stranger. Therefore, by using the root חוס, God was in effect telling Jonah, 'You are grieved by the loss of the *kikayon* because your comfort required it. I, too, would be grieved by the destruction of a city which is essential to the smooth functioning of My creation.'

Thus, the repentance of Nineveh, while short of perfection (see *Overview*), was worthy of evoking God's mercy.

It may be further argued that, by implication, God was telling Jonah that the shelter of the *kikayon* was not necessarily something to which Jonah was *entitled*. He had neither made it nor worked for it; that it was given him was a manifestation of God's mercy. He had neither the right to insist upon it *before* it was created nor to complain about it *after* it was taken away. Nevertheless, he was disturbed by its loss. Why, then, should he complain if similar mercy was shown to Nineveh, which represented so substantial an 'investment' in human and animal life?

Scripture does not record Jonah's response, but *Yalkut Shimoni* gives a moving conclusion to the narrative:

בְּאוֹתָהּ שָׁעָה נָפַל עַל פָּנָיו וְאָמַר הַנְהֵג עוֹלָמְךָ בְּמִדַּת רַחֲמִים, דִכְתִיב לַאדֹנָי אֱלֹהֵינוּ הָרַחֲמִים וְהַסְּלִחוֹת.

At that moment he [Jonah] fell upon his face and said, 'Conduct Your world according to the Attribute of Mercy as it is written: To HASHEM, our God, are mercy and forgiveness' (*Daniel 9:9*).

תם ונשלם שבח לאל בורא עולם

Meir Zlotowitz
27 Tammuz, 5738
Brooklyn, New York

Bibliography/ Biographical Sketches

Bibliography
of Authorities Cited in the Commentary

Italics are used to denote the name of a work. ***Bold italics*** *within the biography indicate the specific work of that author cited in the commentary.*

Akeidas Yitzchak

See *Arama, Rav Yitzchak.*

Albo, Rav Yosef

Spanish philosopher of the fifteenth century. Author of ***Sefer halkkarim.***

Little is known about his life. The dates of his birth (1380) and death (1444) can only be conjectured. He was a student of Rav Chasdai Crescas, and according to some historians, he was a student also of Rav Nissim Gerondi (The *'Ran')*.

His most famous work, ***Sefer halkkarim***, ('Book of Principles'), is an important treatise on Jewish philosophy and faith. The book is divided into four parts the first of which was originally intended to be an independent work. The other three parts which elaborate upon the first part, were added later. The entire work was completed in Castile in 1425.

The work was first printed in 1485, and having achieved great popularity, has been reprinted many times since.

Alkabetz, Rav Shlomo haLevi:

[b. 1505-Salonica; d. 1576 Safed]

One of the greatest Kabbalists and mystical poets of his day. Author of the Piyyut *'L'cha Dodi'* recited every Friday evening. He was a contemporary and friend of Rav Yosef Karo, author of *Shulchan Aruch.*

He is often cited by early commentators, by whom he is referred to in various ways: 'Rashba haLevi'; 'Rav Shlomo haLevi ; 'Harav ibn Alkatetz haLevi.'

He wrote commentaries on most of the Bible, the Passover Hagaddah, on Kabbalah, and was a noted Paytan.

In his Piyyut, *'L'cha Dodi'*, he speaks of the sufferings of the Jewish people and their aspirations for Redemption. Probably no other Piyyut has reached the popularity of *'L'cha Dodi'*; it is recited every Friday evening by all Jewish congregations throughout the world.

Almosnino, Rav Moshe:

Distinguished Rav and commentator. Born in Salonica, 1516, died in Constantinople about 1580.

His family dwelt originally in Aragon. Rav Moshe's grandparents were burned at the stake during the Inquisition, and his parents escaped and settled in Salonica, where he was born.

He was Rav of the Neve Shalom Spanish community in that city, and later of the Livyas Chen community.

Rav Almosnino was famous for his erudition and knowledge in both Torah and secular matters. In 1565 he represented the Jewish community before their Sultan Selim II petitioning for the confirmation of their civil rights. After six attempts, the Sultan acceded to his request and issued a proclamation guaranteeing equal rights to Jews.

He published many works — both in Hebrew and Spanish. Some were published posthumously. Many of his works are extant in manuscript form, others have been lost.

Among his works are: *Tefilah l'Moshe* on *Chumash; Yedei Moshe* on the *Five Megillos; Pirkei Moshe* on *Avos; M'ametz Koach*, a collection of sermons; *Regimento de la Vida* (Way of Life) in Spanish. His commentary to *Jonah* was printed in the *Kehilloth Moshe* Bible; Amsterdam 1724.

Alshich, Rav Moshe:

[Also spelled Alshekh]

Rav, Posek and Bible Commentator. Born in Andrionople in 1521; studied Torah there in Yeshiva of Rav Yosef Karo. Settled in Safed where he spent most of his life and was ordained there by Rav Karo with the full *Semichah* reintroduced by Rav Yaakov Berav. Among his pupils was Rav Chaim Vital, whom he ordained in 1590.

He died in Damascus, where he was travelling, before 1600.

He wrote Commentaries on most of the Bible, and published a collection of 140 of his *halachic* Responsa.

The abridged form of his commentary appearing in many editions of the Bible as *'Kitzur Alshich'* was edited by Rav Eleazer Tarnigrad, Amsterdam, 1697. Tarnigrad added much original material into this abridgement which he attributed to the Alshich but which cannot be found in the Alshich's commentary. Alshich's commentary to ***Jonah, Mar'os HaTzoveos*** was originally published in 1608.

Alter, Rav Yehudah Aryeh Leib:

(1847-1903)

Gerrer Rebbe; known by his work 'Sefas Emes.'

His father, Rav Avraham Mordechai, a great but chronically ill man, died when Yehudah Leib was only 12 years old. His upbringing fell to his grandfather, the illustrious *Chidushei haRim.* Yehudah Aryeh would study eighteen hours a day as a youth. It became widely known that a fitting successor was being groomed for the *Chiddushei haRim.*

He was 19 years old when his grandfather died and, despite the pleas of the chassidim, insisted he was unworthy to become Gerrer Rebbe. Several years later, after the death of Rav Henach of Alexandrow, he acceded to their wishes and molded Ger into the largest chassidus in Poland.

A prodigious and diligent scholar, he nevertheless found time to counsel tens of thousands of disciples every year and to become an effective leader in Torah causes. His discourses were distinguished for profundity and originality. Although he never wrote for publication, his writings were posthumously published as ***Sefas Emes***, separate volumes of novellae on Talmud, and chassidic discourses on Torah and festivals.

Altschuller, Rav Yechiel Hillel

Bible commentator of 18th century.

In order to promote the study of the Bible Reb Yechiel Hillel's father, Reb David, planned an easy-to-read commentary of *Neviim* and *Kesuvim* (Prophets and Hagiographa) based on earlier commentators. His commentary to *Psalms, Proverbs* and *Job* was published before he died in 1753.

Rav Yechiel edited his father's remaining manuscripts and completed the missing books himself. By 1780, the entire completed commentary was published. It consisted of two parts: ***Metzudas Zion*** which explains individual words; and ***Metzudas David***, which provides a running commentary to the text [both parts are cited in our commentary as **Metzudos.**] Due to their simple and concise language, the dual commentaries have become almost indispensable aids in Bible-study. They have attained great popularity and have been reprinted in nearly every edition of the Bible.

ARIzal

see *Luria, Rav Yitzchak.*

Avnei Nezer

see *Borenstein, Rav Avraham.*

Bachrach, Rav Yehoshua:

Contemporary Bible scholar on Israeli scene.

Educated in Lithuanian Yeshivos, the first of which was the Yeshivah of Rav Shimon Shkop in Grodno.

He is senior lecturer in *Neviim Rishonim* at the Jerusalem College for Women (Michlalah). He published a monumental study of David and Saul; a book on *Ruth* entitled *Ima Shel Malchus (Mother of Royalty); and a commentary on Esther.* His commentary on *Jonah* entitled ***Yonah ben Amittai and Eliyahu***, is a poetically profound synthesis of *p'shat* (plain meaning) and *d'rash* (homiletical interpretation).

R' [=Rabbeinu] Bachya ben Asher:

[Also pronounced R' B'chayyai.]

Served as *dayyan* and rabbi in Saragossa, Spain, mid 13th century.

He was one of the foremost students of Rav Shlomo ben Aderes [Rashba.] His most famous work is his commentary on the Torah written in 1291. In this work, written in clear, flowing style, R' Bachya draws on many sources from Talmudic and Midrashic to exegetic and kabbalistic.

His ***Kad HaKemach*** on the foundations of faith had wide circulation. Included in the Yom Kippur section of this work is a verse by verse exegetical commentary on Jonah which is drawn almost verbatim from the philosophic work, ***Hegyon HaNefesh***, by **Rav Avraham bar Chiyyah** who lived in Barcelona and died about 1136.

An annotated edtion of R' Bachya's ***Kad HaKemach*** was published by Rav Ch. B. Chavel in ***Kisvei R' Bachya***, 1970.

Beis Elokim:

See *Rav Moshe ben Yosef of Trani.*

Bereishis Rabbah:

The ***Midrash Rabbah*** to Genesis.

Borenstein, Rav Avraham:

(1839-1910)

Author of ***Eglei Tal*** and ***Avnei Nezer***, he was the son-in-law of Rabbi Mendel of Kotzk and one of the leading scholars and chassidic rebbes of Poland. Aside from his personal accomplishment he left his stamp on future generations through his yeshivah where he educated a generation of leaders who combined outstanding Torah knowledge and Chassidic fervor. For the last 27 years of his life, he was rabbi of Sochaczev. Much of his chassidic and homiletical thought is preserved in ***Shem miShmuel*** by his only son, and in ***Neos heDesheh***, a collection of his writings.

Borenstein, Rav Shmuel:

(1856-1926)

The only son and the successor of the author of ***Avnei Nezer***, Rabbi Shmuel succeeded his father as rabbi of Sochaczev in 1910. He continued the family tradion of outstanding accomplishment in Torah and in chassidic leadership. Rabbi Shmuel edited and published his father's responsa, ***Avnei Nezer***, on the four sections of **Shulchan Aruch.** His own major work, ***Shem miShmuel*** contains his Sabbath and festival discourses. It cites much of his father's thought upon which Rav Shmuel often based his own development of widely varied concepts.

Cordovero, Rav Moshe:

(1522-1570)

Known by his acronym: RaMaK.

Leading Kabbalist in the period before the ARI. He lived in Safed and studied Torah from Rav Yosef Caro, author of the *Shulchan Aruch.* He was ordained with the full Semichah re-introduced by Rav Yaakov Berav.

Ramak was the brother-in-law of the Kabbalist Rav Shlomo Alkabetz who initiated him into the mysteries of Kabbalah — then being propogated in Safed. His stature was such that even the ARIzal referred to him as 'my master and mentor.'

One of Ramak's most important works was his ***Pardes Rimonim,*** elucidating the tenets of Kabbalah.

He is also the author of ***Tomer Devorah***, the famous *mussar* work which is widely studied even today.

Daas Soferim:

Contemporary commentary to most of Scripture stressing the literal sense of the text by the noted Israeli Bible scholar and lecturer, Rabbi Chaim D. Rabinowitz.

Daas Tevunos:

See *Luzatto, Rav Moshe Chaim.*

Derech Hashem:

see *Luzatto, Rav Moshe Chaim.*

Dessler, Rav Eliyahu Eliezer:

(1891-1954).

One of the outstanding personalities of the Mussar movement. He was born in Honmel, Russia.

In 1929 he settled in London. He exercised a profound influence on the teaching of Mussar, not only because of the profundity of his ideas, but also on account of his personal, ethical conduct.

In 1941 he became director of the Kollel of Gateshead Yeshiva in England.

In 1947, at the invitation of Rav Yosef Kahaneman, he became *Mashgiach* of Ponovez Yeshiva in Bnei Brak, Israel, and there remained until his death.

His teachings reflect a harmonious mixture of Mussar, Kabbalah, and Chassidus. Some of his ideas were published by his pupils in ***Michtav me-Eliyahu*** (3 vols. 1955-64).

Eidels, Rav Shmuel Eliezer ben Yehudah HaLevi:

(1555-1631).

(Known as Maharsha — 'Moreinu haRav Shmuel Eliezer').

One of the foremost Talmud commentators, whose two-fold commentary on the halachic and homiletical passages in the Talmud is included in almost every editon of the Talmud.

Born in Cracow, he moved to Posen in his youth. In 1614 he became Rav of Lublin, and in 1625 of Ostrog, where he founded a large Yeshivah.

Einhorn, Rav Zev Wolf:

Rav in Vilna, end of 19th century.

Author of ***Peirush Maharzu***, comprehensive and well-detailed commentary to *Midrash Rabbah* appearing in the Romm edition.

Rav Eliezer of Beaugency:

[Hebrew: Rav Eliezer miBelgentzy.]

Among the earliest Bible commentators.

Lived in North France during the twelfth century. A contemporary, and according to some a student, of *Rashbam*, Rashi's grandson.

Little is known about his life. From references in his own work and those of his contemporaries, notably Rav Yosef B'chor Shor, Rav Eliezer wrote commentaries to much of Scripture. However, only those on *Isaiah* [published in 1879], on *Ezekiel*, and the *Twelve Prophets* [published 1907-13] have been preserved.

Rav Eliezer, in following his predecessors, Rashi, Rashbam and Mahari Kara, stressed *p'shat,* the literal exegesis of the Bible, and shied away, wherever possible from *d'rash*, Midrashic interpretation.

Frankfurter, Rav Moshe:

(1672-1762).

Dayyan and printer in Amsterdam.

Little is known about his life. He wrote *Nefesh Yehudah*, a commentary on *Menoras HaMaor; Zeh Yenachameinu*, a commentary on the *Mechilta;* glosses to *Choshen Mishpat* entitled *Ba'er Heitev* patterned after the Rav Ashkenzi's *Ba'er Heitev to the other three parts of the Shulchan Aruch.*

Rav Moshe also edited a new edition of the famous *Mikraos Gedolos* Bible *'Kehillas Moshe'* [Amsterdam, 1725-27] adding 16 previously unpublished commentaries to the various books of the Bible. In *Jonah,* he added the commentaries of *Sforno* and *Almosnino*, as well as his own commentary entitled ***Minchah Gedolah.***

Hegyon HaNefesh:

By *Rav Avraham bar Chiyya.* See *R' Bachya.*

Hirhurei Teshuvah:

Commentary and novellae to Rambam's *Hilchos Teshuvah* by Hagaon Rav Mordechai Gifter, Rosh Yeshiva Telshe-Stone Jerusalem.

Published 1977, Mesorah Publications.

Hirsch, Reb Mendel:

(1833-1900).

Eldest son of Rav Samson Raphael Hirsch.

For many years continued the educational work begun by his father.

Inspired by his father's commentary on the Torah, Reb Mendel authored a German translation and commentary on the *Haftaros* [1896]; on the *Twelve Prophets* [1900]; and on *Lamentations* [1903.]

His work on the *Haftaros* — in which a commentary to ***Maftir Yonah*** is included, was translated into English by his nephew, Dr. Isaac Levy 1966, and is published by Judaica Press.

Hirsch, Rav Samson Raphael:

(1808-1888).

The father of modern German Orthodoxy.

He was a fiery leader, brilliant writer, and profound educator. His greatness as a Talmudic scholar was obscured by his other monumental accomplishments. After becoming Chief Rabbi and member of Parliament in Bohemia and Moravia, he left to revitalize Torah Judaism in Franfurt-am-Main which he transformed into a Torah bastion.

His best known works are the classic six-volume ***Commentary on Chumash*** noted for its profound and brilliant philosophical approach to Biblical commentary; his ***Commentary to Psalms***, and ***Horeb***, a philosophical analysis of the mitzvos.

Ibn Ezra, Rav Avraham:

(Born 1089 in Toledo; died 1164).

Famous poet, philosopher, grammarian, astronomer — and above all — Biblical commentator.

In all his Bible commentaries he strived for the plain, literal meaning of the verse. His aim was to explain the etymology of difficult words within their grammatical context. Next to Rashi, his commentary on the Torah is one of the most widely studied, and appears in almost all large editions of the Bible.

In France, he met Rav Yaakov Tam ['Rabbeinu Tam'] — grandson of Rashi, and a deep friendship between the two followed.

According to some, he married the daughter of Rav Yehudah haLevi, and had five sons.

Legend has it that he once met the Rambam and dedicated a poem to him on the day of his death.

Ibn Janach, Rav Jonah:

Born in Cordova, c. 985; died in Saragossa, first half of 11th century.

One of the foremost *'Baalei Dikduk'* (grammarians and philologists) of the early middle ages. Little is known of his life.

He published one of the first Biblical grammar books and dictionaries, the earliest to have come down to us in its entirety. It was originally written in Arabic and later translated into Hebrew by Rav Yehudah ibn Tibbon. It is divided into two parts: *Sefer haRikmah;* and ***Sefer haShorashim.***

He is often quoted by later Bible commentators and Hebraists such as: Ibn Ezra; Ibn Daud; Kimchi; and Mizrachi.

The notable exception is *Rashi* who seems to have been unacquainted with his work (or who may have chosen not to quote him).

Ibn Janach was also a physician and he published several treatises on medicine, which have been lost.

Kara, Rav Yosef:

['Mahari Kara'.]

French Bible commentator, c1060-1130. [Not to be confused with Rav Yosef Caro, 15th century author of *Shulchan Aruch.*]

Rav Yosef was the student of his illustrious uncle, Rav Menachem Chelbo, whom he often cites in his commentary.

Rav Yosef resided in Troyes, the same city in which Rashi lived, and he frequented Rashi's house, where he made the acquaintance of Rashi's grandson, *Rashbam.*

Rav Yosef wrote a commentary on Torah — based upon Rashi's commentary which he enlarged and expanded upon. He also added glosses to Rashi's commentary which Rashi himself agreed with and later incorporated into his own manuscript.

Rav Yosef also wrote an independant commentary to most of Tanach, including *The Five Megillos.*

In his commentaries he followed the general style of Rashi but was not as brief. Sometimes whole sentences are translated into French. He cares more for the sense of the whole sentence than for the grammatical dissection of a single word. Although he prefers *p'shat,* the simple meaning of the text, he does not altogether hold aloof from haggadic interpretation — which he held was an adornment of the text and was necessary to 'render Torah great and glorious.'

Kimchi, Rav David:

French grammarian and commentator; known by his acronym 'RaDaK'.

Born in Narbonne, 1160; died there in 1235.

His father, Rav Yosef, also a grammarian, died when Rav David was a child, and he studied under his brother, Rav Moshe, who had also published several volumes on grammer.

Radak's ***commentary on Prophets*** is profound, and is included in most large editions of the Bible.

Many have applied to him the saying from Pirkei Avos: 'Without *kemach* ['flour' i.e., *'Kimchi'*] there is no Torah'; such was his great influence.

One of his main works was the *Michlol,* the second edition of which came to be known independently as the *Sefer haShorashim* (not to be confused with a work by the same name by Ibn Janach).

In his commentary, he stressed the *derech hap'shat,* the plain sense, wherever possible, striving for clarity and readability.

Luria, Rav David:

(1798-1855; Known as RADAL).

Lithuanian Rav and *posek.* Student of Rav Shaul Katzenellenbogen of Vilna.

After the death of his mentor, the Vilna Gaon, Radal was considered one of the Torah leaders of his generation.

His scholarly writings embrace almost all of Torah literature. Among his works are his commentary to the Midrash, *Chidushei Radal,* printed in the Romm edition of the *Midrash Rabbah,* as well as his extensive commentary to ***Pirkei d'Rabbi Eliezer.***

Luria, Rav Yitzchak:

[Known as *ARIzal* (from the initials of ha**E**loki **R**abbi **Y**itzchak, **z**ichrono **l**ivrachah).]

The fountainhead of modern *kabbalistic* thought.

Born in Jerusalem, 1534, to his father, Rav Shlomo Luria, a relative of Maharshal.

While still a child, he lost his father. His mother moved the family to Egypt, and he was brought up by his wealthy uncle Rav Mordechai Francis in Cairo.

He studied at the Yeshivah of Rav David ben Zimra (Radvaz) who was his teacher *par excellence* in Torah and *kabbalah*. He was a student and comrade of Rav Betzalel Ashkenazi (author of *Shittah Mekubetzes*) who himself was a student of Radvaz.

ARIzal was beloved by his uncle, and at the age of fifteen, was given his cousin in marriage.

His holiness manifested itself at an early age and students flocked to him extolling his virtues and saintly qualities.

In 1570, at the age of 36, he moved to Eretz Yisrael and settled in Safed where he formed a circle of *kabbalists* among whom were Rav Shlomo Alkabetz; Rav Yosef Caro; Rav Moshe Alshich; Rav Yosef Chagiz.

His circle widened and his influence grew greatly. He was regarded by all who knew him as a profound *Tzaddik* who had the power to perform miracles.

He entrusted his *kabbalistic* teachings to his disciple Rav Chaim Vital, who, according to ARIzal, possessed a soul which had not been soiled by Adam's sin.

After the ARIzal's death in 1572, Rav Chaim Vital collected notes which the ARIzal's students had made of their master's teachings, and published them. Among the works so published were: *Eitz Chaim; Hadras Melech; Marpei Nefesh; Tikkunei Shabbos; Commentary to Zohar Chadash;* and *Shulchan Aruch* of the ARIzal incorporating his halachic customs. These customs are quoted extensively by later halachic authorities, and his influence is immense.

ARIzal revealed many of the sepulchres of Sages whose locations had been forgotten until his time. He is also credited with composing the Sabbath *Zemiros*: Azamer Bish'vachin, Asader leSudasa and Bnei Heichala.

He died in Safed, 1572, at the young age of 38.

Luzatto, Rav Moshe Chaim:

(1707-1746).

Kabbalist, author of ethical-Mussar works, and poet. (Known by his acronym 'Ramchal').

Born in Padua, Italy, Rav Moshe Chaim was regarded as a genius from childhood, having mastered *T'nach, Midrash* and *Talmud* at an early age. He later went on to delve into Kabbalistic and ethical studies.

He is most famous for his profound ethical treatise, ***Mesillas Yesharim*** ('The Path of the Upright') which has, alongside the *Chovos haLevavos* of Rav Bachya ibn Paquada and *Shaarei Teshuvah* of Rabbeinu Yonah, become the standard ethical-Mussar work.

Among his Kabbalistic works were: *Razin Geneizin, Megillas Sesarim; Maamar HaGeulah;* ***Derech Hashem;*** and ***Daas Tevunos*** which studies in detail the aim of creation, sin, justice, the Next World, prayer and *mitzvos*.

In 1743, he emigrated to Eretz Yisrael. He lived a short time in Acre, and died there, with his family, in a plague.

Mahari Kara:

See *Kara, Rav Yosef.*

Maharsha:

See *Eidels, Rav Shmuel Eliezer.*

Malbim:

(1809-1879).

Rav, Darshan, and Biblical commentator.

The name Malbim is an acronym of Meir Leibush ben Yechiel Michel.

He was born in Volhynia, and was a child when his father died. He studied in his native town until the age of 13. He then went to Warsaw where he was known as the *'iluy* [prodigy] from Volhynia.' He was Rav in several cities but he suffered much persecution because of his uncompromising stand against Reform, leading to his short-term imprisonment on a false accusation. He wandered much of his life, serving as rav in several cities for several years at a time — even serving for a short while as Chief Rabbi of Rumania.

His fame and immense popularity rests upon his commentary to the Bible which was widely esteemed. His first published commentary was on *Megillas Esther* (1845). His commentaries to the remaining books of the Bible were published between then and 1876. His commentary to *Jonah* is entitled **Gei Chizayon.**

His commentary on the Bible [as the author sets forth in his introduction to *Isaiah*] is based upon three fixed principles: in the text of the Torah and the figurative language of the prophets there are no repetitions of mere synonyms; consequently, every word in a sentence is essential to the meaning in accord with the rules of language, despite the fact that they seem to be mere synonymous repetitions. Every statement conveys a sublime thought; all metaphors are of importance and replete with wisdom for they are the words of the living God.

Mechilta:

The earliest Midrashic commentary on the *Book of Exodus* by the school of the second century *tanna,* Rabbi Yishmael. First printed in Constantinople, 1515.

Mesillas Yesharim:

see *Luzatto, Rav Moshe Chaim.*

Metzudos:

[Metzudas David; Metzudas Zion.]

See *Altschuller, Rav Yechiel Hillel.*

Midrash Lekach Tov:

Commentary to various Books of the Bible attributed to *Rav Toviah ben Eliezer* 11th century. The work has achieved great popularity and is quoted by many *Rishonim* such as Rabbeinu Tam, Rambam, Baal haIttur, *Or Zaruah, Shibolei haLeket.* Ibn Ezra also refers to it in his commentary.

This *'Midrash'* has been published at separate times on the various books of the Bible as the manuscripts have been re-discovered.

Midrash Rabbah:

[Lit. 'The Great Midrash'.]

The oldest Amoraic classical *Midrash* on the *Five Books of the Bible* and the *Megillos.*

Rav Moshe ben Maimon:

(1135-1204).

Known by his acronym: RAMBAM; Maimonides.

One of the most illustrious figures in Judaism in the post-Talmudic era, and among the greatest of all time. He was a rabbinic authority, codifier, philosopher and royal physician. According to some, he was a descendant of Rav Yehudah haNasi.

Born in Cordoba; moved to Eretz Yisrael and then to Fostat, the old city of Cairo, Egypt.

At the age of 23 he began his *Commentary on the Mishnah,* which he wrote during his wanderings. His main work was ***Mishneh-Torah/Yad HaChazakah***, his codification of the spectrum of *Halachah* until his day. This was the only book he wrote in Hebrew, all his other works having been written in Arabic, a fact he is said to have regretted later in life.

He is also know for his profound and philosophic ***Moreh Nevuchim ('Guide*** *for the Perplexed')*, and for his many works in the field of medicine, hygiene, astronomy, etc.

Truly it may be said 'from Moshe to Moshe there arose none like Moshe.'

Rav Moshe ben Yosef of Trani:

(1500-1515).

[Known by his acronym: HaMaBIT.]

Born in Salonika, where his family had emigrated from Italy. He later moved to Safed, the largest Torah center in Eretz Yisrael, where he studied under Rav Yaakov Berav, and was one of the four disciples ordained by him. [Among the others was Rav Yosef Caro, author of the *Shulchan Aruch.]*

After the death of Rav Yosef Caro, the Mabit was appointed the spiritual head of the entire community of Safed.

Among his works were *Bais Elokim*, a philosophical work dealing with prayer, repentance, and principles of Jewish belief.

Minchah Gedolah:

See *Frankfurter, Rav Moshe.*

Ohel David:

Novellae on Scripture by the distinguished contemporary Talmudic scholar, Rabbi David Cohen, Brooklyn, New York.

PdRE:

See *Pirkei d'Rabbi Eliezer.*

Peirush Maharzu:

see *Eihorn, Rav Zev Wolf.*

Pirkei d'Rabbi Eliezer:

[Abbreviation PdRE.]

Ancient Midrashic work attributed to the first century *Tanna*, Rabbi Eliezer ben Hyrcanos 'Hagadol.' [See also *Luria, Rav David.]*

Radak:

See *Kimchi, Rav David.*

Rambam:

See *Rav Moshe ben Maimon.*

Rashi:

See *Rav Shlomo ben Yitzchak.*

Seder Olam:

Early systematic Midrashic-chronological work, tracing world history from the time of Adam till the destruction of the Second Temple.

In parts it is an exegesis of Biblical verses and in parts engenders ancient chronological oral traditions.

Seder Olam is mentioned in the Talmud *(Shab.* 88a; *Yev.* 82b et al) and is ascribed to the *Tanna* Rav Yose ben Chalafta, mid 2nd century.

The Vilna Goan published glosses to *Seder Olam.*

An excellent edition is that of Harav Moshe Yair Weinstock (Jerusalem 1967) containing his extensive chronological commentary and tables.

Sefas Emes:

See *Alter, Rav Yehudah Aryeth Leib.*

Sefer Chassidim:

See *Rav Yehudah HaChassid.*

Sforno, Rav Ovadiah:

(1470-1550).

One of the greatest Italian commentators and literary figures of the Renaissance period.

Little is known of Ovadiah's youth, except that he excelled in Torah studies and at an early age his halachic opinions were sought by many. His decisions are quoted by Rav Meir Katzenellenbogen (Maharam Padua) where he is referred to with great esteem.

Sforno studied medicine, which profession he followed.

He finally settled in Bologna where he was a major force in organizing the religious life of the town and established a *bais medrash* which he headed until his death.

Sforno's great fame, however, rests with his commentary to most of the Bible, in which he tries to explain the text literally, usually regarding the verse as a complete entity rather than philologically dissecting it. He usually avoids esoteric or kabbalistic interpretations. His commentary to the Chumash was edited by his brother Chananel after his death. The ***Commentary to Jonah*** was first published in the Kehilloth Moshe Bible, Amsterdam 1724.

Shem MiShmuel:

See *Borenstein, Rav Shmuel.*

Rav Shlomo ben Yitzchak:

(Known by his acronym RASHI).

Leading commentator on the Bible and Talmud.

He was born in Troyes, France in 1040 — the year in which Rabbeinu Gershom Me'or haGolah died. According to tradition, Rashi's ancestry goes back to Rav Yochanan haSandlar and to King David.

The summit of Rashi's commentaries was on the Talmud — an encyclopaedic and brilliant undertaking. Nothing can be compared to the impact this commentary has had upon all who study the Talmud. Rashi's commentary has opened to all what otherwise would have been a sealed book. Without his commentary, no one would dare navigate the 'Sea of Talmud.' Every word is precise and laden with inner meaning. Rashi's corrections of the Talmud text were, for the most part, introduced into the standard editions and became the accepted text.

Rashi's ***Commentary to the Bible***, too, made a similar impact — and virtually every printed Bible contains his commentary which is distinguished by its conciseness and clarity.

Rashi is considered the "Father of the Commentators," and the study of *Chumash* has become synonymous with *Chumash-Rashi.*

Many halachic works form the 'School of Rashi' have come down to us: *Sefer haOrah; Sefer haPardes; Machzor Vitry; Siddur Rashi;* and responsa.

Rashi died on Tammuz 29, 1105. His burial place is not known.

Tanchuma:

[Or: *Midrash Tanchuma Yelamedeinu.]*

Ancient Midrash on the whole of the Torah attributed to the 4th century C.E. *Amora*, Rav Tanchuma bar Abba.

Many of its *sedarim* open with a distinctive proem using the formula *Yelamedeinu Rabbeinu* ['Teach us our master.']

In 1885, S. Buber published an Oxford manuscript of *Midrash Tanchuma* on the whole of *Chumash*, which differs considerably from the standard printed text, but has all the characteristics of the former, such as the frequent mention of Rav Tanchuma. Many post-Talmudic citations from *Tanchuma* not found in the standard edition, are found in the Buber edition.

Targum:

The ancient, authoritative Translation of the Bible into Aramaic.

The *Targum* to *Chumash* is by Onkelos the proselyte [1st century C.E.] who is identified in *Midrash Tanchuma* 41a as the nephew of Hadrian, while in the Talmud he is identified as the nephew of Titus [see *Gittin* 56b.] According to *Megillah* 3a, Onkelos undertook his translation under the guidance of the *tannaim* R' Eliezer and R' Yehoshua.

The *Targum* to the rest of Scripture — called *Targum Yonasan* — is by the first century *tanna*, R' Yonasan ben Uziel, 'from the mouth of Haggai, Zechariah, and Malachi' . . . and who defended his undertaking this translation as being not for the sake of his personal honor, 'but in order that disputes shall not multiply in Israel' [*Megillah* 3a.]

Tomer Devorah:

See *Cordovero, Rav Moshe.*

Yalkut Shimoni:

The best known and most comprehensive Midrashic anthology covering the entire Bible.

It is attributed to Rav Shimon haDarshan of Frankfort who lived in the 13th century.

The author collected *Midrashim* from more than 50 works, arranging them into more than 10,000 statements of *Aggadah* and *Halachah* according to the verses of the Bible.

Rav Yehudah haChassid:

(c. 1150-1217).

One of the main teachers of the 'Chassidei Ashkenaz' and one of the most profound ethical teachers to have lived.

Author-editor of ***Sefer Chassidim***, a profound ethical/halachic treatise which has come down to us in two separate editions. The book has achieved great popularity and was reprinted many times.

Rav Yehuda's father, Shmuel, was a renowned Rosh Yeshiva in Speyer, and Rav Yehudah studied under him. His saintly life was revered by all.

Among his illustrious students were: Rav Eliezer of Worms *(Baal Rokeach)*; Rav Yitzchak of Vienna *(Or Zarua).*

His contemporaries said of him: 'Had he lived in the time of the prophets, he would have been a prophet; in the time of the *Tannaim*, he would have been a *Tanna*; in the time of the *Amoraim*, an *Amora . . .'*

Yerushalmi:

The Jerusalem Talmud, as distinguished from the Babylonian Talmud.

לעילוי נשמת דודי היקר

ר׳ יונה ב״ר חיים צבי ע״ה

ע״ה JAMES PASTER

איש יקר ועדין-רוח

שקיים מצות כבוד אב ואם בחיבה יתירה

נפ׳ עש״ק יא סיון התשל״ח

ת נ צ ב ה